The Treasures of Darkness

Head of a statue of Ninurta, god of the thundershowers and floods of spring. The statue was found in ancient Eshnunna (modern Tell Asmar) by the Iraq expedition of the Oriental Institute of the University of Chicago and dates from shortly after 3000 B.C.

The Treasures of Darkness

A HISTORY OF MESOPOTAMIAN RELIGION

THORKILD JACOBSEN

YALE UNIVERSITY PRESS, NEW HAVEN AND LONDON, 1976

Designed by Sally Sullivan
and set in Baskerville type.
Printed in the United States of America by
The Murray Printing Co., Westford, Massachusetts.

Published in Great Britain, Europe, Africa, and Asia
(except Japan) by Yale University Press, Ltd., London.
Distributed in Latin America by Kaiman & Polon, Inc.,
New York City; in Australia and New Zealand by Book & Film
Services, Artarmon, N.S.W., Australia; in Japan by John
Weatherhill, Inc., Tokyo.

Permission to quote has been given by the following:
The E. M. Forster Literary Estate and The Hogarth Press for
a short extract from *Anonymity: An Enquiry* by E. M.
Forster; The University of Chicago Press for translations
from *The Intellectual Adventure of Ancient Man* by H. and
H. A. Frankfort, John A. Wilson, Thorkild Jacobsen, and
William Irwin (copyright by the University of Chicago Press,
1946), and from *The Burden of Egypt* by John A. Wilson
(copyright 1951 by the University of Chicago); The Oriental
Institute, University of Chicago for translations from *Most
Ancient Verse* by Thorkild Jacobsen and John A. Wilson
(University of Chicago Press, 1963).

Thanks are due to the Trustees of the British Museum, the
Directorate General of Antiquities, Baghdad, and the Oriental
Institute, University of Chicago, for permission to publish
photographs of objects in their collections.

To Katryna

Contents

Illustrations

1
Ancient Mesopotamian Religion: The Terms

"Men do mightily wrong themselves when they refuse to be present in all ages and neglect to see the beauty of all kingdoms" says Traherne, and some such adventurous spirit is clearly called for if one is to venture into ages and kingdoms as far away as those of ancient Mesopotamia.

A measure of caution, however, may not be amiss either; and so we may well begin by attempting to clarify what the terms of our subject actually imply and which particular aspect or aspects of them we may most profitably address.

"Religion" as Response

The Numinous

Basic to all religion — and so also to ancient Mesopotamian religion — is, we believe, a unique experience of confrontation with power not of this world. Rudolph Otto[1] called this confrontation "Numinous" and analyzed it as the experience of a *mysterium tremendum et fascinosum,* a confrontation with a "Wholly Other" outside of normal experience and indescribable in its terms; terrifying, ranging from sheer demonic dread through awe to sublime majesty; and fascinating, with irresistible attraction, demanding unconditional allegiance. It is the positive human response to this experience in thought (myth and theology) and action (cult and worship) that constitutes religion.

Since the Numinous is not of this world it cannot in any real sense of the word be "described"; for all available descriptive terms are grounded in worldly experience and so fall short. At most, as Otto points out, it may be possible to evoke the human psychological reaction to the experience by means of analogy, calling upon the suggestive power of ordinary worldly experiences, the response to which in some sense resembles or leads toward the response to the Numinous, and which thus may serve as ideograms or metaphors for it.

The Religious Metaphor

Such metaphors, since they constitute the only means of communicating the experience of the Numinous, occupy a central place in religious teaching and thought. They form a bridge between direct and mediate experience, between the religious founders and leaders and their followers; and they furnish a common bond of understanding between worshipers, and are the means by which religious content and forms are handed down from one generation to the next. In the metaphors, therefore, all that is shared by the worshipers of an individual culture or cultural period in their common response to the Numinous is summed and crystallized, and in the summation what is specific and characteristic

3

in the response will stand out. For in its choice of central metaphor a culture or cultural period necessarily reveals more clearly than anywhere else what it considers essential in the numinous experience and wants to recapture and transmit, the primary meaning on which it builds, which underlies and determines the total character of its response, the total character of its religion.

For the study of religions the central metaphors are thus of basic importance and our present inquiry, accordingly, will focus specifically on the major religious metaphors of the ancient Mesopotamians, seeking to understand and evaluate them and to trace their development from period to period as new metaphors were found and joined to existing ones. In concentrating attention on the religious metaphors it will be well, however, to bear constantly in mind their double nature as pointing beyond themselves to things not of this world, and yet being and remaining very much of the world, wholly human and culturally conditioned. Neither of these aspects can be overweighted without danger of the metaphor being credited with either too much or too little.

Suggestiveness

It is easy, for example, to think the religious metaphor far more representative than it in fact is and can be, however widespread and dominant it may seem. In attempting to interpret it, one must seek to bring out as fully as possible its powers to suggest and recall the Numinous. But such optimal suggestiveness can clearly not be assumed to have been the general invariable effect of the metaphor in ancient times. Then, as now, people's responsiveness will in fact have varied from moment to moment, and from one person to the next; moments of great religious openness and sensitivity will have alternated with moments when the soul was closed in secular or even profane moods. Then as now one person will have differed very markedly from another in religious sensitivity and understanding. Also, cultural attitudes change, and what to one generation is fresh and powerful may to another seem old and trite. All of this variety in the response must be allowed for, much as a history of literature tacitly allows that groundlings and pedants of all periods will have missed a good many of the values the historian seeks to bring out. For as the historian of literature deals only, or primarily, with the high literary achievements of a period, so the task of the historian of religion must be to present evidence of the highest religious achievement in the data with which he is concerned and to seek to convey all it contains of depths and insights. And as the historian of literature is guided throughout by considerations of literary merit, so the historian of religion will be guided by considerations of religious merits. He must seek in his materials what best and most truly shows awareness of the Numinous, what is, in fact, their specifically religious achievement.

Literalness

As it is easy to overrate the suggestive powers of religious metaphor and assume it to be more generally representative of its period and culture than could actually have been the case, so it is equally easy to overweight the human nature of the religious metaphor and forget that its purpose is to point beyond itself and the world from which it was taken. In a way such a tilt is invited by the necessity to explicate the literal meaning of the metaphor, its character and role in life, and the value-structures adhering to it, before one can grasp its powers as a metaphor for the Numinous. But such attention to literalness, to human purposes and values, may create a sense that all has been explained and is understood, that that is all there is to it.

And that, in fact, is so — on the literal level. But the whole purpose of the metaphor is a leap from that level, and a religious metaphor is not truly understood until it is experienced as a means of suggesting the Numinous.

What is asked for, then, is a degree of openness and religious sensitivity that will make such a leap, such an experience of the metaphor as religious metaphor, possible. As only literary judgment can guide one to what is authentic and genuine in literature, so religious judgment must be the guide to the authenticity of religious data in suggesting the Numinous. Not only must it be the guide to authenticity but also to the degree of understanding a given metaphor is able to suggest. For metaphors differ greatly in what they attempt and in how they are aimed. Their human, often all too human, character is apt to limit them to that narrow aspect of the Numinous that answers human needs or fears: for economic well-being, for security, for freedom from guilt. But this does not rule out their potential as vehicles of true religious response, as will be clear if we compare prayers such as: "give us this day our daily bread," "deliver us from evil," and "forgive us our trespasses." In fact, man's recognition of his utter dependence upon power not of this world, a profound aspect of his response to the Numinous, may well in these forms have found its true religious expression as transcendent hope and trust. Thus, again, openness to a potential may be of the essential.

"Mesopotamian"

Immanence

Moving from a general consideration of the term *religion* to the qualification *Mesopotamian* and asking what in ancient Mesopotamian religion seems specifically Mesopotamian, one cannot but note a tendency to experience the Numinous as immanent in some specific feature of the confrontation, rather than as all transcendent. The ancient Mesopotamian, it would seem, saw numinous power as a revelation of indwelling spirit, as power at the center of something that caused it to be and thrive and flourish.

We may turn for contrast to the world of the Old Testament, which sees the Numinous as transcendent, and consider the experience of Moses with the burning bush as it is told in Exodus 3 : 1–5:

> Now Moses kept the flock of Jethro his father-in-law, the priest of Midian: and he led the flock to the backside of the desert, and came to the mountain of God, even to Horeb. And the angel of the Lord appeared unto him in a flame of fire out of the midst of a bush: and he looked, and behold, the bush was not consumed. And Moses said, I will now turn aside, and see this great sight, why the bush is not burnt. And when the Lord saw that he turned aside to see, God called unto him out of the midst of the bush, and said, Moses, Moses, and he said, Here am I. And he said, Draw not nigh hither: put off thy shoes from off thy feet, for the place whereon thou standest is holy ground. Moreover he said, I am the God of thy father, the God of Abraham, the God of Isaac, and the God of Jacob. And Moses hid his face; for he was afraid to look upon God.

The story makes it clear that God is totally distinct from the bush out of which he chose to speak to Moses. God happened, as it were, to sojourn there; but he is altogether transcendent, and there is nothing but a purely situational, ephemeral, relation with the bush.

An ancient Mesopotamian would have experienced such a confrontation very differently. He too would have seen and heard numinous power, but power of, not just in, the bush, power at the center of its being, the vital force causing it to be and making it thrive and flourish. He would have experienced the Numinous as immanent.

Name and Form

Because of this characteristic manner of experiencing the Numinous both the name and the external form given to encountered numinous power tended in earliest Mesopotamia to be simply the name and the form of the phenomenon in which the power seemed to reveal itself.

Whereas the power speaking to Moses in the desert disassociates itself from the bush, and identifies itself as the god of Moses' fathers, numinous power speaking to the Mesopotamian Enkidu in the Gilgamesh Epic[2] does not choose to disassociate itself from its locus and so needs no introduction. The Gilgamesh Epic simply states: "The sun god heard the word of his mouth; from afar, from the midst of heaven, he kept calling out to him." The power is here seen as immanent in the visible sun, is what animates it and motivates it, is the god who informs it.

The Gilgamesh Epic is written in Akkadian and the word both for sun and for the numinous power in the sun is *šamšum*. Similarly, in Sumerian the corresponding word u t u denotes the visible sun as well as the invisible power in it, the sun god. The Sumerian word a n denotes the sky, the visible blue dome overhead, which turns black and full of stars that make their way across it at night. It is also, however, the name of the numinous power in the sky, its power and its will to be, the sky god. The word n a n n a is both the word for "moon" and the name of the moon god; and e z i n u, the grain goddess, is the grain when the farmer drops it in the furrow, just as she is the green stalks "standing in the furrow like a lovely young girl."

To some extent, of course, the form given to numinous encounter may adjust to the content revealed in it. It may be abbreviated to a single salient feature, as when Inanna, the numinous power in the storehouse, assumes the form of the characteristic gatepost emblem of the storehouse, rather than the storehouse as a whole. Sometimes the form-giving imagination reads details and meaning into a form beyond what is given in simple observation: the numinous power in the thunderstorm, Imdugud, developed from the dark thundercloud into an enormous black eagle floating on outstretched wings; but since the mighty roar of the thunder could not well be imagined as issuing from other than a lion's maw, this bird was in time given a lion's head.

Somewhat similarly the god Ningishzida, "Lord of the good tree," who represented the numinous power in trees to draw nourishment and to grow, had as his basic form that of the tree's trunk and roots; however, the winding roots, embodiments of living supernatural power, free themselves from the trunk and become live serpents entwined around it.

At times such form-giving imagination does not stop at a single interpretation but rings the changes on a basic meaningful form in a whole series of variations, each expressing the underlying numinous content in a different way. As an example we may quote a section of a hymn to the moon god, Nanna,[3] which celebrates the god as source and provider of fertility and plenty in the universe. The hymn as such is quite late, but it retains or reflects very early attitudes. The god's basic shape, that of the new moon, is allowed to call up a whole series of suggestive variant images, all expressive of its power to wax, to produce and yield. We quote the section as a whole before discussing its images one by one:

> Father Nanna, lord, conspicuously crowned,
>   prince of the gods,
> Father Nanna, grandly perfect in majesty,
>   prince of the gods;
> Father Nanna (measuredly) proceeding in noble raiment,
>   prince of the gods;
> fierce young bull, thick of horns, perfect of limbs,
>   with lapis lazuli beard, full of beauty;

fruit, created of itself, grown to full size,
   good to look at, with whose beauty one is never sated;
womb, giving birth to all, who has settled down
   in a holy abode;
merciful forgiving father, who holds in his hand
   the life of all the land;
Lord! — (the compass of) your divine providence,
   (vast) as the far-off heavens, the wide sea,
   is awesome (to behold).

The golden horns of the waxing moon are here first seen by the
worshiper as the horns of a horned crown, emblem of authority, and so fill
out to the image of a ruler, a "lord" or e n, a charismatic leader magically
responsible for producing fertility and plenty for his subjects. The image
is held in the two following lines, which contemplate the majestic progression of the moon across the heavens:

Father Nanna, lord, conspicuously crowned,
   prince of the gods;
Father Nanna, grandly perfect in majesty,
   prince of the gods;
Father Nanna, (measuredly) proceeding in noble raiment,
   prince of the gods.

Then the image changes: the horns become bull's horns and call up the
image of a young bull, embodiment of power to engender, create new life,
and multiply the herd:

fierce young bull, thick of horns, perfect of limbs,
   with lapis lazuli beard, full of beauty.

A new image, emphasizing that the moon is in the process of waxing,
shifts to that of a fruit growing to ripeness, embodiment of the power in
the orchards to grow, ripen, and yield a rich harvest:

fruit, created of itself, grown to full size,
   good to look at, with whose beauty one is never sated;

The image of the fruit yields to yet another way to express the filling out
of the moon, the swelling body of a pregnant woman; and the moon god
becomes a womb, pregnant, producing, lifegiving — and an available
power, near, part of the community, having chosen to live with man and
have his house, his temple, among men:

womb, giving birth to all, who has settled down
   in a holy abode.

With this the poet returns to the human form, first celebrating the god
as a kind father, responsible for the life of his family; and then again the

"lord" used in the first line, a lord of all, whose responsibilities for the welfare of man are so vast that they fill one with profoundest awe:

> merciful forgiving father, who holds in his hand
>   the life of all the land;
> Lord! — (the compass of) your divine providence,
>   (vast) as the far-off heavens, the wide sea,
>   is awesome (to behold).

The situationally determined, nonhuman, forms that we have observed here are all original or old forms or — as in the hymn to the moon god — survivals into a later age. They appear to have had their floruit in Protoliterate or earlier periods, that is to say, during the fourth millennium B.C. Even then, however, the human form would seem to have been an alternative, or perhaps a competing, possibility; and with the beginning of the third millennium, from Early Dynastic onward, the human form came to dominate almost completely, leaving to the older forms the somewhat ambiguous role of divine "emblems" only.

This victory of the human over the nonhuman forms was won slowly and with difficulty. To the latest time the older forms retain a curious vitality, seeming to lurk under the human exterior ready to break through it to reveal the true essence of the divine power and will: rays pierce through the human body of the sun god from within, ears of grain grow out through the human shoulders of the grain goddess, serpent heads through those of Ningishzida, and when Gudea sees the god Ningirsu in a dream the god still has the wings of his old form, the thunderbird Imdugud. He retains those wings in Assyria in representations carved as late as the first millennium.

Also — and importantly — on crucial occasions it was in their old forms as "emblems" that the gods elected to be present to follow and guide the army to victory, or to be brought out to witness and guarantee the making of oaths.

Intransitiveness

As the tendency to see numinous power as immanent led the ancient Mesopotamian to name that power and attribute form to it in terms of the phenomenon, so it also determined and narrowed his ideas of that power's function. The numinous power appeared fulfilled in the specific situation or phenomenon and did not reach out beyond it. The deity made no demands, did not act, merely came into being, was, and ceased being in and with its characteristic phenomenon. Elsewhere we have called this immanence in, and being bound within, a phenomenon "intransitiveness." It is characteristic for all older figures and strata in the Mesopotamian pantheon and contrasts strikingly with the younger "transitive" ruler gods, who, though they too may be the power in a specific phenomenon, have interests, activity, and will beyond it.

We may illustrate the "intransitive" character of the older divine figures by the figure of Dumuzi, the power for fertility and new life in the spring. In all we know of Dumuzi from hymns, laments, myth, and ritual, there is no instance in which the god acts, orders, or demands; he merely is or is not. He comes into being in the spring, is celebrated as bridegroom in the cult rite of the sacred marriage, is killed by powers of the netherworld, and is lamented and searched for by his mother and young widow; any action, any achievement, any demands by the god are absent altogether.

Another example is Nidaba, the goddess of the grasses, of grain, and of reeds, who is what the grain and the reeds are and serve for, who is where they are and is not where they are not, who acts not and wills not beyond them. This section from a hymn to her[4] describes her well:

> Nidaba, (re)builder of abandoned (dwelling) places,
>   (re)establisher of abandoned [shrines?],
> who restores fallen (images of) gods,
>   the able housekeeper of An,
> lady, whose approaching a place sets creation going.
> Nidaba, you are having (people) wash (their) heads
>   and hands (for you), you are treated right.
> Milady, you are the one who sets (her) hand
>   to the well-made (writing) tablets of the land,
> who counsels where the reed-stylus is (wielded).
> You are the one who makes Enlil's heart happy,
> milady, you are the food of (his temple) Ekur,
> you are the drink of (the temple) Eanna,
> you are the joy of Ekur, Enlil's temple,
> (as for) the great gods, you are the life's breath
>   of their father.
> O milady, you are firmly established by Enlil,
> Nidaba, you are the beer — far more than bread,
> Nidaba, you are the firmer of the foundations
>   of kingship.
> . . . .
> Nidaba, where you are not heaped up
> people are not settled, cities not built,
> no palace is built, no king is raised to office,
> the gods' handwashings (before offerings)
>   are not performed correctly
> Nidaba, where you are not near
> no cattle pen is built, no sheepfold constructed,
> and the shepherd soothes not the heart with his reed pipe.

As these lines make clear Nidaba is in the reeds, essential for rebuilding houses and cities. She is in the reed when it is fashioned into a reed stylus, making it work well and fulfill its purpose; and she is in the grains, providing sustenance for the temples, and bread — the staff of life — for the gods. With abundance and plenty she insures a stable reign for kings. The building of cities and palaces, stability of rule, offerings for the gods, construction of pen and fold — even the simple pleasure of the shepherd's pipe — depend on her presence, her will and power to cause reed and grain to be, thrive, and flourish in their full potential.

For contrast, an example of the later "transitive" aspect of deity in Mesopotamia may be quoted, a few stanzas of a hymn to the god Enlil[5] which also emphasizes the contributions which the god makes to human life. However, with Enlil these contributions are not merely by being, as with Nidaba, they are a consequence of the god's planning and ordering, his rule:

> Enlil, by your skillful planning in intricate designs —
>   their inner workings a blur of threads
>   not to be unraveled,
> thread entwined in thread, not to be traced by the eye —
> you excel in your task of divine providence.
>
> You are your own counselor, adviser, and manager,
> who (else) could comprehend what you do?
>
> Your tasks are tasks that are not apparent,
> your guise (that of) a god, invisible to the eye.
>
> You are lord: An, and king: Enlil, (in one),
> judge and decision maker for (both) heaven and earth,
> you know no rescinder of your great decrees,
>   they being as respected as is An. . . .

As Enlil here skillfully governs the universe, so his son Ninurta in the great epic telling of his deeds, L u g a l - e u d m e - l á m - b i n i r - ǧ á l, sails off to war in his boat, wages battle, and afterward judges his defeated enemies; while on the human plane, under his other name Ningirsu, he is party to a boundary treaty between his city of Girsu and the neighboring Umma, a treaty which he later finds necessary to defend with weapon in hand against the encroachments of Umma.

Plurality and Choice

The characteristic Mesopotamian boundness to the externals of situations in which the Numinous was encountered not only tended to circumscribe it and give it intransitive character, it also led to differentiation. The Numinous was the indwelling spirit and power of many phenomena and situations and it differed with each of them. Thus ancient Mesopotamian religion was conditioned to a pluralistic view, to polytheism, and to the multitude of gods and divine aspects that it recognized.

Plurality of numinous power requires the ability to distinguish, evaluate, and choose; and here also the ancient Mesopotamian leaned heavily on external situation. Was the power and will which he met in a numinous encounter a power and will for good or for evil? A power to be sought or a power to be avoided? There is in the experience of the Numinous both dread and fascination, and on the more primitive levels dread tends to predominate.

The word *god* in Akkadian (*ilu*) associates itself easily with the notion of paralyzing fear, as when Gilgamesh in the Gilgamesh Epic wakes and says to his friend Enkidu:

> My friend, you did not call me,
>   why, then, am I awake?
> You did not touch me, why am I startled?
> No god went by, why are my muscles paralyzed?[6]

Only understanding the total situation could reveal what the feeling of eeriness and dread in the presence of the wholly other boded and how one ought best respond to it.

The Mesopotamian concept of the personal god, for instance — a concept with which we shall deal in more detail later on — would seem to have its origins in that sense of supernatural power which often accompanies "uncannily" good luck. Such a power, once encountered, would obviously be sought again by the individual who had benefited from it and would thereafter command his particular allegiance and worship.

But it is not only great good luck that can be felt as uncanny and unnatural. The sudden realization of having come to harm — for instance the onset of illness and pain — may carry the sense of supernatural intervention. Such negative powers were "evil," a god or demon to be avoided and shunned, one against whom man defended himself by incantations and other magical means; no allegiance was invited, no allegiance was offered, no cult developed; the power took its place among the innumerable other destructive numinous powers — demons, evil gods, evil spirits — who were inimical to man:

> They are gloomy, their shadow dark,
>   no light is in their bodies,
> ever they slink along covertly,
>   walk not upright,
> from their claws drips bitter gall,
>   their footprints are (full of) evil venom.[7]

They have nothing in common with us, nothing to which one could appeal, they are purely a dread, unreachable, wholly other:

> Neither males are they, nor females,
> they are winds ever sweeping along,

they have not wives, engender not children,
know not how to show mercy,
hear not prayer and supplication.[8]

As indicated by their various names, these demons are forms given to the numinous power experienced in sudden illness and pain or in other terrifying situations. Sometimes they are described as winds and storms, sometimes they are ghosts who cannot find rest in the netherworld, sometimes they have the names of specific illnesses. They are supernatural wills and powers who will evil things into being:

The shivers and chills (of death)
  that fritter the sum of things,
  spawn of the god of heaven,
  spawned on an evil spirit,
the death warrants, beloved sons of the storm god,
  born of the queen of the netherworld,
who were torn out of heaven and hurled from the earth as castoffs,
  are creatures of hell, all.

Up above they roar, down below they cheep,
they are the bitter venom of the gods,
they are the great storms let loose from heaven,
they are the owl (of ill omen) that hoots in the town,
spawn spawned by the god of heaven, sons born by earth
  are they.

Over high roofs, over broad roofs like a floodwave
  they surge,
from house to house they climb over,
Doors do not hold them, locks do not restrain them,
through the doors they glide like snakes,
through the hinge boxes they blow like wind.

From the man's embrace they lead off the wife,
from the man's knee they make the child get up,
and the youth they fetch out of the house of his in-laws,
they are the numbness, the daze,
  that tread on the heels of man.[9]

A Local Habitation

We have dealt so far with the ancient Mesopotamian's response to the Numinous in thought and have seen how the set toward immanence conditioned his ideas of name, form, direction of will, and diversity of power. With the more total reactions of evaluating a numinous situation, however, we touch on response also in action. Response to a power considered bad was to defend against it and to ward it off; to one considered good it was to cleave to it and try to insure its presence. In this response, too, the ancient Mesopotamian was governed by the conviction that numinous power was immanent, was bound up with the phemone-mon in that it lay at its very center and caused it to be. Bringing the phenomenon into being was therefore also and necessarily bringing into being its power and will; and the creation of the outer form, the external habitation, was inviting — or magically enforcing — the presence of the power within.

Prominent among such efforts at insuring the presence of numinous power, of providing it with habitation, are the cult drama, the fashioning of appropriate divine images, the religious literature, and the building of temples. We may consider them in order.

The purpose and meaning of the ancient Mesopotamian cult dramas was first clarified by Pallis, who in his study of the Akîtu festival[10] in Babylon compares it with similar dramas elsewhere: in the rite, man — in the person of the leader of the community — represents the god, literally re-presents him, for by acting the god, by presenting his external form, he becomes the god, the form fills with its content, and as the god he performs the acts that fulfill the divine will with all its beneficent results for the community.

The three most important cult dramas known to us were the "sacred marriage" which bound the powers of fertility to the divine representative of the community storehouse, the yearly lamentations for the death and disappearance of the power of fertility at the onset of the dry season, and the battle drama in which a primeval contest for world order against the forces of chaos was refought and rewon. To these three may be added a variety of travel rites in which one deity journeyed to visit another at a different locality for ritual purification, investment, or reinvestment with powers and benefits.

Just as the cult drama sought to bring about the god's presence through ritual representations of him, so the fashioning of images of the god sought and achieved his lasting presence. We have evidence of such cult images from the Uruk period down to the latest times of ancient Mesopotamian civilization. The earliest of these images would seem to have shown the gods in their nonhuman forms; later on images in human form became prevalent and the older nonhuman images were considered mere "emblems" though, as we have mentioned, they were still the form under which the gods accompanied the army in battle and the form under which they validated oaths.

Besides representations in the round — the proper cult images — there would seem to have been, especially in older times, magico-religious representations in relief and in wall painting. These representations, which have as their subject important cult rites, appear to have served — much like the cult image proper — to achieve lasting presence of the cult rite, and thus of the god and his blessing actualized in it. As examples of such representations we may mention the famous Uruk Vase with its relief showing the rite of the sacred marriage and various seal impressions with the same cultic motifs. As Frankfort observed, the motifs found on the seal cylinders are monumental motifs, unsuitable to the small scale of the seals. It may be that they were copied from wall paintings now lost.

Poetry was another means of invoking the presence of the powers, for word pictures, too, created the corresponding reality. This is clear in the incantations, which often used the form of command, to exhort evil forces to go away. But mere statement was often enough. A sufferer might declare that he was heaven and earth, and through that statement of identity become filled with the purity of heaven and earth and impervious to evil. An impotent man might call himself a buck or some other animal of sexual prowess and thus be imbued with potency. Materials such as water or salt that were used in magic rituals were blessed. By enumerating their pure origins and sacred powers their powers were, so to speak, recharged to their highest peak of magical efficacy.

The creative power of the word underlies all Mesopotamian religious literature. It may be assumed to have been most clearly and strongly felt in earliest time, and it probably varied with use in rituals, for instructive purposes, or for entertainment. The older religious literature shows a basic division into works of praise (z a g - m í = *tanittum*) and works of lament, each having its own specialist performer, the "singer" (n a r = *narum*) for the literature of praise, the "elegist" or "lamentation-priest" (g a l a − *halûm*) for the songs of lament.

The literature of praise included hymns to gods, temples, or deified human rulers, as well as myths, epics, and disputations. It activated power already present or at least near at hand. The literature of lament, on the other hand, was directed to powers lost, difficult or impossible to regain: the dead young god of fertility in the netherworld, the destroyed temple, the dead king or ordinary human. In the lament the vividness of recall and longing was an actual magical reconstitution, an attempt to draw back the lost god or temple by recreating in the mind the lost happy presence. Progressively, however, under the influence of sociomorphism, the aspect of magical forcing seems to have lessened, yielding in the classical periods to petition. In its new aspect praise literature was primarily aimed at blessing the ruling powers and thereby making them favorably inclined to human petition. The laments were aimed at influencing and swaying the divine heart by reminding the god of past happiness, rather than by magically recreating that past.

Lastly the efforts to achieve and insure divine presence took the form of building temples. The Sumerian and Akkadian words for temple are the usual words for house (é = *bîtum*). They imply between the divine owner and his house not only all the emotional closeness of a human owner and his home, but beyond that a closeness of essence, of being, amounting more nearly to embodiment than to habitation. In some sense the temple, no less than the ritual drama and the cult image, was a representation of the form of the power that was meant to fill it.

Like a human dwelling, the temple was the place where the owner could be found. Its presence among the houses of the human community was visible assurance that the god was present and available, that he — as the hymn to the moon god expressed it — "among the (creatures) in whom is breath of life has settled down in a holy abode."

Like a human dwelling, too, the temple called for a staff, for organization and management. The daily service was that of other great houses: the priests were house servants presenting the god with his daily meals, changing his clothes, cleaning his chambers, making his bed for him. Outside were lands belonging to the god and cultivated by other human servants, the god's retainers. Thus the god — because the temple was his home — was not only near and approachable, he was involved with the fortunes of the community and committed to maintaining it.

Unlike a human dwelling, though, the temple was sacred. The ancient Mesopotamian temple was profoundly awesome, sharing in the tremenum of the Numinous. It carried "awesome aura" (n í) and awesome "nimbus" (m e - l á m). The temple of Nusku in Nippur was a "temple laden with great awesome aura and angry nimbus."[11] Also in Nippur was Enlil's temple: "Ekur, the blue house, your (Enlil's) great seat, laden with awesomeness, its beams of awe and glory reach toward heaven, its shadow lies upon all lands."[12] As it participated in the tremendum of the Numinous, so also in its fascinosum and its mysterium. The temple was "covered with loveliness"[13] but set apart from secular activities; it was a "secret house,"[14] its holy of holy, the god's private apartment shrouded in darkness, was the "dark room" (i t i m a = kiṣṣum) which "knows not daylight,"[15] its ritual vessels "no eye is to see."[16]

To this general sacred character of the temple comes a specific closeness of essence with the power inhabiting it, which made every temple different from another. This distinction may take the form of an acknowledgment of the nature, function, or mood of the power within. The temple of a god in bovine form is seen as his "pen."[17] The temple É - b a b b a r, "house rising sun," of the god Ningirsu is seen as the place where Ningirsu rises like the sun god and judges.[18] Ningirsu's temple É - h u š, "terrifying house," is the place where the god is to be found when he is angry.[19] Sometimes it is difficult to say whether the function is more a function of the temple or one of the god. When Naramsîn destroyed Ekur in Nippur it had immediate consequences for all the country: as the temple bowed its neck to earth like a felled young warrior, so did all lands; as grain was cut in its "Gate-in-Which-Grain-Must-Not-Be-Cut" grain was cut off from the hands of the country; as hoes struck into its "Gate-of-Peace" the peace of all lands became enmity.[20]

The identity may even be total, making of the temple — as we have suggested — more nearly an embodiment than a habitation. Thus the temple of the god Ningirsu in Girsu was known as É - n i n n u, "the house Ninnu." Ninnu (perhaps "Lord Universe") is but another name for the god. The identity of temple and god is further elaborated in the full form of the temple name: É - N i n n u - ^{d}I m - d u g u d^{mušen}- b a r$_6$ - b a r$_6$, "É-ninnu, the flashing thunderbird," or ^{d}I m - d u g u d^{mušen}- a n - š á r - r a - s i g$_4$ - g i$_4$ - g i$_4$, the "thunderbird roaring on the horizon," in which the temple is identified with the original nonhuman form of the god, the thunderbird Imdugud.[21]

In view of this identity of god and temple it is not surprising that the ruler Gudea, before attempting a rebuilding, realized that he needed an authoritative revelation by the god of his innermost nature before he could know what was "the proper thing" in shaping the bricks, or that — when he was granted such a revelation — he impressed the god's thunderbird form on the bricks.

There are a number of other instances of identity between temple and god expressed in their names: É - k u r, "house mountain (kur)," of the god Enlil, also called K u r - g a l, "great mountain (k u r)"; É - b a b b a r, "house rising sun (b a b b a r)," of the sun god Utu, also called B a b b a r, "rising sun"; É - ğ i š - n u$_5$ - ğ á l, "house causing light (ğ i š - n u$_5$)" of the moon god; É - a n - n a, "house of the date clusters (a n n a)," of (N) i n a n n a (k), "Lady of the date clusters (a n n a)"; É - m e s - l a m, "house thriving m ē s u tree (m e s - l a m)," of Nergal, also known as M e s l a m t a e a, "He who issues forth from the thriving m ē s u tree (m e s - l a m)"; and so forth.

"Ancient"

The word *ancient* raises the question of distance in time, absolutely, in terms of the thousands of years that separate us from the things we deal with here, and relatively, in terms of the long span of time that may separate one group or aspect of our data from another.

Ancient to Us

Considering first the absolute distance in time from the end of ancient Mesopotamian civilization shortly before the beginning of our era to the present, it may be noted that it is not only a distance but a clean break. No living cultural tradition connects us with our subject, spans the gap between the ancients and us. We are almost entirely dependent on such archaeological and inscriptional data as have been recovered and upon our own contemporary attempts at interpreting them. These data are, unfortunately, incomplete and somewhat haphazard as sources for the total culture to which they testify; and the languages of the inscriptional materials are still far from being fully understood. The concepts denoted by their words and the interrelations of these concepts, moreover, are not infrequently incongruent with, or accented differently from, anything in our present-day culture and outlook, so that misunderstanding and even failure to comprehend altogether are constant stumbling blocks.

Formidable as our difficulties are, they are no cause for dismay or for ceasing our efforts to understand. If they were, then earlier generations of scholars, the generation of discoverers and decipherers above all, should have been the ones to give up, for they had far greater difficulties and far less help than we have. Actually, the very realization that difficulties exist often goes a long way toward overcoming them by forcing upon us the necessity of other ways of thinking and evaluating than those to which we are accustomed. We may become alert to the dangers of too easy generalization, may doubt accepted translations and search for more adequate meanings of a word. We have dealt in the preceding sections with data deriving their inner coherence and meaning from an unexpected, and to us unusual, view of form and content as belonging so closely together as to imply, almost to compel, each other. We saw this when the characteristic inner form of a power broke through its human guise, when it imposed itself on its temple, when the imitation or representing of a power in the cult rite by a human actor actually made the power present. The clue to understanding in these cases lies in a disinterestedness of the ancients to distinguish as we feel the need to distinguish. To them things are — and so to speak have to be — what they seem, and they evoke immediate, unanalyzed total reactions accordingly. But once this is realized the way is also open for us to recognize occasional similarly unanalyzed total reactions in ourselves. Were anybody, for instance, to attempt to deface the photograph of someone we loved we could hardly fail to respond with resentment and anger — not so much because of what he was actually doing, destroying a piece of cardboard, but out of a vague but hot and angry sense that an attack on the picture was in some sense an attack on the one it represented. In similar ways under emotional pressure the sense of inherent oneness of specific form and specific content may have shaped ancient thinking. If a man in a state of religious transport momentarily sensed a temple as one with the cosmic thunderbird roaring on the horizon, he would be likely to feel this was a more profound insight, more true, than his everyday experience of it as just a sacred structure.

Ultimately, the coherence of our data must be our guide. True meanings illuminate their contexts and these contexts support each other effortlessly. False meanings jar, stop, and lead no further. It is by attention to such arrests, by not forcing, but by being open to and seeking other possibilities, that one may eventually understand — recreate, as it were — the world of the ancients. For the world of the ancients, was, as all cultures, an autonomous system of delicately interrelated meanings in which every part was dependent on every other part and ultimately meaningful only in the total context of meaning of the system to which it belonged. Understanding it is not unlike entering the world of poetry, and E. M. Forster puts that wittily and well when he says: "Before we begin to read the *Ancient Mariner* we know that the Polar Seas are not inhabited by spirits, and that if a man shoots an albatross he is not a criminal but a sportsman, and that if he stuffs the albatross afterwards he becomes a naturalist also. All this is common knowledge, but when we are reading the *Ancient Mariner* or remembering it intensely, common knowledge disappears and uncommon knowledge takes its place. We have entered a universe that only answers to its own laws, supports itself, internally coheres, and has a new standard of truth."[22]

Ancient to Them

Besides considering the distance in time between us and our data we must take account also of the distance that often separates one group or aspect of these data from another. For our data come from a cultural continuum of well over four thousand years and cultures continually change and develop from period to period, often in very intricate and complex ways. It is not only that older elements disappear and are replaced with new; often the old elements are retained and exist side by side with the new; and often too, these older elements, though seemingly unchanged, have in fact come to mean something quite different, have been reinterpreted to fit into a new system of meanings. To illustrate with an example from our own Western cultural tradition, the story of Adam and Eve is retained unchanged since Old Testament times, but the simple folktale of Genesis has been progressively reinterpreted by St. Paul, by St. Augustine, and by Milton (not to speak of modern theologians) so that it has come to carry a wealth of theological and anthropological meaning relating to the essential nature of man, very different from what the story could possibly have meant in its earlier simple cultural setting.

In approaching ancient Mesopotamian materials, it should be kept in mind that the older elements of culture survive, and that they may be reinterpreted over and over; for we find among these materials religious documents, myths, epics, laments, which have been handed down almost unchanged in copy after copy for as much as a thousand or fifteen hundred years, and it is often difficult to say with certainty whether a document originated in the period from which it seems to come, or whether it was in fact from earlier times.

To present a coherent picture on the basis of materials in which meanings and reinterpretations of many periods are thus telescoped is not easy; unless we can reconstruct — at least in outline — the development they have gone through, and come to see them within a perspective of time.

To achieve such a perspective, and obtain a reasonably comprehensive framework, we have made use of a combined typological and historical approach. One can recognize three major religious metaphors in which the gods were seen and presented:

1. As élan vital, the spiritual cores in phenomena, indwelling wills and powers for them to be and thrive in their characteristic forms and manners. The phenomena are mostly natural phenomena of primary economic importance.
2. As rulers.
3. As parents, caring about the individual worshiper and his conduct as parents do about children.

Of these three different ways of viewing and presenting the gods, the first one would appear to be the oldest and most original; for it is the one which is never absent. Characteristic boundness to some phenomenon — what we have termed "intransitiveness" — is a basic aspect in all Mesopotamian gods. That this way of viewing the divine is in fact old is also indicated by our earliest evidence, for in sources from the Protoliterate period and earlier, the gods are still shown largely in nonhuman forms, forms linking them closely with the specific phenomenon of which they are the indwelling power (the lionheaded bird shape for Ningirsu/ Ninurta of the roaring thundercloud, the gate emblem for Inanna, numen of the storehouse), or they hold in their hands the emblem of the phenomenon in which they are the power, as when Dumuzi, god of fertility and crops, is pictured carrying an ear of barley.

The second metaphor, that of the ruler, appears to be later. It is less common, and where it occurs it is intimately bound up with social and political forms of relatively advanced character. Our earliest evidence for this metaphor dates from the outgoing Protoliterate, the so-called Jemdet Nasr period, and the following Early Dynastic period when divine names composed with e n "lord" begin to appear: E n - l í l, "Lord Wind" and E n - k i (. a k), "Lord of the soil." The rather elaborate political mythology associated with this metaphor with its general assembly of gods meeting in Nippur would appear to reflect historical political conditions not earlier than Early Dynastic. Nippur itself seems to date as a major site from just before Early Dynastic I and so the political mythology connected

with it is most likely to be placed in the period of transition from Early
Dynastic I to II.

The third metaphor, that of the parent, centers in the penitential
psalms, a genre not much in evidence before Old Babylonian times; after
which time it spreads and takes hold more and more in our materials.

Applying this general chronological framework, we can distinguish
three major aspects or phases of ancient Mesopotamian religion, each
phase roughly corresponding to, and characterizing, a millennium; each
reflecting the central hopes and fears of its times. In our presentation we
shall consider therefore:

1. An early phase representative of the fourth millennium B.C. and
centering on worship of powers in natural and other phenomena
essential for economic survival. The dying god, power of fertility and
plenty, is a typical figure.
2. A later phase, representative approximately of the third millennium
which adds the concept of the ruler and the hope of security against
enemies. This phase has as typical figures the great ruler gods of the
Nippur assembly.
3. Lastly, there is a phase representative of the second millennium B.C.
in which the fortunes of the individual increase in importance until they
rival those of communal economy and security. The typical figure is the
personal god.

In the latter half of the second millennium and in the following first
millennium a dark age closed down on Mesopotamia. The old framework
within which to understand the workings of the cosmos survived, but it
moved from the interplay of many divine wills to the willful whim of a
single despot. The major gods became national gods, identified with
narrow national political aspirations. There was a corresponding coarsen-
ing and barbarization of the idea of divinity, no new overarching concepts
arose, rather doubts and despair abounded. Witchcraft and sorcery were
suspected everywhere; demons and evil spirits threatened life unceas-
ingly. We will treat this period in an epilogue only for contrast, after
presenting the last great conceptions of an ordered cosmos: Enûma elish
and the slightly older Gilgamesh Epic with its moving treatment of the
question of life and death.

2

Fourth Millennium Metaphors. The Gods as Providers: Dying Gods of Fertility

The Uruk Vase, found by the German archaeological expedition to Uruk (modern Warka). It dates from the end of the fourth millennium B.C. and depicts the rite of the sacred marriage. At the top left, Amaushumgalanna, the god of the date palm, is shown approaching the gate of his bride at the head of a long retinue bearing his wedding gifts. Receiving and opening the gate to him is his bride, the goddess of the storehouse, Inanna. Behind her is the sanctuary in her temple with its altar and sacred furniture, including vases. Scholars believe the Uruk Vase may once have stood in that sanctuary.

The Dumuzi Cult as Representative

It would have been most satisfactory if we could have based our account of the oldest form of Mesopotamian religion solely on evidence from the fourth millennium B.C.

However, that is not possible. It is not only that contemporary evidence is scanty — some temple plans, a few representations of deities and rites on seals and on reliefs — or that it is spotty, coming from a few sites only and telling little about the country as a whole, it is rather that it fails in what one had most hoped for, it fails to be self-evident.

The contemporary evidence is, unfortunately, only understandable and recognizable as religious evidence, through what we know from later times. At most it can attest to the early roots of later traditional forms. For any general impression of what powers were worshiped in the country as a whole, and for any attempt to visualize the form of such worship in detail, we must turn to the more fully documented survivals and try to discern what is old and original in them. Our main criteria and our combined typological and historical approach we outlined in the preceding chapter.

Fortunately, we may turn with some degree of confidence to the chief deities of the oldest ancient Mesopotamian cities, for they, their temples, and their cult are likely to have their roots in the very founding of the settlements, as in Eridu where the Enki temple can be traced through rebuilding after rebuilding to the earliest beginnings.

The various city gods in whom the early settlers trusted appear to be powers in the basic economies characteristic of the region in which their cities were situated. Thus in the south we find a group of city gods closely related to marsh life and its primary economies, fishing and hunting: Enki, god of the fresh water and of vegetable and animal marsh life in Eridu in the west, and, in the east, Nanshe, goddess of fish; Dumuzi-abzu, the power to new life in the watery deep; and others in Nina and Kinirsha. Along the lower Euphrates deities of orchardmen alternate with deities of cowherders. There lie the cities of Ningishzida, "Lord of the good tree"; Ninazu, "The Lord knowing the waters"; and Damu, "the child," power in the sap that rises in trees and bushes in the spring. But here also are the bull god Ningublaga, city god of Kiabrig; the bull god and moon god Nanna in Ur; and, in Kullab, Ninsûna, "Lady of the wild cows," with her husband Lugalbanda. Farther north, in a half-circle around the central grassland of the *Edin* lie the cities of the sheepherders (Uruk, Bad-tibira, Umma, and Zabalam) with their chief deities, Dumuzi the shepherd and his bride Inanna. To the north and east lie cities of the farmers, Shurup-pak and Eresh, with grain goddesses like Ninlil, Ninshebargunu, and Nidaba; Nippur with Enlil, wind god and god of the hoe, and his son Ninurta, god of the thundershowers and of the plow. Under the local name of Ningirsu, Ninurta was worshiped also in Girsu to the southeast.

25

It is understandable that numinous experience in situations connected with basic life-sustaining activities would assume special significance and call for special allegiance. Thus the earliest form of Mesopotamian religion was worship of powers of fertility and yield, of the powers in nature ensuring human survival.

To try to visualize what such a fertility cult would have been like we must turn, as has been mentioned, to materials bearing on specific myths and rituals which on external and internal evidence can be assumed to hark back to early times. Those bearing on the cult of the dying god Dumuzi recommend themselves. The great age of this cult is attested by the Uruk Vase of the outgoing fourth millennium B.C., which depicts the central event of the rite of the sacred marriage. Its reliefs show the bride, Inanna, meeting her groom, Dumuzi, at the gate to admit him and his servants who carry the bridal gifts, an endless abundance of edibles of all kinds. In addition to this evidence, the Dumuzi cult shows itself as early through its old-fashioned "intransitive" conception of the god. He is little more than the élan vital of new life in nature, vegetable and animal, a will and power in it that brings it about. Lastly, the Dumuzi cult is well documented in Sumerian literature so that a remarkably detailed and rounded picture can be drawn of the cult as it survived. For reasons of simplicity we shall present these materials as if they were a connected whole, beginning with the young god's courtship and wedding, moving on to his early death and the lament for him, and ending with the search for him leading to the netherworld. In actual fact this full pattern is not to be found in any single cult; rather the figure of the god tends on closer view to divide into different aspects, each with the power in a particular basic economy emphasized and each with its own characteristic segment of ritual events. We can distinguish the form of Dumuzi called Dumuzi-Amaushumgalanna, who appears to be the power in the date palm to produce new fruit. The name Amaushumgalanna means "the one great source of the date clusters" (a m a - u š u m . g a l - a n a (. a k)) and refers to the so-called heart of palm, the enormous bud which the palm tree sets each year. This is the lightest and happiest of all the forms of the god. The cult celebrates his sacred marriage only, not his loss in death — presumably because the date is easily storable and endures. His worship among the shepherds and cowherds has greater range. The shepherds know him as Dumuzi the Shepherd and he is considered son of Duttur, the personified ewe, while among the cowherds he is son of Ninsûna, the "Lady of the wild cows." The cult comprises both happy celebrations of the marriage of the god with Inanna (who originally, it seems, was the goddess of the communal storehouse) and bitter laments when he dies as the dry heat of summer yellows the pastures and lambing, calving, and milking come to an end. A few texts suggest the existence of still another form of the god which one might call "Dumuzi of the Grain," a form which sees the god as the power in the barley, particularly in the beer brewed from it, and which clearly belongs with the farmers. Lastly, there is the cult in which the god is worshiped under the name Damu, "the child." This form, which may originally have been independent of the Dumuzi cult, still preserves a good many distinctive traits. Damu, who seems to represent the power in the rising sap, appears to have had his original home among orchard growers on the lower Euphrates. He was visualized, not as a young man of marriageable age, but as a small child; where the figures around the other forms of Dumuzi are his bride, his mother, and his sister, only the latter two appear in the Damu cult. Also the rite of search for the dead god, which takes the mother and sister into the shadows of the netherworld, is special to this cult.

Courtship

Considering first the texts dealing with Dumuzi's courtship and wooing of young Inanna, we note at the outset that all of them appear to be purely literary in nature, not connected with any rituals, serving only the purpose, as far as one can see, of entertainment. They are lightweight stuff, popular ditties such as would be sung by women to while away the time at spinning or weaving, or perhaps as songs to dance to.

A first example, only partly preserved, might be called "The Sister's Message," for in it Dumuzi's sister, Geshtinanna, has exciting news to tell. She has just been with young Inanna (here as elsewhere called Baba), who confided to her as one girl to another how smitten she was with love for Dumuzi and how she now suffers all of love's pangs. Geshtinanna, with a teenager's sense for the dramatic, duly relates it all to her brother:[23]

> As I was strolling, as I was strolling,
> as I was strolling by the house
> my (dear) Inanna saw me.
> O (my) brother, what did she tell me,
>   and what more did she say to me?
> O (my) brother, (of) love, allure,
>   and sweetest of sweet things,
> my (dear) adorable Inanna on her part
>   disclosed things to me!
> When I was addressing myself to some errand
> she came across (you) my beloved man,
> and took to you and delighted in you
>   (at) first (glance).
> O (my) brother, she brought me into her house
> and had me lie down in the honey(-sweet softness)
>   of the bed;

and when my sweet darling had lain down
   next to my heart,
(we) chatting, one after the other,
   one after the other,
she, O my good-looking brother,
   wore herself out moaning to me,
and I was fetching (things) for her the while,
   as for someone (very) weak,
and a disposition to tremble, from the ground up —
   exceedingly much — befell her.
O my brother, smiting her hips (in anguish)
does my sweet darling pas the day.

Dumuzi is not slow to take the hint, but not wanting to be too obvious he pretends he has to go to the palace:

"Let me go! O my sister, let me go!
Please my beloved sister, let me go
   to the palace!"

Geshtinanna is not taken in, she can guess where he is headed, and waggishly imitating a pompous father she answers:

"To my paternal eye you are verily (still)
   a small child;
yonder, Baba may know (you for) a man,
   I shall let you go to her!"

and he is off.

   Another song,[24] which could be called "The Wiles of Women," assumes, we take it, that Dumuzi and Inanna have met and fallen in love the evening before. The day of the song the lovers have been separated — Dumuzi most likely has been working — and Inanna has whiled away the long hours with play and dancing, longing for the evening when Dumuzi is free, and hoping he will show up. He does so as she is on her way home:

I, a damsel, having whiled away the time
   since yesterday,
I, Inanna, having whiled away the time
   since yesterday,
having whiled away the time, having danced,
having sung ditties all day to evening,
he met me! He met me!
The lord, the peer of An met me.
The lord took my hand in his,
Ushumgalanna put his arm around my shoulders.
Where (are you taking me)? Wild bull,
   let me go, that I may go home!

> Peer of Enlil, let me go, that I may go home!
> What fib could I tell my mother?
> What fib could I tell Ningal?

Dumuzi, impetuously, thinks of nothing but lovemaking and takes her compliance for granted. Inanna thinks of marriage, and balks. She would love to go with him, she implies, but there is her mother: how could she ever get away with staying out late? Dumuzi, unaware of what goes on in her mind, takes the excuse at face value and shows how young he is by offering himself as an expert on stories girls tell to explain why they are late — Inanna must have smiled:

> Let me teach you, let me teach you,
> Inanna, let me teach you the fibs women (tell):
> "My girlfriend, she was strolling with me
>   in the square,
> to the playing of tambourine and recorder
>   she danced with me,
> our sad songs were sweet — she crooned to me —
> the joyous ones were sweet — and time went by!"
> With this as (your) fib confront your mother;
> (as for) us — O that we might disport ourselves
>   in the moonlight!
> Let me spread for you the clean and sweet
>   couch of a prince,
> Let me pass sweet time with you in joy
>   and plenty.

How Inanna both fends off this proposition and induces her swain to propose is unfortunately lost in a small lacuna. That she successfully did so is clear from the text when it resumes, for it shows that Dumuzi is now following her home to her mother to formally ask for her hand. Inanna already speaks for "our" mother and is so excited she can hardly keep from running. Her only worry is whether the house will be presentable enough for the occasion; she wishes she could send a messenger ahead to warn her mother:

> He has decided to stop at the gate of our mother,
> I am fairly running for (sheer) joy!
> He has decided to stop at the gate of Ningal,
> I am fairly running for (sheer) joy!
> O that someone would tell my mother,
> and she sprinkle cedar perfume on the floor;
> O that someone would tell my mother, Ningal,
> and she sprinkle cedar perfume on the floor!
> Her dwelling, its fragrance is sweet,
> her words are all joyful ones.

Inanna is certain that her choice will be approved and that her mother will
be delighted to accept Dumuzi as her son-in-law. He is of noble family,
rich, and a good provider; and so she enjoys in anticipation what she
imagines will be her mother's welcome to Dumuzi, hailing him as Suen's
— and her own — son-in-law and delighting in his worthiness to be
Inanna's husband:

> My lord, you are indeed worthy of the pure embrace,
> Amaushumgalanna, son-in-law of Suen.
> Lord Dumuzi, you are indeed worthy of the pure embrace,
> Amaushumgalanna, son-in-law of Suen!
> My lord, your riches are sweet,
> your herbs in the desert are all of them sweet,
> Amaushumgalanna, your riches are sweet,
> your herbs in the desert are all of them sweet.

Inanna loves, as will be seen, wisely, rather than too well. Her joy is in
finding security with a good provider no less than delight in a beautiful
youth. And Dumuzi, the very embodiment of fertility and yield, is the
provider par excellence.

While Inanna in this song chose her husband herself, in other songs she
is more conventional and leaves the choice, as custom dictates, to her older
brother, the sun god Utu. The question whether he has chosen well causes
some anxiety in both brother and sister, and their mutual nervousness
when he is to tell her forms the theme of a third ditty which might be
termed "The Bridal Sheets of Inanna."[25]

When the song begins Utu has already made binding arrangements for
Inanna to marry Dumuzi and all that remains is for him to tell her.
Intending to lead up to his news gently and diplomatically Utu begins by
suggesting that new linens may be needed, but without letting on that it
will be for Inanna's bridal bed and her new home.

> The brother decided to tell his younger sister,
> the sun god, Utu, decided to tell his younger sister:
> "Young lady, the flax is full of loveliness,
> Inanna, the flax is full of loveliness,
> (like) barley in the furrow
>   full of loveliness and attraction.
> Sister, a piece of linen large or small is lovely.
> Inanna, a piece of linen large or small is lovely,
> let me bundle for you and give it to you,
> young lady, let me bring you flax!
> Inanna, let me bring you flax!"

This roundabout way of broaching things does not, of course, deceive
Inanna for a moment, if anything it puts her on guard. She senses that her
bridegroom has been chosen, but who is he? The right one, or somebody

else? She is afraid of the answer and tries to push the whole thing away; she is young, delicate, refined, knows nothing of menial, domestic tasks:

> Brother, when you have brought me the flax,
> who will ret (?) for me, who will ret for me,
> who will ret its fibers for me?

But Utu is not to be discouraged, he is set on getting her the linen:

> My sister, already retted let me bring it to you,
> Inanna, already retted let me bring it to you.

And Inanna fends off the gift once more:

> Brother, when you have brought it to me
>   already retted,
> who will spin for me, who will spin for me,
> who will spin its fibers for me?

Once again Utu is all helpfulness, he will bring the flax already spun, and again Inanna tries to have nothing to do with this linen business and to push it away from her: if Utu brings the flax already spun, who then will double up the thread for her? And so it goes: who will dye the doubled up threads, who will weave them, who will bleach[26] the finished piece? But when Utu in his terrifying helpfulness offers to bring the linen sheet already bleached, Inanna is at her wit's end, she can think of no more to be done to it, no more evasions, and so she takes the plunge: "Who is it?"

> "Brother, when you have brought it to me
>   already bleached,
> who will lie down thereon with me? Who will
>   lie down thereon with me?"
> "With you will lie down, will lie down,
> with you will lie down a bridegroom,
> with you will lie down Amaushumgalanna,
> with you will lie down the peer of Enlil,
> with you will lie down
>   the issue of a noble womb,
> with you will lie down
>   one engendered on a throne-dais!"

So at last the tension is broken, and broken by joyous certainty. Utu chose the right one:

> It is true! He is the man of my heart,
>   he is the man of my heart,
> the man my heart told me!
> Working the hoe, heaping up piles of grain,
> bringing the grain into the barn,
> the farmer whose grain is of hundreds of piles
> the shepherd whose sheep are laden with wool.

As in the preceding ditty, Inanna's "Mr. Right" is, above all, the good provider, the embodiment of fertility and yield. Which kind of yield is no longer important: in the previous ditty he was a shepherd with rich grazing grounds in the desert, here he is both a farmer and a shepherd. Inanna herself is more complex: rich, noble, rather spoiled, too precious for ordinary household tasks, occupying her day with play and dancing only, ready to fall in love — but with someone who can maintain her as she wishes to be maintained.

From the courting texts it is only a short step to the texts that deal with Dumuzi and Inanna's wedding; but while the courting texts were all popular ditties, the wedding texts comprise compositions which must be considered belletristic and compositions which are ritual in nature and closely relate to communal worship.

Wedding

It will be convenient to begin with an almost novelistic tale from Nippur[27] which throws a good deal of light on Sumerian wedding ceremonies generally. The story — which we shall call simply "Dumuzi's Wedding" — opens with a list of Inanna's four "bridal attendants," that is, the bridegroom and his three best men. They are the shepherd, the farmer, the fowler, and the fisherman. The shepherd, Dumuzi, who heads the list, is the prospective bridegroom. Inanna, when all is ready for the wedding, sends messengers to these four bidding them to come to honor her with their gifts, and so the shepherd loads himself with fresh cream and milk, the farmer brings the sweet new grain from the furrow, the fowler brings choice birds, and the fisherman offers carps, which at this time of year, the spring, swim up into the rivers in flood.

After arriving at Inanna's parents' house, Dumuzi calls out, asking Inanna to open the door to him — but Inanna is in no hurry, she has lots of things to do yet. First, she goes as a dutiful daughter to her mother to be instructed in how she is to conduct herself with her new family-in-law and is told that her father-in-law must be obeyed as if he were her own father, and her mother-in-law as if she were her own mother.

Dumuzi, out in the street, is still calling for her to let him in, but Inanna cannot yet be bothered. Her mother has told her to have a bath and the girl douses herself with water and scrubs herself thoroughly with soap, then she puts on her best garment, takes her mascot-bead, straightens the lapis lazuli beads on her neck, and takes her cylinder seal in the hand — at long last she is ready to receive Dumuzi:

> The young lady stood waiting.
> Dumuzi pushed (open) the door,

> and like a moonbeam she came forth to him
>   out of the house,
> he looked at her, rejoiced in her,
> took her in his arms and kissed her.

A lacuna at this place leaves us uncertain about what happened next. Conceivably the text told about the consummation of the marriage, a wedding feast, and the newlyweds stay of some days in Inanna's parents' house. When the text resumes (in column three) Dumuzi and Inanna are apparently on the way to his parental home. They stop to visit the temple of Dumuzi's personal god and Inanna is asked to lie down to sleep before the god (perhaps to obtain a dream message), but the text is not well preserved and the meaning is not clear.

After another lacuna column four describes how all of these new and strange events have frightened Inanna: is there, perhaps, even an expectation that she will be of some use in the house, will she have to work? Dumuzi has his hands full trying to pacify and cheer her: she will have an honored position in the household and will have to do no weaving, no spinning, no exertion whatever. She is to continue being the refined, protected, little rich girl we know so well already:

> The shepherd put his arm around the young lady:
> "I have not carried you off into slavery!
> Your table will be the splendid table,
>   the splendid table,
> at the splendid table I eat.
> Your table will be the splendid table,
>   the splendid table,
> you will eat at the splendid table.
> My mother eats at the beer vat,
> Duttur's brother eats not at it,
> my sister Geshtinanna eats not at it,
> (but) you will dip in (your) hand
>   at the splendid table!
> O my bride, cloth you shall not weave for me!
> O Inanna, threads you shall not spin for me!
> [O my bride,] fleece you shall not ravel for me!
> [O Inanna,] warp you shall not mount for me!

And so begins — Inanna clearly having the advantage — their short life together according to this humorous and harmless little tale.

Rather different in both style and tenor are those wedding texts that have a specific ritual background or setting. As a first example we may choose a text that seems to come originally from Uruk and that clearly deals with the wedding of Dumuzi-Amaushumgalanna and Inanna as it was celebrated in that city. It describes the various cult acts in a sort of running commentary as if related by a favorably placed onlooker and we may call it, for convenience, the "Uruk Text."[28] Conceivably, the composition, by reporting the cult acts in songs, helped to enhance a sense of participation in the assembled worshipers on the outskirts of the crowd and enabled them to follow what was going on.

The commentator first — after two obscure lines — reports that a date-gatherer is to climb a date palm for Inanna, and he expresses the hope that the date-gatherer will bring fresh dates down for her. This the date-gatherer does, piling his clusters in a heap which the commentator names "the gem-revealing heap." It appears this is an apt name, for the date-gatherer and Inanna proceed to collect lapis lazuli from its surface:

> A date-gatherer is to climb(?) the date palm,
> a date-gatherer is to climb(?) the date palm
>   for holy Inanna.
>
> May he take fresh ones to her! May he take
>   fresh ones to her, dark early-ripening ones,
> may he take fresh ones to Inanna besides,
>   light-colored early-ripening ones.
>
> The man has decided to take them,
>   the man has decided to take them,
>   has decided to take them
>   to the gem-revealing heap;
> the man has decided to take them,
>   O maiden Inanna, the man has decided to take them
>   to the gem-revealing heap.
>
> On the surface of the heap he is gathering
>   lapis lazuli,
> on the surface of the heap he is gathering
>   lapis lazuli for Inanna.
>
> He is finding the "buttock beads,"
>   is putting them on her buttocks!
> Inanna is finding the "head beads,"
>   is putting them on her head!
> She is finding the roughcut clear blocks of lapis lazuli,
>   is putting them around her neck!
> She is finding the narrow gold braid(?),
>   is putting it in her hair! . . .

The gems and ornaments collected are catalogued and reported one by one by the commentator. They form a complete array of queenly treasures, comprising, in addition to what has been mentioned, two sets of earrings (one of gold, one crescent-shaped of bronze), eye ornaments, nose ornaments, ornaments for her navel, a hip flask, ornaments of alabaster for her thighs, ornaments covering her vulva, and, finally, shoes for her feet. It seems obvious that these various cult acts taken together represent the ceremonial dressing of Inanna before she goes to open the door to her bridegroom. We already know of this dressing of Inanna after her bath and before she opens the door to Dumuzi from the tale of "Dumuzi's Wedding." The rather puzzling additional features found in the Uruk Text, such as the curious origin of the finery — all of it being "found" on the mysterious "gem-revealing heap" — we shall leave unexplained for the moment.

The ceremony of dressing Inanna precedes her opening the door — the central ceremony in a Sumerian wedding, which concluded the marriage and immediately preceded its consummation — and so we find our commentator reporting in his next song her meeting with her bridegroom at the door:

> The lord has met her of the lapis lazuli (gems)
>   gathered on the heap!
> Dumuzi has met Inanna, her of the lapis lazuli (gems)
>   gathered on the heap!
> The shepherd of An, the groom of Enlil
>   has met her!
>
> In Eanna the herdsman of An, Dumuzi,
>   has met her,
> at the lapis lazuli (ornamented) door
>   that stands in the Giparu,
>   the lord has met her!
> at the narrow door
>   that stands in the storehouse of Eanna,
>   Dumuzi has met her!
>
> Him, whom she will lead back
>   to the surface of the heap,
> him, whom Inanna will lead back
>   to the surface of the heap,
> (him) may she, caressing and amid her croonings,
>   take(?) into (?) its clay plaster (covering).
>
> The maiden amid cries of joy
>   has sent someone to her father!
> Inanna, moving as in a dance (for joy),
>   has sent someone to her father, (saying):
>
> O that they rush into my house,
>   (into) my house for me!
> O that they rush into my house, (into) my house,
>   for me whom am the mistress,
> O that they rush into my house, the Giparu for me!
>
> (And) when they have set up my pure bed for him,

O that they spread thereon
  my lustrous lapis lazuli (hued) straw for me.
O that they have the man of my heart
  come in to me,
O that they have my Amaushumgalanna
  come in to me,

O that they put his hand in my hand for me,
O that they put his heart next to my heart for me.
Not only is it sweet to sleep hand in hand with him,
sweetest of sweet is too the loveliness
  of joining heart to heart with him.

The meeting at the door is acceptance. Messengers are sent to have the house readied, the bridal bed set up, and the groom led in to the bride. The opening of the door, the conclusion of the marriage, is followed immediately by preparations for its consummation.

The sequence of the nuptial drama is thus clear, but a great deal of the meaning of the text remains dark and unexplained. What, for example, is the odd "gem-revealing heap"? Why do Inanna's ornaments come from it? And why is Dumuzi-Amaushumgalanna to be taken back to it? To understand this we must understand what the powers stand for, and here it would seem that the bride, Inanna (earlier Ninanna(k), "Lady of the date clusters") represents the numen of the communal storehouse for dates, that "storehouse of Eanna" which she opens for Dumuzi in the text. Her emblem — that is to say, her preanthropomorphic form — confirms this, for it is, as Andrae has shown, a gatepost with rolled up mat to serve as a door, a distinguishing mark of the storehouse.

Correspondingly, the bridegroom, Amaushumgalanna, represents what is to be stored in the storehouse. As indicated by his name, which means "the one great source of the date clusters," he is the personified power in the one enormous bud which the date palm sprouts each year, and from which issue the new leaves, flowers, and fruits. Dumuzi-Amaushumgalanna is thus a personification of the power behind the yearly burgeoning of the palm and its producing its yield of dates; he is, in fact, the power in and behind the date harvest.

That these two powers are wed means that the power for fertility and yield has been captured by the numen of the storehouse — and so by the community — and has become its trusty provider for all time. Amaushumgalanna is safely in the storehouse, and the community revels in abundant food and drink, release from anxiety and fear of starvation, blissfully secure from want. Inanna expresses the communal feeling precisely: not love or the raptures of passion mark her wedding night, but a gently glowing sense of inner and outer bliss in trust and security:

> Not only is it sweet to sleep hand in hand with him,
> Sweetest of sweet is too the loveliness
>   of joining heart to heart with him.

Seeing Inanna as the numen in the date storehouse and Dumuzi-Amaushumgalanna as the power in and behind the date harvest gives us a background against which the underlying ritual of the Uruk Text becomes more understandable. That a heap of fresh dates should furnish the ornaments for Inanna is logical since freshly harvested dates are the pride and adornment of the bare shelves of a storehouse for dates. In the text, however, the relationship between harvest and storehouse has been overlaid with anthropomorphic imagery. The date clusters that are to adorn the shelves of the storehouse become ritually experienced as traditional feminine adornments and jewelry such as would be suitable for decking out a human bride, and the heap from thich they are taken comes close to becoming a jewel shrine of sorts. Its original nature reasserts itself, however, later in the text when we hear that Dumuzi-Amaushumgalanna is to be taken to that heap, under its clay plaster covering, as soon as he has entered her house, the "storehouse of Eanna."

A wedding text somewhat similar in mood to the Uruk Text forms a part of a long hymn to Inanna which, for the sake of convenience, we may term the "Iddin-Dagan Text"[29] since that king figures in it as ritual embodiment of Dumuzi. The exact location of the rite is unfortunately not clear, even though the text seems quite specific, but the most likely place is probably the royal palace in Isin. In the ritual sequence it takes up the thread where the Uruk Text leaves off, that is to say, with the setting up of the bridal couch after Dumuzi (embodied in the king) has been admitted by Inanna — here called by her epithet, Ninegalla, "The queen of the palace." The section begins:

> In the palace, the house that administers the nation
>   and is a (restraining) yoke
>   on all (foreign) lands,
> the house (called) "The River-ordeal,"
>   (therein) has the dark-headed people,
>   the nation in its entirety,
> founded a dais for Ninegalla.
> The king, being a god, will sojourn with her on it.
>
> That she take care of the life of all lands,
> that on the day for her to lift the head
>   and take a good look (at the bridegroom),
> on the day of going to bed together,
>   the rites be performed to perfection,

has it (i.e., the nation) at New Year,
   the day of the ritual,
set up a bed for milady.

Halfa-straw they have been purifying with cedar perfume,
have been putting it on that bed for milady,
over it a bedspread has been pulled straight for her,
a bedspread of heart's delight to make the bed
   comfortable.

Then, when all is ready, Inanna prepares herself for the night:

Milady bathes in water the holy loins,
for the loins of the king she bathes them in water,
for the loins of Iddin-Dagan she bathes them in water.
Holy Inanna rubs (herself) with soap,
sprinkles the floor with cedar perfume.

Next Amaushumgalanna enters the chamber:

The king goes with lifted head to the holy loins,
goes with lifted head to the loins of Inanna,
Amaushumgalanna goes to bed with her,
has truly to praise the woman in her holy loins:
" O my one of holy loins! O my holy Inanna!"
After he on the bed, in the holy loins
   has made the queen rejoice,
after he on the bed, in the holy loins,
   has made holy Inanna rejoice,
she in return soothes the heart for him
   there on the bed:
"Verily, I will be a constant prolonger of Iddin-Dagan's
   days (of life)."

At this loving promise the text leaves the divine couple alone, resuming its tale when on the next morning the bridegroom enters his palace to prepare the wedding feast, his arm fondly around the shoulders of his young bride. The divine couple then take their place on the royal dais, a lavish feast is set before them, the musicians and their soloist intone a song of joy, and the king gives the signal to begin eating:

The king has reached out for food and drink,
Amaushumgalanna has reached out for food
   and drink,
The palace in in festive mood, the king is joyous,
the nation is passing the day amidst plenty;
Amaushumgalanna is come in joy,
long may he remain on the pure throne!

Particularly notable in this text is its formulaic statement of the purpose of the rite of the sacred marriage. The bridal couch is set up for the celebration of the sacred marriage between harvest and storehouse in the hope that the bride, having her first close look at the bridegroom, will become enamored of him so that the hymeneal rites of the bridal couch will come off satisfactorily. For the success of their union means that Inanna, the storehouse, can "take care of the life of all lands."

Full emphasis on the security from want that the sacred marriage ensures, the security that is implicit in the successful harvest, meets us in the description of the lavishness of the wedding banquet:

> Abundance, deliciousness, plenty is brought
>   straight to him,
> a feast of sweets is set up for him.

A notable point in this text, and fully as important as the formulaic statement of ritual purpose it gives, is the clarity with which it shows that the divine bridegroom was represented in the rite by the human king — in this case by Iddin-Dagan of Isin — in such a way as to imply complete identity of the two: "The king, being a god," says the text, and also,

> The king goes with lifted head to the holy loins,
> goes with lifted head to the loins of Inanna,
> Amaushumgalanna goes to bed with her.

And Inanna can turn to her divine spouse and use his human name:

> "Verily I will be a constant prolonger of Iddin-
>   Dagan's days (of life)!"

Iddin-Dagan and Dumuzi-Amaushumgalanna are one.

As the human king could take on the identity of the god of fertility and yield, so the queen or perhaps a high priestess would probably have assumed in the ritual the identity of Inanna, embodying the numen of the storehouse.

This ability of humans to incarnate gods and powers is momentous, implying that they can act as these powers and so commit them; in the rite of the sacred marriage the commitment is one of the love and bonds of marriage: to have and to hold forever the power that provides and maintains, Dumuzi.

A curious — and apparently fairly new — feature of the Iddin-Dagan Text should be mentioned: subtle shift in emphasis from Dumuzi to Inanna as the source of the sought-for blessing. This shift may be connected with the growing political and religious importance of Inanna in historical times, which would tend to make her significantly overshadow Dumuzi; but it is also possible that the king who embodied him would

increasingly be felt as the representative of the human community par
excellence and therefore the one to seek, rather than to dispense, abundance and plenty.

Very close to the Iddin-Dagan Text in general tenor, and with even
more pronounced shift to Inanna as the source of the blessings of general
fertility and yield, is another wedding text that we may suitably call "The
Blessing of the Bridegroom."[30] It begins — the first line is unfortunately
damaged — with a rapt description of the beauty of the temple Ezida, in
which the sacred marriage is to be consummated:

> The . . . of (the temple) E-temen-ni-guru,
> the good management of the Temple of Eridu,
> the cleanness of the Temple of Suen,
> and the (firmly) planted (protective) gateposts
>   of Eanna,
> were verily (all) given as gifts
>   into the hands of the house.
> My (dear) Ezida ("the good house") floats like a cloud
>   (high up on its terrace)

The narrator then turns to the preparations for the night, the readying
of the bridal suite by a trusty servant, who reports to Inanna:

> The pure (bridal) bed, a very semblance of lapis lazuli,
> which Gibil (the firegod) was purifying for you
>   in the Irigal (temple),
> has the caretaker — greatly fit for (ministering to) queenship —
> filled with his halfa straw for you;
> In the house that he has cleaned for you with his reed cuttings,
>   he is setting up the laver for you!

All is thus in readiness and the time to retire is drawing near;

> The day is (the one) named, the day is (the one) appointed,
> The day (for the bride) to view (the bridegroom)
>   on the (bridal) bed,
> that day for the king to arouse (desire in) a
>   woman.
> O grant life to the king!
> Grant to the king (to wield) all shepherds' crooks!

The narrator's reminder seems to have the desired effect. The bride,
Inanna, indicates her wish to go to bed.

> She has called for it! She has called for it!
>   She has called for the bed!
> She has called for the bed of heart's delight!
>   She has called for the bed!

> She has called for the bed for sweetening the loins,
>   she has called for the bed!
> She has called for the royal bed!
>   She has called for the bed!
> She has called for the queenly bed!
>   She has called for the bed!

As the conscientious wife she intends to become, Inanna puts the final touches to the bed herself:

> In her making it comfortable, making it comfortable,
>   making the bed comfortable,
> making the bed of heart's delight comfortable,
>   making the bed comfortable,
> making the bed for sweetening the loins comfortable,
>   making the bed comfortable,
>
> in her making the royal bed comfortable,
>   making the bed comfortable,
> making the queenly bed comfortable,
>   making the bed comfortable,
>
> she spreads the bedding out (evenly) for the king,
>   spreads the bedding out (evenly) for him,
> she spreads the bedding out (evenly) for the beloved one,
>   spreads the bedding out (evenly) for him;
>
> to the couch made comfortable by her
>   she calls the king,
> to the couch made comfortable by her
>   she calls the beloved one.

In answer to the summons her handmaiden, Ninshubur, who has been awaiting the call, goes to fetch the royal bridegroom (looking his best with his wig on) and leads him in to the bride. As she brings him in she indulges, as trusted servants will, in a veritable flood of well-meant, loquacious good wishes which flows on and on — actually she is reeling off a long, standard formula which would seem to belong originally to the Damu cult:

> Ninshubur, the good handmaiden of Eanna,
> stays awake at her goodly duties,
> she leads him bewigged in
>   to the loins of Inanna:
>
> "May the lord, the choice of your heart,
> may the king, your beloved bridegroom,
>   pass long days in your sweet thing, the pure loins!
> Grant him a pleasant reign to come!

Grant him a royal throne, firm in its foundations;
grant him a sceptre righting (wrongs in) the land,
    all shepherds' crooks;
grant him the good crown, the turban that
    makes a head distinguished.

From sunrise to sunset
from south to north
from the Upper Sea to the Lower Sea,
from (where grows) the *huluppu*-tree, from
    (where grows) the cedar-tree,
and in Sumer and Akkad,
    grant him all shepherds' crooks,
and may he perform the shepherdship
    over their dark-headed people.

May he like a farmer till the fields,
may he like a good shepherd make the folds teem,
may there be vines under him,
    may there be barley under him,
may there be carp-floods in the river under him,[31]
may there be mottled barley in the fields under him,
may fishes and birds sound off in the marshes under him.

May old and new reeds grow in the canebrake
    under him,
may shrubs grow in the high desert under him,
may deer multiply in the forests under him,
may (well) watered gardens bear honey and wine
    under him,
may lettuce and cress grow in the vegetable plots
    under him,
may there be long life in the palace under him.

May the high flood rise (?)
    in the Tigris and Euphrates under him,
may grass grow on their banks,
    may vegetables fill the commons,
may the holy lady (of the grains), Nidaba,
    gather grainpiles there!
O milady, queen of heaven and earth,
    queen of all heaven and earth,
may he live long in your embrace!

After this long speech follows the stereotypical formula for reporting
the union of the divine couple:

The king goes with lifted head to the holy loins,
goes with lifted head to the loins of Inanna,

> the king going with lifted head,
> going with lifted head to milady
> . . . .
> puts his arms around the holy one . . .

and with that the text breaks off.

Curious in this version, as we have mentioned, is the odd reversal of roles between Inanna and Dumuzi-Amaushumgalanna, but also noteworthy is the scope of the blessings expected. They range from the yields of farmers and shepherds to the take of fishermen and fowlers, from the wildlife in woods and marshes to the produce of vineyards and gardens. This contrasts strikingly with the first cultic wedding text we dealt with, the Uruk Text. There the god, Dumuzi-Amaushumgalanna (consonantly with his name), was the power in the fertility and yield of the date palm only, and the underlying ritual was a date harvest ritual and nothing else. This concentration on a single major economy is, we should judge, an original feature, but as the cities drew a variety of economies into their orbit — Uruk, for instance, seems to have united several settlements of date growers, oxherders, and shepherds — the purview of the cult broadened so as to make its god stand for a general fertility and yield. Such a broadening is already suggested on the Uruk Vase of the outgoing fourth millennium where the bridal gifts brought by the god include not only dates but ears of grain and sheep heavy with wool. In the marriage story where Dumuzi is a shepherd, the broadening is deftly handled by having the farmer, the fisherman, and the fowler act as wedding attendants, bringing gifts of their produce to supplement what the shepherd provides. In other texts, such as "The Bridal Sheets of Inanna," Dumuzi has to figure — a little awkwardly — as both shepherd and farmer in Inanna's eulogy of him.

The broadening of purview — more and more pervaded by a sense that all the fertility powers were but one divine figure, Dumuzi — does not curiously enough affect the materials we possess so as to obliterate or blur the originally distinct economic settings. It is, rather, an inconsequential and external addition to forms already crystallized or an accretion from elsewhere as rituals lose their original meaning and become vague and generalized.

How incisively a particular economic setting may determine the meaning of a rite may be illustrated by a last ritual wedding text[32] which one could call the "Herder Wedding Text" since it presents the rite of the sacred marriage as it took form in a herding environment. It differs in basic aspects from the wedding texts we have considered, texts which on the whole may be classed as Amaushumgalanna or date harvest texts.

The "Herder Wedding Text" does not use the name Amaushum-

galanna, but calls the god by his herder names, Dumuzi or "Wild Bull
Dumuzi." "Wild Bull" was a Sumerian metaphor for "shepherd" — originally, probably for "cowherd." The beginning lines are unfortunately badly
damaged, but as the text gradually becomes better preserved it would
appear that we are following Inanna as she is being escorted to the bridal
chamber by attendants and girlfriends who exchange erotic pleasantries
with her and not too subtle double entendres inspired by the occasion.
Attempting a restoration of the lacunas one may perhaps render the first
lines as follows:

> *(Inanna:)*
> "The words of my mouth are all pure,
> I am directing the country rightly!"
> *(Girlfriends:)*
> "As sweet as your mouth are your parts,
> they befit princely state,
> they befit princely state indeed!"
> *(Inanna:)*
> "Subduing the rebellious countries,
> Looking to having the nation multiply,
> I am directing the country rightly!"

To begin with, as may be seen, Inanna seems most concerned with pride
in her power, royal duties, and riches. She goes on to speak of her jewelry
and her palatial dwelling, but eventually she enters into the spirit asking
who will irrigate her field, "The Hillocks," and the girlfriends are ready
with the answer: Damuzi, the bridegroom, is hastening to irrigate for her,
he will irrigate "The Hillocks." The mention of Dumuzi makes Inanna
cast her mind back to the day she first decided upon him as her future
spouse; she tells of her reasons for the choice, of the ready acceptance of
him by her parents, and of her having now bathed and arrayed herself in
her best clothes for him:

> *(Inanna:)*
> "I had in view having the nation multiply,
> chose Dumuzi for (personal) god of the country.
> For Dumuzi, beloved of Enlil,
> I made (his) name exalted, gave him status.
> My mother always held him dear,
> my father sang his praises,
> I have bathed for him, rubbed (myself) with soap
>   for him,
> and when the servant had brought the pitcher
>   with the bath water
> she laid out my dress correctly like a two-ply dress,
> and I (wore) two-ply for him the grand queenly robe!"

The end of column one and the beginning of column two of the text are again rather badly damaged, but when the text becomes understandable Inanna's pride appears focused at last on her own bodily charms, so much so indeed that she wants them celebrated in a song. She calls upon the girl singer and girl elegist who accompany her and orders them to weave her praise of her charms into a song for all to sing:

> *(Inanna:)*
> "My heart has pondered what I am about to let you know,
> and what I advisedly let you know I will have you reveal
> — I, Inanna of the grand dress, the two-ply dress —
> the elegist will weave it into a song,
> the singer will extoll it in a lay,
> my bridegroom will thereby rejoice in me,
> the shepherd, Dumuzi, will thereby rejoice in me;
> whoever has a mouth
>   will take the words into his mouth,
> whoever hears it
>   will teach the song to a youngster.
> When it has soared (to full chorus)
> it will be (like) Nippur
>   (celebrating a) festival,
> when it has settled down it will softly. . . .

The elegist complies:

> The young lady was praising her parts
> and the elegist was weaving it into a song,
> Inanna was praising them,
> had her parts extolled in song.

In the song Inanna, glorying in her young body, which has just attained puberty, sings the praises of her pubic triangle with its as yet sparse growth of hairs, comparing it first to a metal enchasement with decorative studs sticking out like linchpins in a cartwheel, then to a ceremonial barge called the "Barge of Heaven" (the recent hairs she sees as mooring ropes holding the barge), and the image leads over into that of the cosmic barge of heaven, the crescent of the new moon. Next her triangle has become a virginal plot in the desert, not yet cultivated, then again a stubble field on which ducks have been put out to be fattened, black hairs dotting it like black ducks against light dun soil, then it is a high-lying field, hillock land, piled up with levees, well watered in readiness for ploughing — she has just bathed in water — and then moist lowlands similarly readied. Since a woman, though she may own fields, cannot herself plough them but must seek a ploughman to do it for her, the song ends with the question of who he should be:

"My enchased parts so nailed down
as (with) linchpins
     attached to a big cart,
(my crescent-shaped) "Barge of Heaven,"
     so (well) belayed,
full of loveliness, like the new moon,
my untilled plot,
     left so fallow in the desert,
my duck field so studded with ducks,
my hillock land, so (well) watered,
my parts, piled up with levees,
     (well) watered
I, being (but) a maiden,
     who will be their ploughman?
My parts, (well) watered lowlands,
I, being (but) a lady,
     who will put (plough) oxen to them?"

And the elegist responds:

"Young lady, may the king plough them for you!
May the king, Dumuzi, plough them for you!"

which is obviously the right answer:

"The man of my heart! The ploughman is the man
     of my heart!"

Again the text is damaged and some lines are completely lost but they
must have led up to Inanna's union with Dumuzi for when the text
resumes it describes the union and tells how it magically awakens new life
through all nature.

At its mighty rising, at its mighty rising,
did the shoots and the buds rise up.
The king's loins! At its mighty rising
did the vines rise up, did the grains rise up,
did the desert fill (with verdure)
     like a pleasurable garden.

From the description of the union and its effects the text moves without
apparent transition to a description of Inanna's joy at living in Dumuzi's
house and of her request of him to make the milk yellow — that is, creamy
and fat — for her. She asks for cow's milk, goat's milk, and even for
camel's milk, all of which Dumuzi readily promises to provide and to place
in his house E-namtila, that is, "the house of life." With a rather long praise
of this house and its contents of milk and other dairy products the text
finally concludes.

The "Herder Wedding Text" ends on much the same note as the other wedding texts, with delight in great abundances of food. Yet, there is one subtle difference. The riches here garnered by Inanna — milk and milk products — are short-term only. They will not, like the more durable riches of the date harvest, last through an approaching dry season and free the community from want until the next season. The sense of having reached security which informs the wedding texts of Amaushumgalanna can have little relevance in the herder's world with its swiftly passing blessings.

That world has, rather, its own set of relevant experiences. In spring the desert fills with green, the herds gambol in the pastures and mate, and from that mating flows the herder's prosperity; increase of flocks and herds, newborn lambs, kids, and calves, plentiful milk from the full udders of the mother animals. In the herder's view the emphasis of the sacred marriage is therefore on its mating aspect. He sees it as a divine engendering which brings into being spring's glorious burst, the sacred cosmic sexual act in which all nature is fertilized.

This emphasis comes through clearly in Inanna's frank praise of her private parts with its central image of the field ready for the fertilizing seed plough — an image, incidentally, which still does not take us outside the herder's world since the plough oxen were provided by the cowherders.

Thus the orchardman's and the herder's rite of the sacred marriage differ fundamentally. The first is a harvest rite binding the date palm's power for fertility and yield to the numen of the storehouse in bonds of marriage and mutual love. The other is a fertility rite uniting — by incarnating them in human actors — the divine powers for fertility and new life in a generative sexual embrace.

Death and Lament

Spring does not last long, and its fecund power wanes and is lost as the dry hot summer sets in. Mythopoeically experienced this means that Dumuzi dies, a victim of the powers of death and the netherworld.

The precise manner of the god's death varies from one text to another: he is set upon by highwaymen in his fold or elsewhere or by a posse of evil deputies from Hades; he is killed, taken captive, or perishes in his attempt to flee. In many versions the death of the god is assumed to have taken place at an earlier time, the text following his young widow, Inanna, his sister, and his mother, as they come to his gutted and ravaged camp in the desert to bewail him.

The larger reasons behind the god's death are mostly left vague. Sometimes it seems to be due simply to the innate bloodthirst and lust for booty in the attackers, but there are occasionally references to orders given them by the dread powers they serve, orders, however, which are never explained further.

Only in one treatment, the long, entirely literary, composition known as the "Descent of Inanna" is a specific reason offered. Here the god is delivered up by his young wife, by Inanna, as a substitute for herself. It seems best to put this highly complex work to one side at first and to begin with another more traditional literary account, closer to that of the cult texts, the one given in the composition called "Dumuzi's Dream."[33]

"Dumuzi's Dream" begins by relating how Dumuzi, grieving because of a premonition of his death, asks all of nature to lament him — the high desert and the swamps, the crayfish and the frogs in the rivers — and he hopes that his mother Duttur will cry out in her grief, "He was (worth) any five! He was (worth) any ten!" If she has not heard of his death, the desert is to tell her. Then the despondent Dumuzi falls asleep, but his dreams are disquieting: he awakens, rubs his eyes, and, half-dazed, calls for his sister, Geshtinanna, who is skilled in such matters, to come and propitiate the dream. But Geshtinanna can do nothing to relieve his anxieties. The dreams are of inexorably bad portent and cannot be propitiated. Dumuzi has dreamt of rushes that rose up against him, which means that highwaymen on a raid will attack him. He dreamt of a lone reed and of two separate reeds that were removed together: they stand for their mother, Duttur, and for Geshtinanna and Dumuzi who will be taken from her. He has also dreamt that water was poured on the embers of his campfire as one does when camp is abandoned, that his churn was removed from its churning pit (?), and his cup was gone from the peg on which it usually hung. He saw his sheep and goats lying in the dust and with them the missing churn and cup. The churn lay on its side, no milk poured from it; the cup lay on its side. He himself lived no more, his fold had been abandoned to the winds. The import is only too clear, he has seen what is soon to befall.

Dumuzi, however, still hopes he may escape his fate. He sends his sister up on a hill as lookout. When she and her girlfriend, the wine-grower goddess, sight the boat with his attackers approaching on the river he tells her and a comrade he will hide in the pastures in the desert, in the large grassy spots, in the small grassy spots, and in the dike of the Aralli desert, and he asks that they not reveal his whereabouts. They both — not content to answer a simple yes — wish that they may be eaten by Dumuzi's shepherd dogs if they ever reveal what has been told them.

When the attackers — a posse made up of deputies from four major cities — arrive in the town, Dumuzi's sister keeps her promise but his comrade proves false. One after the other he tells Dumuzi's hiding places, adding in each case that he does not know where he is; but the deputies relentlessly search each place and eventually find Dumuzi in the Aralli canal dike. Dumuzi, seeing them approach, realizes what has happened:

> In town my sister helped me stay alive,
>   my comrade caused my death!

Assuming that the attackers have killed both his sister and his comrade or taken them away as booty, he thinks of their orphaned children.

> If (my) sister has to let a child wander the streets
>   may someone (love and) kiss it,
> if (my) comrade has to let a child wander the streets
>   may no one kiss it!

The attackers surround him and bind him securely, but Dumuzi turns in his anguish to the sun god, reminding him that as Inanna's husband he is his brother-in-law, and asking Utu to change him into a gazelle. The sun god hears his prayer, changes him into a gazelle, and Dumuzi escapes his captors, fleeing to a locality with a long difficult name known so far only from this text. The evil deputies, however, continue in pursuit and capture him once more. Again Dumuzi appeals to Utu, again he is changed and escapes; this time he seeks refuge in the house of the wise woman Belili. As he nears the house he calls for water and for flour that he may quickly drink and eat and tells her that he is no mortal but a goddess' husband. Belili comes out to him but the pursuers see her and guess that Dumuzi is there. They surround and bind him.

One last time Dumuzi appeals to Utu, is changed, and escapes. This time he seeks refuge in his sister's sheepfold in the desert, but the fold is no protection. The attackers enter one by one, wreaking havoc on their way. The destruction of the sheepfold that Dumuzi had seen in his dream now comes to pass. As the churn and the cup run dry where they were carelessly flung by the invaders, Dumuzi ceases to live; the fold is abandoned to the winds, he himself has fallen at "the festival of the young men" as the text says, using an old kenning for battle.

Turning from the literary treatment in "Dumuzi's Dream" to the handling in the cult texts, one notes a similarity of underlying theme and myth in the text we shall call "The Most Bitter Cry."[34] The latter differs, however — apart from details of the myth — in its more forceful style and greater emotional participation. The text begins with compassion for the bereft young widow:

> The most bitter cry (of commiseration) — because
>   of her husband,
> (the cry) to Inanna, because of her husband

to the queen of Eanna, because of her husband,
to the queen of Uruk, because of her husband,
to the queen of Zabalam, because of her husband.
Woe for her husband! Woe for her young man!
Woe for her house! Woe for her city!
For her captive husband, her captive young man,
for her dead husband, her dead young man,
for her husband lost for Uruk in captivity,
lost for Uruk and Kullab in captivity,
lost for Uruk and Kullab in death. . . .

After further lines of condolence the lament is taken up by Inanna herself:

Inanna weeps bitter tears for her young
   husband:
"The day the sweet husband, my husband,
   went away,
the day the sweet young man, my young man,
   went away,
you went — O my husband — into the early
   pastures,
you went — O my young man — into the later
   pastures.
My husband, seeking pasture, was killed in
   the pastures.
My young man, seeking water, was delivered
   up at the waters.
My young husband nowise departed town
   like the (decently) shrouded corpses,
O you flies of the early pastures!
   He nowise departed town
   like the (decently) shrouded!

The text then tells what has happened. Seven evil deputies of the netherworld have crept up on Dumuzi's fold where he lies asleep. Like all razzias in the desert this one was made by night. The attackers gain entry into the fold and demolish everything in their insolent lust for destruction. The seventh deputy comes to Dumuzi and awakens him rudely:

The seventh deputy, entering the fold,
   roused the chief shepherd,
   who lay asleep,
roused Dumuzi, the chief shepherd,
   who lay asleep,
roused holy Inanna's husband,
   the chief shepherd, who lay asleep:
"My master has sent us for you,
   get up, come along,

Has sent us for you, Dumuzi,
   get up, come along!
Husband of Inanna, son of Duttur,
   get up, come along!
Ululu, brother of mistress Geshtinanna,
   get up, come along!
Your ewes are taken, your lambs driven off,
   get up, come along!
Your goats are taken, your kids driven off,
   get up, come along!
Take the holy crown off your head,
   get up bareheaded;
take the holy royal robe off your body,
   get up naked;
lay aside the holy staff in your hand,
   get up emptyhanded!
Take the holy sandals off your feet,
   get up barefooted!

But somehow Dumuzi manages to escape the hands reaching for him and gets out of the fold safely. He flees toward the river where he flings off his clothes, hanging some on thorns and leaving others on the ground, before plunging into the water to swim to the other bank where his wife Inanna and his mother Duttur await him. His pursuers, not daring to follow, seek other plunder in the desert. But Dumuzi, unfortunately, has not gauged the current in the river, which is rising in flood. The swirling waters carry him past Duttur and Inanna as they look on from the bank. He reaches out his hands toward them in a futile gesture:

As he reached for the lap of Duttur, his
   mother who bore him,
Duttur, his mother who bore him,
   (his) compassionate mother
   was filled with pity for him,
Inanna (!) his wife, his compassionate wife,
   was filled with compassion for him,
as he reached for the lap of Inanna, his bride,
did Inanna shriek to him
   like the howling (!) storm.

But they are helpless:

At the appletree of the great dike
   in the desert of Emush,
there did the boat-wrecking waters
   carry the lad into Hades,
did the boat-wrecking waters
   carry Inanna's husband into Hades.

The text ends with a brief description of Dumuzi's existence in the netherworld, a world devoid of real substance, a realm of shades, of unreal things:

> (Yonder) he shares in food that is no food,
>   shares in water that is no water,
> (yonder) are built cattle pens
>   that are no cattle pens,
> (yonder) are wattled over
>   what are no sheep sheds;
> deputies (of the netherworld), not his trusty
>   spear, are at his side.

The narrative section in "The Most Bitter Cry," which recalls the similar (but not altogether comparable) narrative sections in the wedding cult texts, is a rarity in the death and lament texts. The tradition is — as we have mentioned — to assume the actual death of Dumuzi to have occurred earlier, and to present his chief mourners — widow, sister, and mother — as they make their way to his raided camp to mourn. This may involve narrative, but the emphasis is on the laments through which the mourners vent their grief.

An example of such a lament is a dirge[35] sung by Dumuzi's young sister, Geshtinanna. She has no thoughts for herself, identifies completely with her slain brother, and grieves, as if she were he, for hopes cut short and fulfillment denied.

> Before a young wife had yet slept
>   in his embrace
> and my mother could raise
>   a (grand) child on (her) knee,
> when he had been chosen by his parents-in-law,
> and he had acquired them as parents-in-law,
> when he sat among fellows as a comrade
>   when he was only a young soldier —
>
> (then) did (the powers) pass sentence upon him,
> on the high, noble, (young) lord;
> and his god let the sentence befall him:
> "A strong one shall hurl the throwstick
>   against you"
>   — when he was only a young soldier —
> "A swift one shall speed against you,
> an angry one shall roar against you,"
>   — when he was (only) a young soldier.

As if Dumuzi had been a mere human, just another young boy, his sister sees his death as a thing decided on by the gods — a decision which his own guardian angel, his personal god, was unable to stay.

To represent the laments that express the sorrow of Dumuzi's young widow, Inanna, we choose one which may be called "The Wild Bull Who Has Lain Down."[36] "Wild Bull" is, as mentioned earlier, a term for "shepherd" and serves as epithet for Dumuzi. Inanna, going to visit Dumuzi in his fold in the desert has found him dead, his fold raided, the young men, women, and flocks of his household killed. She asks the mountains for news of him, only to be told that "the Bison" has led him (that is, his shade) into the mountains, which is to say into the realm of the dead, for to the Sumerians k u r, "the mountains," represented Hades. Wild animals now roam where Dumuzi's camp was. Our rendering omits a long litany of titles and epithets of Dumuzi between the first and second stanza:

> The wild bull who has lain down, lives no more,
>   the wild bull who has lain down,
>   lives no more,
> Dumuzi, the wild bull, who has lain down,
>   lives no more,
> . . . the chief shepherd, lives no more,
> the wild bull who has lain down, lives no more.
>
> O you wild bull, how fast you sleep!
>   How fast sleep ewe and lamb!
> O you wild bull, how fast you sleep!
>   How fast sleep goat and kid!
> I will ask the hills and the valleys
> I will ask the hills of the Bison:
> "Where is the young man, my husband?"
>   I will say;
> "he whom I no longer serve food?"
>   I will say;
> "he whom I no longer give drink?"
>   I will say;
> "and my lovely maids?"
>   I will say,
> "and my lovely young men?"
>   I will say.
>
> "The Bison has taken thy husband away
>   up into the mountains!
> The Bison has taken thy young man away,
>   up into the mountains!"
>
> "Bison of the mountains, with the mottled
>   eyes!
> Bison of the mountains with the crushing
>   teeth!
> Bison! Having taken him up away from me,
>   having taken him up away from me,

having taken him I no longer serve food
  up away from me,
having taken him whom I no longer give
  drink up away from me,
having taken my lovely maids up away
  from me,
having taken my lovely young men up
  away from me,
the young man who perished from me
  (at the hands of) your men,
young Ababa who perished from me
  (at the hands of) your men:
May you not make an end to his lovely look!
May you not have him open with quaver (of
  fear) his lovely mouth!

On his couch you have made the jackals lie down,
in my husband's fold you have made the raven dwell,
his reed pipe — the wind will have to play it,
my husband's songs — the north wind will have to sing
  them."

From the laments in which the bereaved mother pours out her heart we choose one called, from its beginning line, "My Heart Plays a Reed Pipe."[37] Dumuzi has sent for his wife, mother, and sister to join him in his fold in the desert, but upon arrival they find that raiders have gutted the fold and killed Dumuzi. The lament begins as a lament by all three but becomes quickly the expression of the mother's feelings only.

A reed pipe of dirges —
My heart plays a reed pipe,
  (the instrument) of dirges,
  for him in the desert,
I, the mistress of Eanna, who lay waste the
  mountains,
and I, Ninsuna, mother of the (young) lord,
and I, Geshtinanna, daughter-in-law of heaven.

My heart plays a reed pipe of dirges
  for him in the desert,
plays where the lad dwelt,
plays where Dumuzi dwelt,
in Aralli, on the Shepherd's Hill —
my heart plays a reed pipe of dirges
  for him in the desert —
where the lad dwelt, he who is captive,
where Dumuzi dwelt, he who is bound,
where the ewe surrendered the lamb —

my heart plays a reed pipe of dirges,
   for him in the desert —
where the goat surrendered the kid.

Treacherous are you, numen of that place,
where, though he said to me,
   "May my mother come to join me!"
   — my heart plays a reed pipe,
   for him in the desert —
he may not move toward me his prostrate hands,
he may not move toward me his prostrate feet.
She neared the desert — neared the desert —
   the mother in the desert, O what loss
   has she suffered!
She reached the desert where the lad dwelt,
   reached the desert, where Dumuzi dwelt,
. . . .
— the mother in the desert, O what loss has she
   suffered!
She looks at her slain (young) bull,
looks at his face —
— the mother in the desert, O what loss has
   she suffered!
How she shudders
. . . .
— the mother in the desert, O what loss has
   she suffered:
"It is you" she says to him,
"You look different" she says to him,
. . . .
— O what loss has she suffered,
in woe for her house, in grief for her chamber.

Before we can leave the texts concerned with Dumuzi's death we must consider briefly a curiously deviant attitude which has found expression in the complex literary composition called the "Descent of Inanna."[38] Here the young wife, instead of lamenting Dumuzi's death, is the instrument of it; she delivers him to the powers of the netherworld to escape herself. Only his sister Geshtinanna remains true to him and she eventually pays for her loyalty with death.

The story begins with a whim, a sudden desire of Inanna for the netherworld, a desire that comes to rule her to the exclusion of everything else:

She set her heart from highest heaven
   on earth's deepest ground,
the goddess set her heart from highest heaven
   on earth's deepest ground,

> Inanna set her heart from highest heaven
>   on earth's deepest ground,
> milady abandoned heaven, abandoned earth,
>   went down to Hades,
> Inanna abandoned heaven, abandoned earth,
>   went down to Hades.

She sets out on her venture in full panoply, gathering the emblems of her powers of office around her and dressing in her most majestic robes and ornaments. As she nears the entrance to the netherworld she is beset by last minute misgivings about her ability to cope with what lies before her, and she decides that it would be wise to have someone seek help in case things went badly. She turns to her trusty maid Ninshubur, and gives her precise instructions about what to do if she does not come back, which gods she is to appeal to and what she must say to them. That done, Inanna approaches the great gate of the netherworld where, imperious young queen that she is, she seeks to gain the gatekeeper's attention by hammering on the gate and rudely demanding to be let in. The gatekeeper, not noticeably impressed, asks her bluntly who she is, and when he learns that she is Inanna, the mighty goddess of the morning star standing in the Heavens at sunrise, he naturally begins to wonder what purpose could have brought her to his uninviting gates:

> Neti, the chief gatekeeper of Hades,
> answered holy Inanna (saying):
> "Who might you be, you?"
> "I am Inanna towards the place of sunrise."
> "If you are Inanna towards the place of sunrise,
> why (then) are you come to the land of no return?
> Onto the road (on which) no traveler returns
> how did your heart lead you?"

Inanna has her explanation ready: she is there on a visit of sympathy. The lord Gugalanna, "The great bull of heaven," husband of her elder sister Ereshkigal who is the queen of Hades, has died, and she has come to see the commemorative statue made of him and to grace with her presence the rites of funerary libations of beer. Her explanation fails to set Neti's mind at rest; he asks Inanna to wait while he goes in to tell Ereshkigal about her. His report is explicit to a fault, not a detail of Inanna's appearance seems to have escaped him; though the reasons she has given for coming he apparently considers pure eyewash, not worth repeating.

Ereshkigal is not happy at the news, she smites her thighs with her hands and bites her lips. Finally, she orders Neti to let Inanna in and to bring her before her crouching and stripped bare.

Neti does as he is told, and as he leads Inanna through the seven gates of the netherworld, a functionary at each gate removes one of Inanna's ornaments or pieces of clothing. Astounded, she asks why this is done and each time she receives the same answer:

> "Be silent, Inanna! It befits the ways of Hades;
> raise not your voice, Inanna, against Hades'
>   customs!"

When she has passed through the seventh gate and come before Ereshkigal completely disrobed, Neti makes the full significance of his answer clear:

> "Be silent, Inanna! It befits the ways of Hades;
> raise not your voice, Inanna, against Hades'
>   customs:
> crouched and stripped bare, man comes to me."

The ancients were laid in the grave naked and in crouched position. Without realizing it Inanna has become like the dead, submitting to, not conquering, the realm of death.

Her purpose still rules her, however, and undaunted, she pulls Ereshkigal up from her throne and sits down on it herself. But she has reckoned without the powerful Anunnaki gods, the seven judges of Hades. They do not concur with her brazen attempt to dethrone her sister, but coldly sit in judgment on her and condemn her to death. When she is killed she turns into a side of meat hung on a peg in the wall; it is not even fresh, but green and tainted. She has been utterly vanquished by death and its grim processes of decay.

In the meantime her handmaiden Ninshubur has been patiently waiting outside the gates. When three days and three nights have gone by it is clear that something has gone wrong and that it is time to carry out Inanna's instructions. Ninshubur follows them to the letter, setting up public laments for Inanna to gather people around and bring the loss home to them, sounding her dirge drum in lordly assemblies, doing the rounds of the gods' houses to call attention to what has happened to Inanna. She herself is a model mourner, with her nails raking her eyes and mouth — her belly too, but modestly, and only when men are not around — and she dresses scantily, in a single garment, like a widow who has no man to look after her. Thus she comes to Enlil in Nippur and pleads with him to help Inanna. The words she uses are those Inanna taught her, their burden is that Inanna is much too precious to be treated as if she were a mortal. Enlil would not let his pure silver be fouled in the dust, or his block of lapis lazuli be cut up along with the ordinary stones of the lapidary, or his precious boxwood be chopped down with the cheap woods of the carpenter. How then can he let his daughter be lumped with mortals and become the spoil of Hades? Enlil, persuasive though the argument may be, is unable to help her. Hades is beyond his domain. All

he can say is that Inanna has brought this upon her own head and there is
nothing anybody can do about it.

> "My child craved highest heaven,
>   craved earth's deepest ground,
> Inanna craved highest heaven,
>   craved earth's deepest ground.
> The ways of Hades — exacting ways,
>   exacting ways — have run their course.
> Who could reach her yonder and claim her?"

Ninshubur leaves Nippur and takes the road to Nanna in Ur. Here she
repeats her plea, but Nanna too considers the case hopeless and answers
her in the same words as Enlil. Her last hope is Enki in Eridu. Making her
way to Eridu she repeats her pleas, and at last gets a more promising
response. Enki feels that he should take a hand:

> Father Enki answered Ninshubur:
> "What has befallen my child?
>   I must exert myself!
> What has befallen Inanna?
>   I must exert myself!"

Out of the dirt under his fingernails he fashions two expert mourners, a
beadle, the *kurgaru,* and an elegist, the *kalaturru,* and sends them to Hades
with instructions as to how they may cunningly ingratiate themselves with
Ereshkigal and find a chance to revive Inanna with the water of life and
the grass of life, which he gives them.

Following Enki's instructions the *kurgaru* and the *kalaturru* take the road
to the netherworld where they slip in unnoticed, flying over the doors like
flies and twisting themselves like lizards under the doorjamb pivots, until
they reach Ereshkigal.

They find her sorrowing as is her wont, raking herself in anguish, sick
with grief for her little children who have died before their time:

> The mother who gave birth, Ereshkigal,
> lay there sick (with grief) for her children,
> her pure limbs no linen veiled,
> her bosom had nothing drawn over it,
> her talons were like a copper rake (?) upon her,
> the hairs on her head were like (spiky) leeks.

As instructed by Enki the two mourning specialists join in her laments.
Whenever she wails, "Woe, alas for my heart!", they say to her, "O you
who are sighing, O our lady, alas for your heart!", and whenever she wails,
"Woe, alas for my liver!", they are ready with an, "O, you who are sighing,
O, our lady, alas for your liver!"

To find such sympathy and pity in her lonely misery touches Ereshkigal — as Enki had calculated that it would — and she asks who these kind beings are to whom she can communicate her heart's sorrows. In her gratitude she promises to speak a good word for them if they are gods, to give them a blessing if they are human. This is just what they have been waiting for. They adjure her to give them the side of meat that hangs on the peg. Taken by surprise, Ereshkigal instead offers them first the river in flood, then the field in grain; but they are adamant. Ereshkigal equivocates by telling them that the side of meat belongs to their mistress (i.e., to Inanna), and so, presumably, is not Ereshkigal's to dispose of, but they are not to be swayed and finally the side of meat is handed over. At once one of the professional mourners throws upon it the grass of life and the other the water of life, and Inanna stands before them. She is about to ascend from the netherworld when the dread Anunnaki gods again interpose. None has ever left Hades scot-free. Inanna must present a substitute to take her place.

> One threw on it the grass of life,
>   one the water of life,
> and Inanna rose up.
> Inanna was about to ascend from Hades
> (but) the Anunnaki seized her (saying),
> "Who of those who ascended from Hades
>   ever did get up scot-free?
> If Inanna is ascending from Hades
> let her give a substitute as substitute for her."

Accordingly, Inanna is released only conditionally, and a detachment of deputies from the netherworld goes along with her to see that she provides the substitute. They insolently take over the prerogatives of her trusty Ninshubur: one walks in front of Inanna with staff in hand, one behind her with a club at his side, and the others around her as numerous as reeds in a thicket. They are a frightening, wild, and ruthless crowd, impervious to proffered gifts, respecting no human ties of love and affection.

The first person to meet them on the way back is the faithful Ninshubur who throws herself at her mistress' feet. The brutish deputies suggest to Inanna that they take Ninshubur back with them to Hades as the substitute. Inanna cannot agree to this; Ninshubur has just saved her life, how can she hand her over to death? They continue the march and come to Umma where the city god, Shara, meets them and throws himself at Inanna's feet. He has been sitting sorrowing in the dust, dressed in mourner's garb because of Inanna. Again, the deputies wish to take him, again Inanna cannot bring herself to deliver up to them someone so loyal and so needed for the services he performs for her. Presently, they come to Bad-tibira where the city god, Latarak, throws himself at her feet in greeting. He, too, has been mourning in the dust. Again the deputies want to get the business over with, and again Inanna balks. And so they continue toward Uruk, or more particularly, toward the maimed apple-tree in the desert of Kullab which is a part of Uruk. It is here that Inanna's young husband has his sheepfold and here that Inanna and the deputies come upon an astonishing sight. The bereaved husband, far from eating his heart out and grieving in sackcloth and ashes like everyone else, seems to be enjoying himself thoroughly, sitting in noble raiment on a noble seat.

The deputies — perhaps sensing what the sight is doing to Inanna — do not ask leave this time but immediately attack:

> The deputies surged into his fold,
> pouring the milk out of its seven churns;
> all seven they were rushing him
>   as were he an interloper
> and began by striking the shepherd
>   in the face with the flutes and pipes.

As for Inanna, she is in the grip of black rage and jealous hurt; one look has been enough for her. She gives the deputies their head:

> She looked at him, it was a look of death,
> spoke to them, it was a word of wrath
> cried out to them, it was the cry of "guilty!"
> "Take this one along!"
> Holy Inanna gave the shepherd Dumuzi into their hands.

For poor Dumuzi there is little hope. The deputies of Hades are ruthless:

> They who escorted him,
> they who escorted Dumuzi,
> knew not food, knew not water,
> ate not (offerings of) strewn flour,
> drank not libations of water,
> filled not with sweetness the loins of the
>   mate,
> kissed not the sweetest child —
> made a man's son get up from (his) knee,
> made the daughter-in-law leave the father-
>   in-law's house.

In his distress Dumuzi can think of no one to turn to except the traditional guardian of justice, the sun god Utu, who is, moreover, his brother-in-law. He lifts his hands to Utu, reminding him of their relationship and asking to be changed into a snake that he may escape his captors.

At this point our main version of the tale breaks off, but the story of "Dumuzi's Dream" and particularly a variant version of "Inanna's Descent" from Ur allow us to surmise that Utu granted his prayer, that he escaped and was recaptured several times, that his sister Geshtinanna was set upon by the deputies and refused to betray him, and that he was finally captured in his own sheepfold. The Ur version breaks at this point, but its last lines suggest that Geshtinanna set out in search of her brother after he had been taken away:

> The sister, on account of her brother,
>   roamed around in the city like a
>   (circling) bird:
> "I will go to the perpetrator of (this) outrage
>   on my brother, I will enter any house."

To be with her brother she is willing to serve in any house where he is captive.

We need to turn to other texts for suggestions about how the story must have continued, particularly to one that tells us that it was the fly that revealed to Geshtinanna where her brother was to be found and led her to the brewery where he dwelt with the wise brewmasters.[39] This introduction of the fly accords with the last section of the main version of Inanna's descent, which we fortunately still have, albeit in battered condition. This section deals with Inanna's determining the fate of the fly — whether for good or bad is not clear — apparently because of something the fly has done. It seems natural to suppose that she is punishing or rewarding it for telling where Dumuzi is. The text relates how she decided to mitigate the fate of Dumuzi.

> Dumuzi wept (saying),
> "My sister has come,
>   she has been delivered up with me!
> Now, alas, her life [is cut short]."

To which Inanna seems to answer

> "You half a year, your sister half a year:
> while you are walking around (alive),
>   she will lie prostrate,
> while your sister is walking around (alive),
>   you will lie prostrate."

Dumuzi and his sister will alternate half-year terms in the netherworld.

The story ends with two more lines that abruptly recall us to what we had forgotten as we followed the fortunes of Dumuzi and Geshtinanna, namely, that the tale is basically about Inanna's challenge to Ereshkigal, a challenge in which the latter emerges victorious, while Inanna barely manages to extricate herself at heavy moral cost:

> Holy Inanna was delivering up Dumuzi
>   as her substitute.
> Holy Ereshkigal! (To sing) your praises is sweet.

What is the meaning of this extraordinary tale or, perhaps better, of the underlying mythical materials on which it builds? The story seems to be composed of no less than three separate myths, each dealing with a dying and reviving deity, which are combined so that the revival of one deity is the cause of, or coincides with, the death of another. The revival of Inanna becomes the cause of the death of Dumuzi, and the revival of Dumuzi — at least for half of the year — depends on the death of Geshtinanna. The clearest component is probably the one relating to Geshtinanna. The fact that here Dumuzi is found in the brewery, the "house of beer" shows that in this part of the story we are dealing with the aspect of the god under which he is the power in grain and in the beer brewed from it and not as elsewhere with his shepherd aspect. His death, accordingly, is when the grain is cut at harvest and then brewed into beer which goes into storage underground: that is to say, into the netherworld.

Geshtinanna herself is the power in the grape and in the wine made from it. This is clear from her name, which means "the leafy grapevine" and her epithet A m a - g e s h t i n n a (in the Eme-sal dialect A m a - m u t i n n a), which means "Root-stock of the grapevine." Thus the powers informing the two principal intoxicating drinks of the ancients, the beer and the wine, were seen by them to be closely related, as brother and sister. Both died, mythopoeically speaking, at harvest time, and both descended into the earth for underground storage. But they did not do so at the same time of year. Grain was harvested in the spring and brewed and stored afterward. The grape was harvested only in the autumn and was made into wine then. It is this difference in the time of death and descent that the myth takes as its theme to explain in terms of timeless happenings in *illo tempora*. When Dumuzi of the beer disappears underground in the spring or early summer, his sister, the wine goddess, seeks him disconsolately until, by autumn, she herself descends into the earth and finds him there in the netherworld. The myth further explains how this difference in the time of living and growing above ground became permanent through divine fiat: Inanna determined as their fate that they were to alternate substituting for her in the netherworld.

More difficult is the myth about Inanna and *her* descent. Tentatively we would suggest that it deals with the time of year when food supplies are at their most critical point, which is late winter when the stores in the storehouse dwindle and finally come to an end. In the humanizing terms of myth that becomes the death of the storehouse and the power in it to function, Inanna; its subsequent replenishment from the pastures in spring correspondingly becomes a revival of its power. If this is true, Inanna's intention in the myth of taking over the netherworld will reflect the way that the underground storeroom looks roomier as it becomes more empty and seems to vie with that other underground space familiar to the ancients, the grave vault. The gradual disappearance of its proper

vestments and ornaments, the stores, may find its mythopoeic counterpart in the disappearance of Inanna's raiment and ornaments as she
moves deeper and deeper into the realm of death. Her actual death, the
final inability of the storehouse to function as food supply, the myth
dramatically symbolizes by the cut of tainted meat into which she is turned
in the netherworld. The empty storehouse in late winter holding only a
last side of decaying meat was undoubtedly an experience familiar to the
ancients, familiar and terrifying in its smell of death and clear and present
threat of starvation.

Inanna's revival, the replenishing of the storehouse, is caused by Enki,
god of the fresh waters, and by the pasture and watering places that he
provides: the grass of life and the water of life. It takes place in the spring,
the time when rains and inundation by floods make the desert into green
pasture land and the time, also, of harvest (Ereshkigal can offer the river
in flood and the field in grain to the emissaries of Enki). Further, the
revival implies the death of Dumuzi the shepherd, for the replenishing of
the stores is at the expense of the flocks and the newborn lambs and kids
that must provide fresh meat to be stored, at the expense of that very
increase of which Dumuzi is the active principle and which ceases at that
time of year. Thus, at its simplest, we would see the death of Inanna in the
emptying of the storehouse, her revival and the resultant death of
Dumuzi in the replenishing of the storehouse with fresh meat when the
flocks return from the desert and its withering pasturage in late spring
and early summer. The last part of the tale, Geshtinanna's search for her
brother, seems to be a myth belonging to Dumuzi under his aspect of
power in the grain and the beer; this was originally a separate myth
concerned with explaining the difference in timing of the grain crop and
the grape crop, of beer and wine.

Search and Return

Geshtinanna's search for her lost brother is dealt with in myths of
Dumuzi in which he is the power in the grain and beer. Such a search by
mother and sister, or by sister alone, is also characteristic of the myths
around Damu, the aspect under which Dumuzi is the power in the sap in
trees and vegetation. Here it is combined with a celebration of the return
of the dead god to the land of the living. The best known treatment of it is
probably the one given in the composition called *Edin-na ú-saĝ-ĝá*, "In the
desert in the early grass," which seems to be basically a Damu text, although materials from the cult of several other Dumuzi figures have
been worked into its sequences. The text begins with a long lament
addressed to the dead god, whose connection with trees and vegetation is
clear — but to us a little monotonous — in lines such as

> (O you) my tamarisk, (fated) not (to)
>   drink water in its garden bed,
> whose top formed no foliage in the plain,
> my poplar, who rejoiced not at its water
>   conduit,
> my poplar torn up by the root;
> my vine, (fated) not (to) drink
>   water in the garden. . . .[40]

The text then moves into the search for Damu by his sorrowing mother and sister.[41] The mother recalls the terrible day when the deputies of the netherworld came to take Damu from her:

> I am the mother who bore (him)!
>   Woe to that day, that day,
>   woe to that night!
> I am the lad's mother!
>   Woe to that day, that day,
>   woe to that night!
> The day that dawned for my (only) support,
> that dawned for the lad, my Damu,
> a day to be blotted out, that I would I
>   could forget!
> Yon night that should never have let it
>   go forth,
> when the brazen deputies entered before me,
> that day bereft me of the lad, . . .
> bereft me of the lad, my Damu. . . .

She asks for her lost son along the road:

> I, the lad's mother, will go
>   from canebrake to canebrake,
> I, mother of the lord, will go
>   from canebrake to canebrake,
> one may show me (where) my provider (is),
> one may show me where my provider,
>   robbed from me, is.[42]

But the canebrake has no comfort to give her:

> Cow, do not low for the calf,
>   turn your face toward me!
> The sheriff's deputy will not give you
>   your son,
> the governor will not give him to you,
> the lord who slew him will not give
>   him to you![43]

The mother continues her lament:

> From me, wailing woman — woe! — what sought
>   the sheriff from me?
> The sheriff of the governor,
>   what sought he from me?
> In Girsu on the bank of the Euphrates,
>   what sought he from me?
> He parted my thighs, robbed me of my husband;
> he parted my knees, robbed me of my son!
> Woe (to that) sheriff, what sought he from me?[44]

She will seek restitution from him:

> At the gate of the sheriff I will stand,
>   will bring to him my tears,
> at the gate of the sheriff I will tread
>   a mournful measure;
> "woe for that lad" in grief I will say,
> "for my lovely one" in grief I will say,
> "I, the mother who bore him, driven
>   like an ox," hotly I will say.
> And when I have spoken my plaint, what can
>   he say to the plaint?
> When I have brought (him) my tears, what
>   can he say to the plaint?
> When I have filled (his gate) with wailing
>   what can he say to the plaint?[45]

At long last she realizes that her son is nowhere in heaven, nowhere on earth; he is in the netherworld and she must seek him there. It is to no avail that Damu himself seeks to warn her from the grave — rather gruesomely referring to the food and water which it was customary to place in the grave with the corpse:

> O you, mother, who gave birth,
>   how could you eat the food,
>   how could you drink that water?
> O, mother, of the lad,
> how could you eat the food,
>   how could you drink that water?
> The looks of that food is bad,
>   how could you eat that food?
> The looks of that water is bad,
>   how could you drink that water?
> The food I have been eating since yesterday,
>   my mother, you must not eat!
> The water I myself have drunk,
>   my mother must not drink![46]

But the mother is set on her course; she cannot be deterred:

> If it is required, O lad, let me walk with you
> > the road of no return.
> Woe the lad! The lad, my Damu!
> She goes, she goes,
> > towards the breast of the hills (of death),
> The day waning, the day waning,
> > toward the hills (still) bright,
> to him who lies in blood and water,
> > the sleeping lord,
> To him who knows no healing lustrations
> to "The Road That Destroys Him Who Walks It."[47]

And so we follow her through the desert, calling her son in vain:

> I am not one who can answer my mother
> > who cries for me in the desert,
> who makes the cry for me echo in the desert,
> > she will not be answered.
> I am not the grass,
> > may not grow up (again) for her,
> I am not the waters,
> > may not rise (again) for her,
> I am not the grass sprouting in the desert,
> I am not the new grass, growing up in the desert.[48]

There are stations on the road where she and Damu's sister stop; there are laments that we only half-understand; there are litanies enumerating the graves in which Damu and his various manifestations rest, among these all the dead kings of the Third Dynasty of Ur and of later dynasties. Toward the end of the composition we seem to lose sight of the mother and it is only Damu's sister who finds him and joins him in the netherworld. He greets her pathetically:

> "O my sister, who must also be a mother to me,
> O Amageshtinna, who must also be a mother to me,
> tears like a child I weep,
> sobs like a child I sob to you!"[49]

She answers — reminding us by her terms of address that underneath the human guise we are dealing with the numinous power of vegetation:

> "O my brother, luxuriantly sprouting in appearance,
> > luxuriantly fruitful in appearance:
> who is your sister? I am your sister!
> Who is your mother? I am your mother!
> The day that dawns for you will also dawn for me
> the day you see, I shall also see!"[50]

The search for Damu is also dealt with in a fragmentary composition where the sister follows him along the bank of a river on which he is carried to the netherworld — the empty riverbed of the dry season:

> The river of Hades lets no water flow —
>> water from it slakes no thirst.
> The field of Hades grows no grain —
>> no flour is milled from it.
> The sheep of Hades carry no wool —
>> no cloth is woven from it.

She calls to him that she has food and drink for him if he is hungry and thirsty, but he cannot answer. When they finally reach the gates of the netherworld she presses her hand against it in a vain effort to open it but has to turn back. Damu now feels truly abandoned — his sister, who has taken care of him and been as a mother to him, has left him:

> "Now it is truly doomful,
>> my mother has turned away from me,
> my mother has turned away from me,
>> my sister has turned away from me,
> my mother has turned away from me!"

Still a third Damu text — originally composed, it would seem, for the tree god Ningishzida with whom Damu is identified — tells how his older and younger sisters find him in a boat ready to sail down to the netherworld. The sisters call to him, one standing at the prow and one at the stern of the boat, and ask to be taken aboard. At first he does not answer, but when the evil netherworld deputy who captains the boat calls his attention to them, he tries to dissuade them by asking why they want to sail with him, by trying to make clear that he goes as a bound prisoner, and by comparing himself to a tree, a tamarisk or a date palm, destroyed before its time. The sisters, however, insist, offering their ornaments and jewelry as ransom and pleading that the food and drink they brought with them has been taken from them by hungry and thirsty ones so that they are at the end of their tether. The evil deputy then halts the boat's departure so that they can join their brother and the boat begins its journey down to Hades. A cry of warning precedes them:

> O (city of) Ur! At my loud cry
> lock your house, lock your house,
>> city lock your house!
> O temple of Ur! Lock your house,
>> city lock your house.
> Against your lord who has gone out
>> of (his house) the Giparu.
> city lock your house!

Eventually the boat arrives in the netherworld where, unexpectedly, it is halted by the son of Ereshkigal, probably Ninazu, who orders the deputy to release his captive. Damu, with tears of gratitude, bathes his head, puts on shoes, and sits down to a tasty meal. He is now an official in the netherworld, not its captive.

The return of Damu to the land of the living is celebrated, as far as we know, only in one composition. However, we have that in three versions, only one of which is reasonably complete.[51] It may, from its beginning line, be named "O Lord, Great Noble Child, Exalted Above and Below!" Its first song is a paean of praise to Damu in which the poet expresses his wish to speak nobly and extol Damu's name in song, then hails him under the names of the various gods with whom he was identified, such as Ishtaran, Igishuba, and others. This initial hymn of praise is followed by one of appeasement, and then by a lament for the destruction of Uruk consequent upon a decision made in the assembly of the gods, announced as usual by An and Enlil. Many parts of these first songs are stereotypical and may well turn out to be later additions. We arrive at the substance of the composition in the fifth song, which is a lament by Damu's mother who is fearful that the god may not return:

> For him of the faraway —
>   the wailing for (fear) that he may not come,
> for my child of the faraway,
>   the wailing for (fear) that he may not come.
> For my Damu of the faraway —
> for my anointed one of the faraway —
> from the holy cedar
>   where I, (his) mother, bore (him),
> from Eanna above and below,
>   the wailing for (fear) that he may not come,
> the wailing in the lord's house,
>   the wailing for (fear) that he may not come,
> the wailing in my lord's city,
>   the wailing for (fear) that he may not come,
> that wailing is verily wailing for the vines;
>   the plot with vines may not give birth to it.
> That wailing is verily for the barley;
>   the furrow may not give birth to it.
>
> . . . .
>
> That wailing is verily for the great river;
>   it may not give birth to its waters.
> That wailing is verily for the field;
>   it may not give birth to the mottled barley.
> That wailing is verily for the marsh;
>   it may not give birth to carp and trout.

> That wailing is verily for the reed thicket;
>   the old reeds may not give birth to (new) reeds.
> That wailing is verily for the woods;
>   they may not give birth to stag and deer.
> That wailing is verily for the gardens;
>   they may not give birth to honey and wine.
> That wailing is verily for the garden beds;
>   they may not give birth to lettuce and cress.
> That wailing is verily for the palace;
>   it may not give birth to long life.

In the sixth song the mother goes to seek her son from a nurse with whom she had placed him:

> O my (good) nurse, from whom I was parted,
>   I put a child to dwell with you,
> a child engendered by An,
> I put a child to dwell with you,
> I put the lad Ususu ("The nourisher"),
>   a child, to dwell with you,
> I put a child to dwell with you,
> I put the lord Ningishzida to dwell with you,
> I put a child to dwell with you,
> I put the lad, my Damu, to dwell with you,
> I put a child to dwell with you,
> I put Ishtaran, Igishuba, to dwell with you,
> I put a child to dwell with you —
> my eyes I have adorned with eyeblack for him,
> my forearms I have adorned with cedar perfume
>   for him,
> my back I have adorned
>   with embroidered cloth and embroidered linen for him,
> my head I have adorned
>   with a splendid turban for him.

She goes on to say that the child lay in the nurse's marrow and bark, that the nurse ate and drank with him; she laments the loss of him as her future provider, her cries of "Woe!" and "Ah!" rising to heaven and going down into the earth. In the seventh song which begins:

> (To please) him who sails the high waters, the flood, . . .
> to please him who comes out of the river,
> I, to please the child who comes out of the river . . .

the mother once again tells how she has dressed in all her finery for the sake of her son. In one of our versions, moreover, she identifies herself as a tree, a cedar. She says:

> My sides are cedar, my breast is cypress,

> O nurse, my limbs are sappy cedar,
> are sappy cedar, are of the Hashur (mountains),
> are black wood of (the island) Tilmun.

After telling about her fine dress she adds that her son was lying asleep in
rushes and trees, but that these have released him to the desert, which is
now guarding him until he may come on the flood:

> My child who lay down to sleep till now,
> the wild bull, who lay down
>   to sleep the treacherous sleep till now,
> Damu, who lay down
>   to sleep the treacherous sleep till now,
> the anointed one, who lay down
>   to sleep the treacherous sleep till now.
>
> my child was lying in the *shuppatu* rush,
>   and the *shuppatu* rush hushed,
> my child was lying in the halfa grass,
>   and the halfa grass hushed,
> He was lying in the poplar
>   and the poplar rustled to him,
> he was lying in the tamarisk
>   and the tamarisk sang lullabies to him,
>
> that child they have released into the high
>   desert,
> released him into the high desert and the low
>   desert;
> the desert kept watch over him at the place,
> like a cowherd over the place of his numerous cows
>   it kept watch over him,
> like a shepherd over the place of his numerous sheep
>   it kept watch over him,
> over him who sails the high waters, the flood.

In the eighth song, a rapturous paean, we have the greeting to the god as
he finally arrives, enchanting the worshipers:

> Noble, noble, that lord is noble!
> Ususu the noble householder,
>   that lord is noble!
> Ningishzida the noble householder,
>   that lord is noble!
> Damu the noble householder,
>   that lord is noble!
> Ishtaran the noble householder,
>   that lord is noble!
> Igishuba the noble householder,
>   that lord is noble!

The mother who bore him is a goddess, Urash (i.e., The tilth),
    that lord is noble!
His father is the wild bull of Eridu (Enki),
    that lord is noble!
His glance is fraught with awesomeness,
    that lord is noble!
His utterance is full of deliciousness,
    that lord is noble!
His limbs are covered with deliciousness,
    that lord is noble!
His word takes precedence,
    that lord is noble!
Noble one, noble one, be at ease with us!
Ususu, noble householder, be at ease with us!
Ningishzida. . . .

The song repeats word for word all it has already said but with the refrain "be at ease with us!" instead of "that lord is noble!"; then it again repeats itself, this time with the refrain "we will appease him!" before it comes to an end.

A short ninth song, apparently an invocation to the ox of the god, perhaps the one towing his boat, is followed by a processional hymn, the ninth song, the worshipers accompanying the god to his father:

You whom I accompany, in whom I rejoice,
walking with speed under the stars in peace;
Ususu, whom I accompany to the father,
    in whom I rejoice,
Ningishzida, whom I accompany to the father,
    in whom I rejoice,
my Damu, whom I accompany to the father,
    in whom I rejoice,
Ishtaran, whom I accompany to the father,
    in whom I rejoice,
Igishuba, whom I accompany to the father,
    in whom I rejoice,
shepherd Ur-Nammu, whom I accompany to the father,
    in whom I rejoice. . . .

With Ur-Nammu, the first king of the Third Dynasty of Ur, the song takes up the series of rulers who during their lifetimes were the god's ritual avatars and who continued to be his incarnations after their death. The litany moves from the kings of the Third Dynasty of Ur through the kings of the Dynasty of Isin, ending with the short-lived ruler Iddin-Eshtar. The character of the god as provider of food stands out clearly in the concluding section of the song:

> The lord of food and drink whom I accompany,
>   in whom I rejoice;
> the lord of food and drink whom I accompany,
>   in whom I rejoice

which continues — unfortunately much damaged — with references to cattle pens, sheepfolds, vines, fields, and irrigation canals.

The composition contains yet three more songs, the eleventh, built on the theme "Great lord, could I but rival you in awe and glory!", the twelfth which repeats the seventh, and the thirteenth and last. Unfortunately, this thirteenth song is much damaged and any reading and restoration is tentative and uncertain. It seems to celebrate the gifts the god brings and may be rendered:

> You come to us laden,
>   you come laden!
> O Ususu! You come to us laden,
>   you come laden;
> Ningishzida, you come to us laden,
>   you come laden;
> my Damu, you come to us laden,
>   you come laden;
> Ishtaran, Igishuba, you come to us laden,
>   you come laden.
> you come to us laden with restoration of temples,
>   you come laden;
> you come to us laden with restoration of cities,
>   you come laden;
> you come to us laden with life(-giving) food,
>   you come laden;
> you come laden with life(-giving) water,
>   you come laden. . . .

This list of blessings continues with some eight more lines, too fragmentary to be reconstructed. The composition is undoubtedly a true cult song meant to accompany a ritual; a ritual, it seems safe to postulate, which began with laments sung at a sacred cedar tree growing in the compound of the temple Eanna in Uruk (mentioned in the fifth song). This sacred cedar not only marked the god's birthplace but was itself considered his mother, and probably the bend in the river where the god was met was nearby. The rite seems to have closed with a triumphant procession that followed the god downstream. The god appears to represent the sap lying dormant in the rushes and trees during the dry season but reviving, to the profound relief and joy of the orchardman, with the river's rise. Representing the sap, a "sappy cedar" growing near Uruk may have been considered Damu's mother; ultimately, however, since the sap derives

from irrigation with waters of the river — Enki, drenching the tilth, Urash
— he was also the son, or descendant, of those two.

The fourth millennium, then, as far as we can grasp it from contemporary sources and later survivals, informed ancient Mesopotamian religion
with its basic character: the worship of forces in nature. These forces were
intuited as the life principle in observed phenomena, their will to be in this
particular form. As the most characteristic trend of the millennium we
may posit the selection and cultivation for worship of those powers which
were important for human survival — powers central to the early
economies — and their progressive humanization arising out of a human
need for a meaningful relationship with them. This led to a growing
preference for the human form over the older nonhuman forms as the
only one truly proper to the gods, and to a preference for organizing the
gods within human patterns of family and occupation. The dominant
figure is the son and provider, whose life from wooing to wedding to early
death expresses the annual cycle of fertility and yield.

While we have considered only one cult, that of Dumuzi and figures
identified with him, there is every reason to assume that this cult was
characteristic and that its ritual and metaphorical patterns of wooing and
wedding, death and lament, were widespread and typical, for traces and
parallels are to be found in the lore of almost every major ancient
Mesopotamian god. Wooing and wedding occur in myth and ritual also
associated with Enlil, Nanna/Suen, and Ninurta/Ningirsu; while near-
death, death, or descent to the netherworld is told (in one form or
another) also of An, Enlil, Enki, Nanna/Suen, Ninurta/Ningirsu, Utu,
Ishkur, and Inanna. They would seem, therefore, to constitute the forms
of approach to the Numinous generally available. In the next millennium
the trend to humanization was to extend from the narrow pattern of
family, occupation, and individual life cycle, to the wider patterns of the
community and the state with its internal and external political forms:
from anthropomorphism and sociomorphism to politicomorphism.

3
Third Millennium Metaphors.
The Gods as Rulers:
The Cosmos a Polity

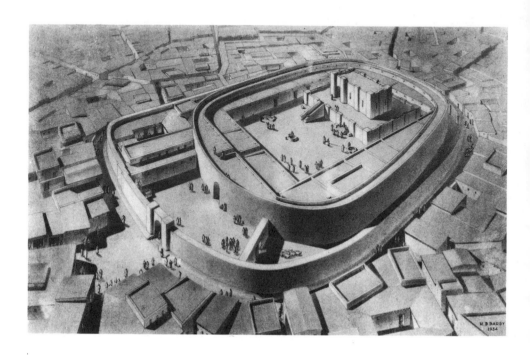

A reconstruction by Hamilton C. Darby of a Mesopotamian temple (Khafajah) from the early half of the third millenium B.C. excavated by the Iraq expedition of the Oriental Institute of the University of Chicago. The temple is enclosed by a solid, oval, defensive wall. Along the inside of this wall were storerooms and craftsmen's shops. On the left-hand side is the Giparu, the dwelling of the high priest or *en*. The temple was dedicated to Inanna, who had her abode high on the central terrace. There is an altar next to the stairs leading to the sanctuary. The excavators even uncovered evidence of animals that were dragged on a rainy day to be sacrificed.

Warlike Times

We have mentioned earlier how human wavering between attraction to and fear of the Numinous introduced an element of choice, of seeking it or avoiding it, and in our discussion of the early fertility cults we saw how this choice tended to become situationally conditioned: the powers whose allegiance was sought were those encountered in situations and phenomena on which life depended, powers holding out the promise of freedom from want.

With the beginning of the third millennium B.C., the ever present fear of famine was no longer the main reminder of the precariousness of the human condition. Sudden death by the sword in wars or raids by bandits joined famine as equally fearsome threats.

As far as we can judge, the fourth millennium and the ages before it had been moderately peaceful. Wars and raids were not unknown; but they were not constant and they did not dominate existence. In the third millennium they appear to have become the order of the day. No one was safe. The quickness with which an enemy could strike — some warlord bound for loot to fill the long boats in which he moved along the network of major canals crisscrossing Mesopotamia — made life, even for the wealthy and powerful, uncertain and insecure: queens and great ladies like their humble sisters faced the constant possibility that the next day might find them widowed, torn from home and children, and enslaved in some barbarous household:

> Alas! that day of mine, on which I was destroyed;
> alas! that day of mine, on which I was destroyed,
>
> . . . .
> For on it he came hither to me in my house,
> for on it he turned in the mountains
>   into the road to me,
> for on it the boat came on my river toward me,
> for on it, (heading) toward me,
>   the boat moored at my quay,
> for on it the master of the boat came in to me,
> for on it he reached out his dirty hands toward me,
> for on it he yelled to me: "Get up! Get on board!"
> For on it the goods were taken aboard in the bow.
> For on it I, the queen, was taken on board in the stern.
> For on it I grew cold with the most shivering fear.
> The foe trampled with his booted feet into my chamber!
> That foe reached out his dirty hands toward me!
> He reached out the hand toward me, he terrified me!
> That foe reached out his hand toward me,
>   made me die with fear.

That foe intimidated me — I did not intimidate him.
That foe stripped me of my robe,
    clothed his wife in it,
that foe cut my string of gems,
    hung it on his child,
I (myself) was to tread (the walks of) his abode.[52]

The queen speaking here is a goddess and the attack she describes cannot be placed in time; but her bitter memories of a "day . . . on which I was destroyed" would have been those of many a noblewoman of the Early Dynastic period.

The intensity of the danger at this time may be gauged by the enormous city walls which ringed every city; only dire necessity could have commanded the staggering investment of labor they attest to. This necessity is also vividly indicated by the new settlement patterns of the time. The investigations of Robert M. Adams in the central regions of Sumer show that the network of small open villages which had earlier characterized the region disappeared with the coming of the Early Dynastic period. Instead, the larger cities of the region grew as the village populations sought protection behind their walls.[53]

The Ruler Metaphor

Amid these dangers men could look for protection only to the now vitally important institutions of collective security, the great leagues and their officers, and particularly to the new institution of kingship as it took form in these years. The evidence suggests that kingship originally was a temporary office: a king was chosen as leader when war threatened and ceased to exercise authority once the emergency was over. Now, the emergency had become chronic, and the office of king had become permanent because of it, so had his army and the manning and maintenance of the city wall. Gradually, leadership in all major communal undertakings devolved on the king and became united in his person. A traditional formula of homage to the ruler of Uruk, preserved for us in a tale dealing with these times, expresses the trust in the king as protector of the walled city and vanquisher of the foe:

(The city) Uruk, handiwork of the gods,
and (its temple) Eanna, temple descended from
    heaven. . . .
It is the great gods (themselves who) made
    their component parts!
As the great wall that (the former) is —
    a stormcloud lying on the horizon —

and as the august abode that (the latter) is —
  one founded by An —
(Uruk and Eanna) are (both) entrusted unto thee,
  thou are the king and defender!

The cracker of heads, the prince beloved by An,
O! how he inspired fear after he had come!
Their troops melted away, scattering from the rear;
their men were unable to face him.[54]

With the new anxiety a new savior-figure had come into being, the ruler: exalted above men, fearsome as warrior, awesome in the power at his command.

The impact of the new ruler concept on contemporary thought can hardly be overestimated. In art the old ritual motifs receded before representations of war and victory; in literature a new form, the epic tale, took its place beside the myth. In the epic, man, represented by the ruler, is the hero, and the tale celebrates his prowess and his cleverness, even to the point of challenging the authority of the gods. Gilgamesh, for example, champions Inanna in one tale, even though her brother, the sun god and god of justice, had refused to do so, and is punished for it by the loss of sporting gear, which in turn leads to the death of his trusty servant Enkidu when the latter seeks to recover it from Hades.[55] In the story of the "Bull of Heaven"[56] Gilgamesh treats Inanna with insolence. In the story of Huwawa he disregards Enlil by killing the latter's forester.[57] In the epic of "Enmerkar and the Lord of Aratta"[58] the human ruler of Aratta bends all his cleverness to frustrate what he knows to be Inanna's will — and succeeds in no small measure. The trend to believe in man and his powers in defiance of the gods continued into the Period of Agade and found its most striking — and most cautionary — expression in the figure of the willful king, Naramsîn, whose defiance of Enlil led to the destruction of Agade and the end of its rule.[59]

Religion met this trend toward hubris and lack of respect for the gods, as the examples just mentioned show, with the assertion that in the long run the gods would not be flouted, that divine retribution was certain. Also — and far more revolutionary — by the insight that this new concept of the ruler, though purely secular in origin, actually provided an approach to central aspects of the Numinous which had not been readily suggestible before: the aspects of tremendum as "majesty" and "energy." In the small, tight-knit society of the village and small town, such as we must suppose for ancient Mesopotamia in the earliest period, there had not been much social differentiation between people, and not much opportunity for feelings of awe and reverence to develop. With the concentration of power in the person of the king, the experience of awe and majesty entered everyday existence. The unique energy that the king represented was new. His was the central will of society in peace and in war; he was its driving force in all things.

Inasmuch as the new concept of the ruler allowed a more profound recall of numinous experience than the older metaphors taken from primary economic situations and focusing mainly on the fascinosum, its extensive application as a metaphor for the divine can be understood. A striking example is the prayer of Gudea of Lagash to Ningirsu. That prayer is later in date than the times with which we are dealing and shows, perhaps, a more effortless blend of the ruler metaphor with the older metaphors taken from nature, than the earliest applications may have attained to. Ningirsu is the power in thunderstorms and the yearly flood when the Tigris is swelled by the reddish brown waters of its rain fed mountain tributaries. He ranks as the firstborn son of the "great mountain," the storm god Enlil, whose title clearly alludes to the eastern mountains from which the tributaries come. Ningirsu has commanded Gudea in a dream to build his temple, but has not yet given specific instructions, and so Gudea prays:

> O my master Ningirsu, lord,
>   seminal waters reddened in the deflowering;
> able lord, seminal waters
>   emitted by the "great mountain,"
> hero without a challenger,
> Ningirsu, I am to build you your house,
> but I have nothing to go by!
> Warrior, you have called for the "proper thing,"
> but, son of Enlil, lord Ningirsu,
> the heart of the matter I cannot know.
> Your heart, rising as (rise the waves in) mid-ocean,
> crashing down as (crash) the breakers,
> roaring like waters pouring (through a breach in a dike),
> Destroying cities like the flood-wave,
> rushing upon the enemy country like a storm,
> O my master, your heart, a torrent (from a breach in a dike)
>   not to be stemmed,
> warrior, your heart, remote (and unapproachable)
>   like the far-off heavens,
> how can I know it?[60]

The ruler metaphor — expressed in the terms "master," "lord," and "warrior" — fits particularly well the unbounded power of the natural phenomenon in which the god is experienced, and the prayer cogently conveys Gudea's awe before a mysterium tremendum, the wholly other, terrifying power in the flood-wave sweeping down from the mountains.

The ruler metaphor — like the ruler concept — could not be lifted out of the social and political context from which it derived its meaning. The new view of the gods as rulers brought the whole political context of the ruler to bear on them and thus — since they were the powers in all the significant phenomena around — on the whole phenomenal world. The universe became a polity.

To form an idea of what the world thus seen and experienced was like, we may begin by considering the role of the gods on the narrowest, local level, rulers of their own temples and towns, and then move on to look at their broader duties and functions as citizens on the national political scene.

Divine Manors

At home the more important gods were simply manorial lords administering their great temple estates, seeing to it that plowing, sowing, and reaping were done at the right times, and keeping order in the towns and villages that belonged to the manor.

Eninnu, the temple of Ningirsu in Girsu, was an example of such a divine manor and we are particularly well informed about its organization from a variety of sources. The manual work in the temple and on its lands was performed under the direction of the ruler of Girsu, similarly, the temple of the god's wife, Baba, was administered by the ruler's wife, and the temples of the god's children were administered by — or in the name of — the ruler's children. The ruler had a large staff of human helpers. Some worked in the temple itself performing the daily rituals of preparing and serving the god's meals, looking after his clothes, and keeping his quarters neat. Others saw to ploughing, sowing, the irrigation works, harvesting, fishing, and looking after the asses, oxen, sheep, and goats of the temple. Milling grain, spinning, and weaving wool were largely in the hands of female personnel, though often there were male overseers. Scribes and accountants kept a close eye on income and expenditures.[61]

Since man, as the Sumerians saw him, was weak and could achieve no success in anything without divine assistance, it was fortunate that all these human workers in and outside the temple could invigorate themselves with divine power. Each group of human toilers had human overseers; but above these there were divine officials to direct the work and infuse success into human efforts. The complete divine staff that served Ningirsu, and through which he managed the affairs of Eninnu, is listed for us in an inscription of Gudea, the ruler of Girsu whose prayer to Ningirsu we already quoted. Gudea tells how he appointed these attendant gods to their offices in the new temple he had built, beginning with Ningirsu's son Igalima who was appointed high constable:

> In order to guide aright the hand of the righteous man, but to put the evildoer in the neck-stock, to make the house just, to make the house plea-

sant, to issue ordinances for his city, the manor Girsu, to set up the throne of
(rendering) verdicts, to place in (Gudea's) hand a long-term sceptre, to make
the shepherd called by Ningursu lift up the head (as proudly) as the yellow
turban (of the moon), and to assign positions in the courtyard of Eninnu to
the skin-clad (fieldhands), the linen-clad (house servants) and (those with)
the head covered (administrators?), he (Gudea) let Igalima, high constable of
Girsu, his (Ningirsu's) beloved son, go about his duties for the lord Ningirsu
in (the cella) Ulnun, as great doorleaf.[62]

The god Igalima, whose name means "the doorleaf of the honored one,"
was a personification of the door to Ningirsu's holy of holies, Ulnun. The
Sumerian mythopoeic imagination gave him the task of guard and made
him Ningirsu's high constable. As head of the constabulary it was his duty
to maintain justice, arrest evildoers, issue ordinances to the city, and when
the ruler sat in judgment, to set up his throne and hand him the symbol of
authority, the sceptre. For this reason the position is also called "throne-
bearer," g u z a l a. Igalima is also in charge of policing the courtyard of
Eninnu where the audience seekers throng and of assigning to each their
place in line.

After Igalima, Gudea lists Ningirsu's oldest son, Shulshagana, and
outlines his duties as steward. We learn that the domestic requirements of
Ningirsu were taken care of by a divine "chamberlain," the goddess
Kindazi, who was in charge of preparing the god's bath and seeing that
there was fresh straw in his bed. Shulshagana, as was customary for the
oldest son in a great household, supervised the meals and carried the
pitcher of water for washing the hands before and after eating. Ningirsu's
shifting moods were humored by two divine musicians, the "singer"
Ushumgalkalama, who inspired the harp of that name and provided
gaiety, and the elegist Lugaligihusham, the spirit of another harp that
brought solace in dark moments. For "handmaidens" Ningirsu had his
septuplet daughters — personifications of the clouds — born to him by his
wife Baba. Their special task was to present petitions to him.

For the official, administrative side of the god's day there was a divine
"counselor," Lugalsisa, whose name means "the king righting (wrongs)."
He served as regent when Ningirsu was away on one of his cultic journeys
to far-off Eridu. Matters calling for the god's attention were not thrown at
him pell-mell, important and unimportant matters alike, but were prepared and winnowed by his "secretary" (s u k k a l) Shakan-shabar, before they were presented to him. To enforce internal law and order the
god had his son Igalima, whose police functions as "high constable" we
have already noted. For outside threats Ningirsu had two "generals," the
gods Lugalkurdub and Kurshunaburuam and he would, of course, himself ride his war chariot at the head of the army.

The war chariot had its peaceful use too; it conveyed Ningirsu all or part of the way to Eridu on his cultic journey there, for one of the asses that drew it was called "The Ass of Eridu." This and Ningirsu's other asses were tended by a divine assherd, the god Ensignun, while another divine herder, Enlulim, served Ningirsu as shepherd.

The extensive lands belonging to Eninnu were mostly situated in a fertile tract called Guedinna, comprising arable lands, swamps, and desert. Here we find Ningirsu's ploughman, the god Gishbare, and the god, Lamar, the "tax gatherer" of fisheries, who looked after the stocking of the marshes with fish and who would send reports to Ningirsu by an envoy, Iminshattam, traveling by packet. Lastly there was the "ranger," Dimgalabzu, whose task it was to protect wildlife on the uncultivated tracts in Guedinna so that birds and beasts might rear their young safely, thrive, and multiply.

The conception of the god shows both continuity and innovation. Ningirsu continues to be the power for fertility in the thundershowers of the spring and the floods of the Tigris; but he takes occupational form from human economic activities as a productive manager of his estate, specifically as "ploughman." This is clearly seen in Nippur where — under his name Ninurta — he is Enlil's "ploughman" in charge of the ploughing of Enlil's temple lands. More significantly new is the god's concern for justice and his role as protector and military leader. These are ruler functions that come to the god with the ruler metaphor.

Mesopotamian kingship (n a m - l u g a l) originated with leadership in war. When attack threatened, a young noble was chosen pro tem to lead the community in battle and was granted supreme powers during the emergency. When the gods came to be seen as rulers it was natural that they should be expected to provide protection against outside foes, and tests from the Early Dynastic period such as Entemena's cones, tell how Ningirsu does battle with Girsu's neighbor and perennial enemy, Umma. The famous Stele of the Vultures shows how the god has cast his net over the foes and cracks their skulls one by one with his mace as a fowler might do to netted birds.

Since the early kingship had been a temporary office, and the king's influence and authority tended to wane with the passing of the emergency, the young kings naturally welcomed opportunities to hold on to their power. Therefore they were eager to engage in the righting of wrongs, as "judges" in the biblical sense which allowed them to reassert their position of power in a morally acceptable way. The ruler metaphor, also applied this concern with justice to the divine, and a ruler such as Uruinimgena of Lagash tells how he entered into a covenant with Ningirsu that he would not give over the waif and the widow to the powerful man.[63] His language is echoed by later rulers such as Gudea, who also tells how he restrained evildoers and heeded the common law of Nanshe and Ningirsu.[64]

The broad and varied concerns with which the ruler metaphor invested the gods made it in many ways less obvious what the gods wanted of man. The older view had seen the Numinous as "intransitive," the force in and behind some phenomenon in nature willing that phenomenon to be. Now the role of the god as ruler, — managing his estate, deciding about war and peace, judging between right and wrong — raised all kinds of problems, and the responsibility for solving them rested on the human ruler. Before acting he had to know — and know for certain — what exactly the gods wanted, and he personally had to see that it was properly carried out lest the community suffer from divine wrath or, almost as bad, divine neglect.

In part such knowledge was, of course, given with tradition. The gods were certain to want their temples looked after, their cult performed correctly, their festivals celebrated at the proper times, and attention and reverence from their people generally. But these — one might call them the "standing" orders — was not all. Situations were bound to develop in which the divine will might not be so clear. Did the god want a new high priest or high priestess and, if so, whom? Did the god wish that his old temple be rebuilt now or later? Or not at all? Did he think one should go to war against an encroaching neighbor, or was he inclined to use diplomatic means? And, of course, the god might harbor a wish that one could not guess, but which nevertheless had to be divined and carried out.

For such cases — one might call them the "specific" orders — the ruler had to rely on messages from the gods in dreams or visions, on signs and portents, or on one of the traditional ways in which one could approach the gods and obtain — if one was lucky — an answer. Gudea, for instance, was told in a dream that he should rebuild Ningirsu's temple. Not satisfied with his own powers of interpretation he took his dream to the divine interpreter of dreams, Nanshe, and asked her to explain its symbolism. Upon her advice he then sought a new dream message from Ningirsu and, having obtained it, checked its validity by slaughtering a kid and reading the will of the gods from the shape of its liver.[65] In view of their importance it is no wonder that the arts of divination flourished and gave rise to a rich and detailed technical literature.

Cosmic Offices

Besides their roles as lords of their manors and leaders in their local communities, most major gods held office and had roles to play on the national, or cosmic, scene.

In many cases these roles were essentially the old ways of the fertility
powers, but they are now less expressions of the gods' innate natures than
charges conferred on them by a high-ranking god such as An or Enlil, or
by the assembly of the gods as a whole. Thus Ningirsu/Ninurta, the power
in the spring thunderstorms is not merely expressing his inner essence, he
is fulfilling his duties in a cosmic office: he is Enlil's "warrior" doing battle
for him with the highlands.[66] Similarly, Enki, god of the fresh waters in
rivers and marshes, is no longer merely the power for fertility in those
waters. He is an official charged by An with such duties as:

> To clear the pure mouths of the Tigris and
>   Euphrates, to make verdure plentiful,
> make dense the clouds, grant water in abundance
>   to all ploughlands,
> to make grain lift its head in furrows
>   and to make pasture abundant in the desert,
> to make young saplings in plantations and in orchards
>   sprout where planted like a forest.[67]

Enlil himself is no longer the power in the wind, "Lord Wind," but has
charge of all winds and has them do his bidding.

The term for these cosmic offices is the same as that used for the more
lowly domestic appointments described by Gudea, *me*, and actually the
organization of the cosmos parallels the organization of an estate with its
varied tasks. In the myth called "Enki and World Order"[68] we hear how
Enki organized the cosmos for Enlil in just such terms. He instituted the
regime of the Euphrates and the Tigris, appointed the god Enbilulu as
divine "inspector of canals," and he arranged the marshes and the sea,
appointing divine officials to take charge of them. Next he organized the
rains and put Ishkur in charge. There followed the instituting of agriculture: ploughing, irrigation, and harvesting, the appointment of the
farmer god Enkimdu and the grain goddess, Ezinu. After agriculture
came brickmaking and the builder's craft under the brick god, Kulla, and
the divine architect, Mushdama; and in similar manner Enki organized
the wildlife of the desert, founded husbandry, fixed boundaries, set limits
for building plots and fields, and instituted weaving — in each case
appointing appropriate gods to the offices of supervision.

The god whom Enki placed in charge of boundaries was the sun god
Utu, god of justice, and the universal scope of his responsibilities is
underlined in the myth by the words "for heaven and earth." The point is
an important one, for it implies that all of the universe was under the same
law and the same judge. This concept, that everybody and everything in
existence is under the law and may be brought to justice, influenced
thinking and acting in many ways. For instance, it gave rise to the "just
war." A war could now be equated with the use of force to enforce a court

verdict. Thus Entemena presents Eannatum's successful boundary war with Umma as undertaken by Ningirsu at the "just" command of Enlil. Originally Enlil had adjudicated the boundary dispute between Girsu and Uma and determined the true boundary between them. This boundary was later violated by the ruler of Umma, and so Enlil ordered Ningirsu to enforce his decree.[69] Similarly, Sargon of Agade, when he had successfully repulsed an attack by Lugalzaggesi and taken him captive, speaks of this as Enlil's "judgment" upon Sargon's law case.[70] Quite technical legal terms were used: when Utuhegal set out on his war of liberation against the barbarous Gutians who had arrogated to themselves the kingship of Sumer he was given a divine "deputy" to accompany him, just as the plaintiff in a law case was given an official "deputy" to look into his complaint.[71]

The possibility of going to law against wrongdoers of any kind is utilized on a cosmic scale by the incantations that deal with the baneful activities of ghosts or demons of illness preying upon the living. In such a case the victim can sue them before the sun god, who judges in the netherworld during the night, or before Gilgamesh and other judges of the netherworld. He can even call upon the deceased members of his family to turn up at the proceedings and help his case. The judges are asked to arrest the evil ghost or demon and return it to the prison in the netherworld from which it has escaped.[72] Going to law also underlies the great *bît rimki*[73] ritual of purifying the king when he is threatened by the evils involved in an eclipse of the moon. The sunrise ritual takes the form of a full-dress lawsuit before Utu and the assembly of the gods. Utu acts as judge and hears the complaint. Enki guarantees that the verdict will be enforced, a function known as "overshadowing" the case.

Ultimate Power: The Assembly of the Gods

The highest authority in the Mesopotamian universe was the assembly of the gods. It met, when occasion arose, in Nippur in a corner of the forecourt of Ekur (Enlil's temple there) called U b - š u - u k k i n n a; and before getting to business the gods would usually fortify themselves with food and drink. Presiding over the assembly was the god of heaven, An. The gods would bind themselves by oath to abide by the decisions the assembly might make; proposals were then placed before them and voted upon, each god indicating assent by saying: h e a m, "so be it!" The decisions of the assembly were cast in their final form by a group of seven "gods of the decrees" and the execution of the decisions usually fell to Enlil.

The matters with which the assembly dealt were basically of two kinds: it served as a court of law judging and passing sentence on wrongdoers, human or divine, and it was the authority that elected and deposed officers such as kings, human and divine. Two examples of its functioning as a court of law are the banishing of Enlil, when, as a young man, he had raped Ninlil,[74] and the indictment of Kingu for fomenting rebellion in Enûma elish. As part of its elective function it chose Marduk as king in Enûma elish, while the many royal hymns of the Isin-Larsa period refer to the role of the assembly in the election of a human king. Its power to depose kings, divine and human, is strikingly depicted in the great "Lament for Ur" in which the goddess of Ur, Ningal, tells how she suffered under her sense of coming doom:

> When I was grieving for that day of storm,
> that day of storm, destined for me,
>   laid upon me, heavy with tears,
> that day of storm, destined for me,
>   laid upon me heavy with tears, on me, the queen.
>
> Though I was trembling for that day of storm,
> that day of storm, destined for me,
>   laid upon me heavy with tears,
> that cruel day of storm destined for me —
> I could not flee before that day's fatality.[75]
> And of a sudden I espied no happy days within my reign,
>   no happy days within my reign.
>
> Though I would tremble for that night,
> that night of cruel weeping destined for me,
> I could not flee before that night's fatality.
> Dread of the storm's floodlike destruction
>   weighed on me,
> and of a sudden on my couch at night,
>   upon my couch at night no dreams were
>   granted me.
> And of a sudden on my couch oblivion,
>   upon my couch oblivion was not granted.
>
> Because (this) bitter anguish
>   had been destined for my land —
> as the cow to the (mired) calf —
>   even had I come to help it on the ground,
> I could not have pulled my people back
>   out of the mire.[76]
>
> Because (this) bitter dolor
>   had been destined for my city,
> even if I, birdlike, had stretched my wings,
> and, (like a bird), flown to my city,
> yet my city would have been destroyed
>   on its foundation,
> yet Ur would have perished where it lay.

Because that day of storm had raised its hand,
and even had I screamed out loud and cried:
   "Turn back, O day of storm,
   (turn) to (thy) desert,"
the breast of that storm
   would not have been lifted from me.[77]

The goddess, unable to bring herself to abandon her city to its fate, tries vainly to intercede for it with An and Enlil. Then, desperate, she makes a last attempt to sway all of the divine assembly from its resolve:

Then verily, to the assembly,
   where the crowd had not yet risen,
while the Anunnaki, binding themselves
   (to uphold the decision), were still seated,
I dragged my feet and I stretched out my arms,
truly I shed my tears in front of An.
Truly I myself mourned in front of Enlil:

"May my city not be destroyed!"
   I said indeed to them.
"May Ur not be destroyed!" I said indeed to them.
"And may its people not be killed!"
   I said indeed to them.
But An never bent towards those words,
and Enlil never with an, "It is pleasing, so be it!"
   did soothe my heart.

(Behold,) they gave instruction
   that the city be destroyed,
(behold,) they gave instruction
   that Ur be destroyed,
and as its destiny decreed
   that its inhabitants be killed.[78]

The city is doomed, and the execution of the terrible decree is left to Enlil. Stating in plain terms what we know happened we could say that wild mountaineers from the East — Elam and the Sua people — invaded Sumer, besieged Ur, and, when eventually the inhabitants surrendered the city, sacked and burned it mercilessly. But plain terms would be entirely inadequate to convey what the Sumerians knew took place. In a cosmic sense it was Enlil's own destructive essence expressed in his element the storm that destroyed Ur. The wild hordes from the mountains were but incidental form in which that essence clothed itself, the reality was Enlil's storm:

Enlil called the storm.
   The people mourn.
Winds of abundance he took from the land.
   The people mourn.

Good winds he took away from Sumer.
    The people mourn.
Deputed evil winds.
    The people mourn.
Entrusted them to Kingaluda, tender of storms.

He called the storm that annihilates the land.
    The people mourn.
He called disastrous winds.
    The people mourn.
Enlil — choosing Gibil as his helper —
called the (great) hurricane of heaven.
    The people mourn.
The (blinding) hurricane howling across the skies —
    the people mourn —
the storm that annihilates the land roaring over the earth —
    the people mourn —
the tempest unsubduable like breaks through levees,
beats down upon, devours the city's ships,
(all these) he gathered at the base of heaven.
    The people mourn.

(Great) fires he lit that heralded the storm.
    The people mourn.
And lit on either flank of furious winds
    the searing heat of desert.
Like flaming heat of noon this fire scorched.[79]

It is this storm that destroys the city:

The storm ordered by Enlil in hate,
    the storm which wears away the country,
covered Ur like a cloth,
    veiled it like a linen sheet.[80]

When it clears away all is over:

On that day did the storm leave the city;
    that city was a ruin.
O father Nanna, that town was left a ruin.
    The people mourn.
On that day did the storm leave the country.
    The people mourn.
Its people('s corpses), not potsherds,
littered the approaches.
The walls were gaping;
the high gates, the roads,
were piled with dead.
In the wide streets,
    where feasting crowds (once) gathered,
jumbled they lay.

In all the streets and roadways bodies lay.
In open fields that used to fill with dancers,
the people lay in heaps.

The country's blood now filled its holes,
    like metal in a mold;
    bodies dissolved — like butter left in the sun.[81]

The assembly of the gods has decided, and the decision has been carried out.

In considering where the ascendancy of the ruler metaphor has led, we note that the whole view of existence appears to have changed. The earlier world in which things happened more or less by themselves and the gods were "intransitive" powers has yielded to a planned, purposeful universe actively administered and ruled by gods who have broadened their concerns far beyond what we call nature: to society as upholders of the legal and moral order, and to politics, deciding about victory and defeat. They have come to control and shape history.

How does this new view account for historical disasters of such magnitude as the fall of Ur? Does it look for sins or faults in the victims that justify their fate? Apparently not. The question of guilt on the part of Ur is raised in another long lament in which the city god Nanna/Suen appeals to his father Enlil on its behalf. He says:

O my father who engendered me!
    What has my city done to you?
    Why have you turned away from it?
O Enlil! What has my city done to you?
    Why have you turned away from it?
The ship of first fruits no longer
    brings first fruits to the engendering father,
no longer goes in to Enlil in Nippur
    with your bread and food-portions!
. . . .
O my father who engendered me! Fold again
    into your arms my city from its loneliness!
O Enlil! Fold again my Ur into your arms
    from its loneliness!
Fold again my (temple) Ekishnugal
    into your arms from its loneliness!
Let renown emerge for you in Ur!
    Let the people expand for you:
let the ways of Sumer,
    which have been destroyed,
be restored for you![82]

Enlil, in his answer, has no fault to find with Ur, but merely points to the fact that there has always been violent change and that the gods had not guaranteed that things would last:

> Enlil answered his son Suen (saying):
> "The heart of the wasted city is weeping,
>   reeds (for flutes) of lament grow therein,
> its heart is weeping,
>   reeds (for flutes) of lament grow therein,
> its people spend the day in weeping.
> O noble Nanna, be thou (concerned) about yourself,
>   what truck have you with tears?
> There is no revoking a verdict,
>   a decree of the assembly,
> a command of An and Enlil
>   is not known ever to have been changed.
> Ur was verily granted kingship —
>   a lasting term it was not granted.
> From days of yore when the country was first settled,
>   to where it has now proceeded,
> Who ever saw a term of royal office completed?
> Its kingship, its term of office, has been
>   uprooted. It must worry.
> (You) my Nanna, do you not worry!
>   Leave your city!"[83]

In reality, then, justice — that is to say, human justice — quails before the absolute authority of the unanimous will of the gods; they are not to be challenged.

4

Third Millennium Metaphors. The Gods as Rulers: Individual Divine Figures

Sunrise depicted on a cylinder seal (Seal of Adda) from the middle of the third millennium B.C. A number of the major divinities are represented. In the center is the sun god, Utu, rising from behind the mountains. To his left stands Inanna, goddess of the morning star, and next to her is Ninurta, god of the thundershowers, with his bow (its arrows typify lightning) and his lion (whose roar typifies thunder). To the right of the sun god is shown the god of the sweet waters, Enki. From his shoulders spring the main rivers of Mesopotamia, the Euphrates and the Tigris. Enki holds the thunderbird on his hand. Behind Enki stands his vizier Isimud.

The gods who formed the assembly of the gods were legion. It is not possible to characterize more than a few prominent ones. We shall base our discussion mainly on materials from Sumerian literary compositions that, while preserved in Old Babylonian copies, reflect views and beliefs of the outgoing third millennium, to which many of them date back. We have not hesitated, however, to cite earlier and later materials to round out our sketches of the individual gods.

An = Authority

The Power in the Sky

An ranked highest among the gods. His name, borrowed by the Akkadians as Anum, is the Sumerian word for "sky," and inherently An is the numinous power in the sky, the source of rain and the basis for the calendar since it heralds through its changing constellations the times of year with their different works and celebrations. Originally, one may surmise, An belonged to the herders' pantheon since he is often visualized in bovine form.

An's spouse was the earth, Ki, on whom he engendered trees, reeds, and all other vegetation. A late Akkadian incantation[84] refers to this when it says: "As the sky impregnated earth (so that) vegetation became plenteous," and in the myth, L u g a l - e, which dates from the end of the third millennium, the opponent of Ninurta, Azag, king of the plants, was so engendered:[85]

> . . . An impregnated the verdant earth (*Ki*)
> and she bore him one unafraid of the warrior Ninurta,
>   Azag.

Another name for Ki — probably an early loan from Akkadian — was Urash, "The tilth."[86] As father of Enki, god of flowing waters, An is paired in the list of gods[87] with the goddess Nammu, who seems to be the power in the riverbed to produce water. There also seems to have been a tradition that saw the power in the sky as both male and female and distinguished the god An (Akkadian Anum) from the goddess An (Akkadian Antum) to whom he was married.[88] According to that view the rains flowed from the sky goddess' breasts, or (since she was usually envisaged in cow shape) her udder — that is, from the clouds.[89]

An had not only engendered vegetation, he was the father and ancestor of all of the gods, and he likewise fathered innumerable demons and evil spirits. Frequently he was envisaged as a huge bull. One of his epithets is "Fecund Breed-Bull,"[90] an apt personification of the overcast skies in spring whose thunder recalls the bellowing of a bull and whose rain

95

engenders vegetation far and wide. As an older form of the god himself we should probably consider the "bull of heaven" which belongs to him and is killed by Gilgamesh and mourned by Inanna and her votaries.[91] The bull is also mentioned as a dying god and husband of Ereshkigal — in the myth "Inanna's Descent" where it is called Gugalanna (i.e., G u (d) - g a l - a n n a (k)) "The great bull of heaven."[92] Its death would stand for the vanishing of the cloudy skies with the passing of spring.   .

Source of Authority

The view of An as a major source of fertility, the "father who makes the seed sprout,"[93] engenderer of vegetation, demons, and all the gods, led naturally to the attribution of paternal authority to him. As a father he presides over the assembly of the gods, his children.

With the developing of social differentiation and the attitudes of growing respect and awe before the ruler, a new sensitivity to the potential in the vast sky for inducing feelings of numinous awe seems to have come into being. The sky can, at moments when man is in a religiously receptive mood, act as vehicle for a profound experience of numinous awe, as may be instanced in our own culture — e.g., by Watts's lines:

> Eternal Power, whose high abode
> Becomes the grandeur of a God,
> Infinite length beyond the bounds
> Where stars revolve their little rounds.[94]

or in this experience of an anonymous writer quoted by William James:

> I remember the night, and almost the very spot on
> the hilltop, where my soul opened out, as it were,
> into the Infinite, and there was a rushing together
> of the two worlds, the inner and the outer. It was
> deep calling unto deep, — the deep that my own
> struggle had opened up within being answered by the
> unfathomable deep without, reaching beyond the
> stars. I stood alone with Him who had made me, and
> all the beauty of the world, and love, and sorrow,
> and even temptation.[95]

To the ancient Mesopotamians what the sky might reveal was An, its own inner essence of absolute authority and majesty — *might* reveal, but would not necessarily reveal, for in everyday moods the sky would be experienced apart from the numinous power in it and would recede into the category of mere things.

The absoluteness of the authority divined in An may be seen clearly in statements that make him the fountainhead of all authority and authoritative commands, whether parental, lordly, or royal. In the myth of the elevation of Inanna the gods address him saying:

What thou hast ordered (comes) true!
The utterance of prince and lord is (but)
    what thou hast ordered, dost agree with.
O An! thy great command takes precedence,
    who could gainsay it?
O father of the gods, thy command,
    the very foundations of heaven and earth,
    what god could spurn (it)?[96]

The passage as we have it probably dates from the second rather than the third millennium B.C. and so may conceivably bring the powers in An to a sharper point than older materials. Yet it is clearly of a piece with them. What it says is that all authority, that of prince or lord, derives from An; he is its source, it carries out his will.

Since human society is not the only structure based on authority and command (the natural world is as well), all things and forces in the polity that is the universe conform to An's will. He is the power that lifts existence out of chaos and anarchy and makes it an organized whole. As a building is supported by and reveals in its structure the lines of its foundation, so the ancient Mesopotamian universe was upheld by and reflected An's ordering will. His command is "the foundation of heaven and earth."[97]

As the ultimate source of all authority An was closely associated with the highest authority on earth, that of kingship. It was he who proclaimed the king chosen by the assembly of the gods and he who was, par excellence, the god that conferred kingship. The royal insignia lie before An in heaven for him to bestow, and with them he conveys not only the general powers of kingship but duties linked to his own cosmic functions: responsibility for the calendar and for carrying out his calendric rites. For example, his new moon festivals, which, as shown by their name, *ezen-èš-èš*, ("all temple festival") were celebrated in all temples, and the New Year festival at which the year seems to have been named from one of the king's accomplishments. Through this mandate, accordingly, the king becomes An's instrument for seeing to it that the times do not get out of joint. When An agreed to make Shulgi king he referred to these central duties as follows:

Let Shulgi, king with a pleasant term of reign,
perform correctly for me, An,
    the rites instituted for kingship,
    let him direct the schedules of the gods for me,

let him offer up to me the things for the New-moon day
and the things for the New Year (festival).
Let him present (?) to me salutations, petitions,
and plaints —
abundance, breaking through the earth like grass and herbs,
I have verily (?) added on for him![98]

A description of An from the Isin-Larsa period as he takes his seat to
confer kingship upon the ruler, Lipit-Eshtar, conveys a sense of the god
and the awe he inspired.

The exalted lord, the leader,
the skillful officiant, the supreme one,
stirps of all lords,

the one with head held high, the surpassing one,
the fecund breed-bull,
(of) honored name, greatly imbued with awe,
whose grandly proclaimed (decrees)
know none who could quash them,
ascended step by step the pure mountain
of (his) office,
took his seat on the great throne-dais,
An, king of the gods.

(From) afar he looked firmly toward him,
looked firmly toward Prince Lipit-Eshtar,
granted long life to him,
granted long life to Prince Lipit-Eshtar,
An's decree, a decree (as good as) carried out,
no god will oppose.

The Anunnaki, the gods in their entirety,
gathered to him at the place of decision-making,
all the great offices he caused to appear —
the gods of heaven stood in attendance on him —
their schedules he directed —
the gods of earth bowed down before him —
from among the exalted offices,
from among the offices of the foremost row,
the kingship, being all things precious,
to Lipit-Eshtar, son of Enlil,
great An granted as a gift.[99]

Enlil = Force

The Power in "Growing Weather"

Next to An in rank, but embodying energy and force rather than the
calm authority of An, is Enlil or Nunamnir. The name Enlil means "Lord

Wind" and the title e n, which stands for "lord" in the sense of "productive manager," shows that it is primarily the power in the moist winds of spring — growing weather — that is aimed at. Further traits suggest that Enlil is that power particularly as seen by the farmer, for he is the creator of the farmer's most versatile implement, the hoe, which, like the plough, comes into play when the humid air of spring makes the soil workable.[100] His throne is D u 6 - k u g , "the holy mound," i.e., the storage pile of grain and wool.[101] His wife Ninlil or Sud is a grain goddess, daughter of the god of stores, Haia, and the barley goddess Ninshebargunu or Nidaba.[102] His son is Ninurta or Ningirsu, god of the plough and of the spring thunderstorms.

The role of Enlil as the spring winds bringing nature back to life is well conveyed by a passage from a hymn in his honor:[103]

> O mighty one, you hold the rains of heaven
>   and the waters of earth,
> Enlil, you hold the halter of the gods
>   (of nature),
> Father Enlil, you are the one
>   who makes the vines grow up,
> Enlil, your (warm) glow brings in the deep
>   the fish to maturity,
> you let the birds in heaven, the fish in the deep,
>   eat their fill.

The picture of him in the closing paean of the myth "Enlil and Ninlil" is very similar:

> You are lord! You are lord!
> Enlil, you are lord! You are lord!
> Nunamnir, you are lord! You are lord!
> A lord of (great) consequence,
>   a lord of the storehouse
>   are you!
> A lord making the barley grow up,
>   a lord making the vines grow up
>   are you!
> Lord of heaven, lord of abundance,
>   lord of earth
>   are you!
> Enlil being lord, Enlil being king,
> Enlil's utterance is a thing unalterable,
> his sagacious word can not be changed.[104]

As Administrator

In time — as the ruler metaphor took stronger hold — the picture of the power in the fertile winds of spring assumed the form of a human

executive gathering all the threads of complex management, making all
major decisions, and communicating his orders through an administrative assistant. The great "Hymn to Enlil" thus describes him:

> When he shines on the throne-dais
>   in (his temple) Imhursag,
> like the rainbow, he, too, circles the heavens.
> like a floating cloud he goes his own way.
>
> He is the one prince of heaven,
>   the only great one of earth,
> he is the exalted tutelary god of the Anunnaki,
> accordingly he makes decisions by himself,
> no god looks on.
> His grand vizier, the leader of the assembly,
>   Nusku,
> can know and discuss with him
> his commands and matters
>   that are in his heart —
> far and wide he will take them for him,
> with a holy greeting in holy office he
>   (Enlil) bids him Godspeed.
>
> Without (warrant of) the great mountain, Enlil,
> no city could be built,
>   no population settled therein,
> no cattle pen built, its sheepfold not set up.
> No king could be raised to office,
>   no lord created,
> No high priest or high priestess
>   designated by the (omen-)kid,
> among the troops no general and lieutenant
>   could be had.
> The water of the carp-flood at its height
>   could not dredge the canals,
> the (flood arriving) after it,
>   would tend to break out (from the bed),
>   could not go straight,
>   not extend (by scouring) the far reaches
>   (of the canals).
> The sea could not give birth
>   to the heavy souther with its rain.
>
> The fish of the deep could not lay their eggs
>   in the canebrake;
> the birds of heaven not spread their nests
>   on the broad earth.
>
> In the sky the rain-laden clouds
>   could not open their mouths,

in the fields the tilth could not sprout
    the mottled barley,
in the desert its green spots could not
    let grass and herbs grow long,
in the orchards the broad trees of the mountains
    could not bear fruit.

Without (warrant of) the great mountain Enlil,
(the birth goddess) Nintur could not
    let die (at birth),
could not slay, the cow could not lose its calf
    in the cattle pen,
the ewe not bring forth a premature lamb
    in its sheepfold.
The wildlife grown numerous by itself,
could not lie down in their lairs and (settle on) their perches,
The (wild) goats and asses, the four-legged (beasts),
    could not be fertile,
    could not (even) copulate.[105]

No wonder that the hymn marvels at the compass of Enlil's responsibilities.[106] His "skillful planning in intricate designs — their inner workings a blur of threads not to unravel — thread entwined in thread, not to
be traced by the eye" makes him a marvel of divine providence. No one
can help him. His decisions must be his own, for nobody could begin to
fathom the intricacies of the problems he deals with.

The Power in the Storm

It may be noted that not all of Enlil's activities are beneficent to mankind. He allows the birth goddess to kill at birth, and he is behind the
miscarriages of cows and ewes. This aspect of Enlil as potentially hostile
corresponds with the two-sided nature of the wind, not only the benign
zephyr, but also the destructive storm. In the storm a brooding violence
and destructiveness in Enlil finds expression:

The mighty one, Enlil,
    whose utterance cannot be changed,
he is the storm, is destroying the cattle pen,
    uprooting the sheepfold.
My roots are torn up! My forests denuded![107]

Thus complains a mourner in Enlil's own city, Nippur. Man can never
be fully at ease with Enlil, can never know what he has in mind:

What has he planned? . . .
What is in my father's heart?
What is in Enlil's holy mind?

What has he planned against me
   in his holy mind?
A net he spread: the net of an enemy;
a snare he set: the snare of an enemy.
He has stirred up the waters
   and will catch the fishes,
he has cast his net,
   will (bring) down the birds too.[108]

Nor can any man say when he will relent:

Until when? Enlil, until when?
Like a cloud on the horizon,
   when can he bring himself
   to settle down?
The great mountain Enlil,
   when can he bring himself
   to settle down?[109]

In his wild moods of destructiveness he is unreachable, deaf to all
appeals:

O father Enlil, whose eyes are glaring (wildly),
how long til they will be at peace again?
O thou who covered up thy head with a cloth —
   how long?
O thou who laid thy head upon thy knees —
   how long?
O thou who closed thy heart like an earthen box —
   how long?
O mighty one who with thy fingers sealed thine ears —
   how long?
O father Enlil, they are being pummeled
   till they perish![110]

As we mentioned in discussing the "Lament for Ur," Enlil's destructive
side often serves the assembly of the gods. With his storm he executes the
decisions of the assembly. At times the storm is the breath issuing from his
mouth; and just as we speak of "breathing a word," so to the Sumerians
the word that Enlil "breathed" could be his annihilating storm. When he
executed decisions voted by the gods in assembly the storm became the
word they all breathed, a destruction decreed by all:

A storm cloud lying on the horizon,
   its heart inscrutable,
His word, a storm cloud lying on the horizon,
   its heart inscrutable;
the word of great An, a storm cloud lying on the horizon,
   its heart inscrutable;

the word of Enlil, a storm cloud lying on the horizon,
   its heart inscrutable;
the word of Enki, a storm cloud lying on the horizon,
   its heart inscrutable;
the word of Asalluhe, a storm cloud lying on the horizon,
   its heart inscrutable;
the word of Enbilulu, a storm cloud lying on the horizon,
   its heart inscrutable;
the word of Mudugsaa, a storm cloud lying on the horizon,
   its heart inscrutable;
the word of Shiddukisharra,
   a storm cloud lying on the horizon,
   its heart inscrutable;
the word of the lord Dikumah,
   a storm cloud lying on the horizon,
   its heart inscrutable;
his word which up above makes the heavens tremble,
his word which down below rocks the earth,
his word wherewith the Anunnaki gods destroy,
his word has no seer (who can foresee it),
   no diviner (who could divine it),
his word is a risen flood-storm,
   it has none who could oppose it.[111]

Myths

The myths about Enlil reflect his complex nature. He is depicted as creative and benevolent in the myth, "Creation of the Hoe,"[112] which tells how he separated heaven from earth so that seeds could grow up, how he fashioned the first hoe and used it to break the hard crust of the earth in U z u m u a, "the flesh producer," in Nippur, and how the vanguard of mankind sprang from the hole made by his hoe, breaking through the earth like plants. His role in the "Dispute between Summer and Winter"[113] is also beneficent; he cohabits with the mountain range, the Hursag, and engenders on it the two opponents of the dispute; the god of summer, Emesh, and the god of winter, Enten.

More tension between the light and dark sides of Enlil's nature shows in the "Enlil and Ninlil"[114] myth which tells how young Ninlil, disobeying her mother, bathes in the canal where Enlil sees her and takes her by force. For this he is arrested as a sex criminal and condemned by the assembly of the gods to banishment from the city, Nippur, the scene of the tale. Enlil, complying with the sentence imposed upon him, leaves Nippur for the netherworld, and Ninlil, pregnant with his child (the moon god Nanna or Suen), follows him at a distance. On the way Enlil, taking the shape of several men they meet, the gatekeeper in Nippur, the man of the river of the netherworld, and the ferryman of the river of the netherworld, persuades Ninlil to lie with him to engender a child who may take Nanna's place in the netherworld and save him for the world above. Thus three more gods are engendered, all chthonic in nature, Meslamtaea, Ninazu, and — if we read the name right — Ennugi. The myth ends with the paean to Enlil quoted earlier, hymning his productive powers and the authoritative character of his word.

Probably this singular tale about the condemnation and death of the god is best seen in relation to the cult of the dying and reviving gods of fertility: Enlil, as the fertile wind of the spring rapes Ninlil, the grain — perhaps a mythopoeic interpretation of wind-pollination — and dies with the passing of spring, as the grain goes underground too in the storage bin.

There is another myth[115] dealing with Enlil's pursuit of Ninlil, but in this one Enlil, though perhaps more impetuous in his advances than polite manners called for, wins her decorously and properly.

Finally, in the "Myth of the Flood" as we have it in Sumerian,[116] in the Akkadian Atrahasīs story,[117] and, secondarily, in the Gilgamesh Epic,[118] Enlil is uniformly unfavorably disposed and is given to extremes of violence when provoked. It is by his hand that the flood is loosed to annihilate man.

Ninhursaga = Productivity

With An and Enlil stands the third in the triad of most powerful deities, the goddess Ninhursaga, also known as Nintur, Ninmenna, Ninmah, Dingirmah, Aruru, and in Akkadian as Bêlit-ilī, Mama, and numerous other names.[119] How many of these names indicate aspects of the goddess that have taken on an identity of their own and how many represent other deities who have merged with Ninhursaga, it is difficult to say. The texts sometimes treat these names as designations of distinct deities, at other times they identify them as appellations of the same goddess.

Numen of the Stony Ground

Her original aspect is probably as the numinous power in the stony soil that rings the Mesopotamian alluvial ground: in the east, the foothills and near ranges of the Iranian mountains, in the west, the stony Arabian desert. This power, called n i n - h u r s a ǧ . a (k), "Lady of the stony ground" or "Lady of the foothills"[120] we meet, minimally personified, in the introduction to the "Dispute of Summer and Winter"[121] where we are told that Enlil in the shape of a huge bull copulated with "the foothills" (h u r s a ǧ) and engendered "summer" (E m e s h), and "winter" (E n-t e n). Elsewhere, as Ninhursaga, she is considered the spouse of Enlil. Their son, Ninurta or Ningirsu, in the myth of L u g a l - e is credited[122] with constructing her domain, the foothills, and furnishing them richly with trees, plants, metal ores, and wildlife. He presented them to her as a gift, giving her on that occasion the name Ninhursaga, "Lady of the foothills"; before that she had been called Ninmah, "August lady."

Parallel to the tradition in which Ninhursaga was the spouse of Enlil runs another more common one according to which she was his sister (n i n₉) and Ninlil was his wife.

Mother of Wildlife

Wildlife, one of the things with which Ninurta furnished the foothills, seems to belong very closely with Ninhursaga. In the tradition which makes her the sister rather than spouse of Enlil her husband is Shulpae, king of the wild beasts of the desert, and in a lament of hers[123] she seems to have been envisaged in animal form, for the son she has lost turns out to be a donkey stallion:

> My choice donkey (stallion) lost in the desert,
> my stallion which the enemy took as booty!

She wails:

> I, the mother who bore (him), I, mated in vain,
> I, kissed in vain,
> I, made with child (?) in vain!
> . . . .
> I gave birth, I gave birth, I gave birth to a freeborn son.
> For what gave I birth?
> I became pregnant, pregnant, pregnant with a freeborn son.
> For what became I pregnant?
> I, the mother who gave birth, my giving birth, my being pregnant,
> what gained I by it?
> I gave birth to . . . it was killed by a thane.
> What gained I by it?
> I gave birth to a . . . , it was killed by a thane.
> What gained I by it?
> I gave birth to a choice donkey (stallion),
> a lord mounted it. What gained I by it?
> I gave birth to a strong mule, a lord hitched it up.
> What gained I by it?[124]

As goddess of the foothills and the stony desert Ninhursaga is specifically mother of the wild animals native to these regions; she loses them when they are killed by hunters or captured and tamed. To domestic animals, on the other hand, her territory may prove fatal if they stray. In a lament by Ninhursaga's daughter Lisina, who was also, it seems, a donkey goddess, the young goddess vainly hopes that

> He will bring it back to me! He will bring it
>   back to me!
> My strong deputy will bring my donkey stallion
>   back to me!
> Will bring my herd, which got cut off from me,
>   back to me!
> Will bring my foal back to me
>   from its destroyed lair!
> Will bring my wild ass,
>   which got cut off in the wood,
>   back to me!
> The canal inspector floating down river (in his boat)
>   will bring it back to me.
> The farmer will bring it back to me,
>   from its flooded field
>   (i.e., where it may be mired).[125]

But she knows that her foal will not be returned, that it has perished, and she blames her mother, the power in the wastelands, who let it die:

> "To whom should I compare her?
>   To whom should I compare her?
>   I, to whom should I compare her?
> My mother let my (only) one die!
>   I, to whom should I compare her?
> My mother who bore me, Ninhursaga —
> my mother let it die!
>   I, to whom should I compare her?
> To the bitch, that has no motherly compassion,
>   let me compare her!"
> Lisina in her grief sits alone.[126]

Yet, in spite of the passionate reproach in this lament, Ninhursaga is usually regarded not only as mother of the wildlife in the foothills and desert, but also as the tender mother of the herd animals.

> To her who is as radiant as Enlil
> low the cow and its calf,
> and Mother Nintur on her part
>   calls plaintively to them,
> Mother Nintur, the exalted queen of Kesh.[127]

She is the mother of man and the mother of the gods, and as Gudea once called her, "the mother of all children."[128] This aspect is in many respects her central one, and may at one time have constituted a separate and independent deity.

Form Giver and Birth Giver

The name most frequently used for her in her character as mother and birth giver is Nintur, which may tentatively be translated "Lady birth hut." The element t u r is written with a sign which seems to have been originally the picture of the birth hut in the cattle pen[129] to which cows were taken when they were ready to calve, and where, presumably, any weak or ill animal might be taken for care. This explains the varying meanings of the sign: "to give birth" (d ú); "child," "young," "weak," "goat kid" (t u r_5); but also "ill" (d u r_x). The sheepfold, Sumerian a m a š, with its birth house t ù r and é - t ù r was used metaphorically to designate the female generative organs:[130] š a g_4 - t ù r, "the 'pen' or 'birth house' of the inside" is the Sumerian term for "womb." Moreover, this term in Akkadian, *šassuru*, actually is one of the names of Nintur.[131] She is also called "The lady of the womb" (*be-lit re-e-me*)[132] and her emblem, shaped like the Greek letter omega (Ω), has been convincingly interpreted from Egyptian parallels as a representation of the uterus of a cow.[133] The fact that the birth of calves, lambs, and kids normally takes place in spring when the herds are pastured in the foothills or the desert may have contributed to seeing the power in birthing as an aspect of the power in the wild, Ninhursaga.

The power in the womb was specifically the power to make the embryo grow and give distinctive form to it. As such Nintur is called "Lady of form-giving":[134]

> Mother Nintur, the lady of form-giving,
> working in a dark place, the womb (lit. "heart");
> to give birth to kings, to tie on the rightful tiara,
> to give birth to lords, to place the crown
>   on (their) heads, is in her hands.

Other terms for her that stress this aspect are "Lady of the embryo" (N i n - z i z n a k), "Lady fashioner" (N i n - d í m), "Carpenter of (i.e., 'in') the insides" (N a g a r - š a g a k), "Lady potter" (N i n - b a h a r), "Copper-caster of the land" or "of the gods" (^{d}T i b i r a - k a l a m m a k, ^{d}T i b i r a - d i n ǧ i r e n e k), etcetera.[135] Occasionally she uses this power capriciously as in the myth about "Enki and Ninmah" where, to show that she can give man good or bad shape at will, she makes a series of misshapen creatures. According to the hymn to Enlil that was quoted above, however, she must have Enlil's permission in order to produce a monstrous lamb.

When the fetus is fully developed and shaped she loosens it, a function
to which she seems to owe her name A - r u - r u, "Germ-loosener." A
hymn to her temple in Kesh tells how:

> Ninhursaga, being uniquely great,
>   makes the womb contract;
> Nintur, being a great mother,
>   sets the birth-giving going.[136]

Correspondingly, in the myth of the "Creation of the Hoe," it is she under
her name of Ninmenna who sets the birth-giving going after the heads of
men have been uncovered by Enlil's hoe.[137]

The time of the shaping of the child in its mother's womb is one during
which it is susceptible to both good and bad influences and so is the
moment of birth; an incautious word then may saddle the child with any
manner of unpropitious fate. Therefore Aruru is the "Lady of silence,"
N i n - s i g₅ - s i g₅.[138] The silence is for the birth helpers only, however;
the goddess herself speaks with a loud voice through the wails of the
woman in labor. In a hymn to her temple, that sacred place is told:

> Your princess is a princess enjoining silence,
>   a great *igizîtu* ("real princess") priestess of An.
> Her word shakes the heavens,
>   her utterance is a howling storm,
> Aruru, the sister of Enlil.[139]

It is to the stopping of blood after birth (or possibly to the ceasing of
menstruation after conception) that her name, ^{d}M u d - k e š d a, "Blood
stauncher" probably refers, just as her names A m a - d ù g - b a d,
"Mother spreading the knees," and A m a - u d ú d a, "Mother who has
given birth"[140] allude to her role as birth giver. A description of her
image as Nintur[141] says that "her bosom is bare; on her left arm she carries
a baby so that it can feed at her breast," and royal inscriptions and royal
hymns abound in assertions that kings and rulers have been suckled with
pure milk by Ninhursaga.

Midwife

As the tendency to see numinous power in human form and social
context gradually asserted itself, it was natural that the power for birth
take the form of birth helper or midwife. Nintur accordingly meets us as
Š a g₄ . z u - d i n ğ i r e n e k, "Midwife of the gods."[142] As such she is
described in the myth "Enki and World Order":

> Aruru, the sister of Enlil,
> Nintur, lady of the foothills,

> verily holds her badge of lordly office,
>   the pure birthstones,
> verily carries on the arm her . . .
>   and the leeks,
> verily holds her lapis lazuli vessel
>   in which the afterbirth is laid,
> verily carries on the arm
>   her (properly) blessed pure water pail.
> Verily she is the midwife of the country.[143]

Her midwife's water pail is also mentioned by Gudea, who provided one of copper for her temple in Girsu.[144]

Source of Kingship

The crowning achievement of the birth goddess was the birth of kings and lords:

> Giving birth to kings, giving birth to lords
>   is verily in her hand.[145]

And she not only gives birth to them, she also has the power to confer on them their insignia of office. Thus in the hymn to one of Ninhursaga/Nintur's temples we have already quoted, it is said that

> to give birth to kings, to tie on the rightful tiara,
> to give birth to lords, to place the crown
>   on (their) heads, is in her hands.[146]

The same is said about a related figure, N i n - m u g, "Lady vulva" in "Enki and World Order."[147]

In the passage about the origin of man in the "Creation of the Hoe" Ninhursaga/Nintur is called "the lady giving birth to lords, giving birth to kings, Ninmenna . . ." which is her name as "Lady of the diadem."[148] Under that name her office was to place the golden crown firmly on the head of the "lord" in Eanna in Uruk according to an Old Babylonian investiture ritual.[149] Correspondingly a date formula of Rîmsîn II traces the royal authority of that ruler to investiture by Nintur/Ninhursaga of Kesh, who is called by her name, Ninmah.[150]

The growing acceptance of the ruler metaphor seems to have affected Ninhursaga's character little if any. Her image was one rooted in the family, the mother, and she had no specific political function. Her importance in the general scheme of things as the rocky ground and the power in birth placed her with An and Enlil as a decisive power in the universe and the scheme of things. She is appealed to in the myths when something new is to be born, but she holds no specified political office and during the

second millennium she lost more and more rank until she seems to have
been completely supplanted by Enki.

Enki = Cunning

A rather persistent rival of Ninhursaga in the triad of ruling gods, An,
Enlil, and Ninhursaga, was Enki (Akkadian Ea).

The Fertilizing Sweet Waters

Enki personifies the numinous powers in the sweet waters in rivers and
marshes or rain. He says of himself:

> My father, the king of heaven and earth,
>   had me appear in the world,
> My older brother, the king of all lands,
>   gathered and gathered offices,
>   placed them in my hand.
> From Ekur, Enlil's house,
>   I brought craftsmanship to my Apsû (of) Eridu,
> I am the true seed emitted by a great wild bull,
>   I am the foremost son of An,
> I am the great storm (clouds) rising out of the netherworld,
>   I am the great good manager of the country,
> I am the irrigation officer for all the throne-daises,
>   I am the father of all lands,
> I am the older brother of the gods,
>   I make abundance perfect.[151]

Later on he specifies his benefactions:

> I am a good manager, am of effective commands,
>   am preeminent,
> at my commands cattle pens are built,
>   sheepfolds fenced in,
> when I draw near unto heaven the rains of abundance
>   rain down from above,
> when I draw near unto the earth, the carp-flood at its height
>   comes into being,
> when I draw near unto the yellowing fields,
>   grain piles are heaped at my command.[152]

and in the hymn to him quoted earlier, his father An assigned him:

> To clear the pure mouths of the Tigris and Euphrates,
>   to make verdure plentiful,
> make dense the clouds, grant water in abundance
>   to all ploughlands,

to make grain lift its head in furrows
and to make pasture abundant in the desert.[153]

Enki is usually pictured with two streams, the Euphrates and the Tigris, flowing out of his shoulders or from a vase he holds. Frequently fish are swimming in these streams. Occasionally he holds an eaglelike bird, the thunderbird, Imdugud, signifying the clouds rising from the waters, and his foot may rest on an ibex, emblem of sweet underground springs, the Apsû.[154]

His name Enki (i.e., e n - k i (. a k)), "Lord (i.e., productive manager) of the soil," reflects the role of water in fructifying the earth. Other names such as L u g a l - i d (a k), "Owner of the river," L u g a l - a b z u (a k), "Owner of the Apsû" and the Akkadian *Naqbu*, "Source," present him as the specific power in rivers or underground waters.[155]

The power in water that makes the soil produce was thought to be of a kind with the engendering power in male semen. Sumerian does not differentiate semen and water: one word stands for both. It is therefore natural that Enki is the power to fecundate. Another connection between productivity and water is the "birth water" which precedes and announces birth. As the power in amniotic fluid Enki is celebrated in a passage that reads:

O Father Enki, go forth out of the seeded country,
    and may it sprout good seed!
O Nudimmud, go forth out of my good ewe,
    and may it give birth to (a good) lamb!
Go forth out of the impregnated cow,
    and may it give birth to a good calf!
Go forth out of my good goat,
    and may it give birth to a good kid!
When you have gone forth out of the drenched field,
    my good field,
    may it heap grain heaps in the high desert.[156]

The Form-giving Sweet Waters

The power to fertilize is not the only power in water. When it moistens clay, it gives it plasticity and the ability to assume and hold all manner of shapes. In Enki, this power finds expression in his name N u d i m m u d, "Image fashioner," god of "shaping,"[157] and seems to underlie his function as god of artists and craftsmen: potters, bronze casters, stonecutters, jewelers, seal cutters, and others.[158] To this side of him belongs his epithet *mummu*, a loan from Sumerian u m u n, "mold," "form." In Akkadian the word stands for "original form," "archetype," and serves as epithet for Ea/Enki, as the name of an emblem of his (a crooked stick with handle in the shape of a sheep's head) and, hypostatized in Enûma elish, as the name of one of his captive foes.[159]

The Cleansing Sweet Waters

The third power of water is to cleanse, and Enki is the god of ritual lustration and purification from polluting evil. A common pattern in Sumerian incantations has Enki's son Asalluhe discover some evil and report it to his father, who then tells him which measures he should take. In the series called "The Bathhouse" (*bît rimki*) used to purify the king from the evil that threatens during an eclipse of the moon, the rite takes — as mentioned earlier — the form of a lawsuit before the assembly of the gods at sunrise with the sun god as judge. Enki has the role of "over-shadowing the case," i.e., of guaranteeing that judgment is executed. This duty he performs as the power in the cleansing waters of the lustrations for which the rite is named.

Myths

The role of executor of judgments which Enki fills in the "Bathhouse" ritual is an unusual one for him, for force is not his way. Rather, he exerts his will through diplomacy or guile. This may reflect the fact that he is the power in the sweet waters, for "the ways of water are devious. It avoids rather than surmounts obstacles, goes around and yet gets to its goal. The farmer, who works with it in irrigation, easing it along from canal to canal, knows how tricky it can be, how easily it slips away, takes unforeseen turns. And so, we may assume, the idea of cunning, of superior intelligence, came to be imparted to Enki."[160]

His most frequent opponent in the myths is Ninhursaga in one form or other: as goddess of the stony ground of the western desert, or as goddess of birth. But though she is outwitted time and again by the clever Enki she oddly enough does not lose dignity, rather, one has the impression that she is, when all is said and done, the more noble and the more powerful deity of the two.

The myth "Enki and Ninhursaga"[161] tells how Enki at the beginning of time, when the two had been allotted the island Tilmun (modern Bahrein), furnished the place with water and made its city a flourishing emporium for her. He then sought to have intercourse with her, but was rejected until he formally proposed marriage. The result of their union was a vegetation goddess N i n - s a r, "Lady Plant," who, when she grew up, wandered down to the riverbank where Enki saw her and united with her as he had done with her mother. She gave birth to a mountain goddess N i n - k u r r a, "Lady of the mountains," to whom, when she matured, the same thing happened that had happened to N i n - s a r. Her child was the spider goddess of weaving, U t t u — the Sumerian counterpart of Arachne. According to another version Enki first engendered the goddess N i n - i m m a, a deification of the female sexual organs, on N i n-k u r r a and then U t t u on N i n - i m m a. When U t t u was born, Ninhursaga, at long last roused to action, warned her against Enki and ensconced her safely in a house. Enki, however, was able to seduce her by promising marriage and offering her various vegetables, which he had helped a gardener grow, as wedding gifts. Ninhursaga, coming to the aid of U t t u after Enki had used and left her, removed Enki's semen from her body. From this semen eight plants grew up. After a while Enki happened upon these plants, gave them names, and ate them. Furious on hearing this, Ninhursaga cursed his name and vowed never to look at him with life-giving eye.

Meanwhile the plants, Enki's semen, developed in his body and — since as a male he was not built to be pregnant — made him deathly ill. The gods were disconsolate at his sufferings but incapable of helping him until the fox offered to get hold of Ninhursaga. It kept its promise. Ninhursaga relented, came running, placed Enki in her own vagina and so was able to give birth, for him, to the eight children that had developed in his body. These children, all goddesses, were named for the various parts of Enki's body where they had developed and were either married off or given means to support themselves by Enki. The myth, which ends with a formula of praise of Enki, seems, in a grotesque primitive fashion, to celebrate the generative power in river water and to attribute to it a variety of other powers, such as those in plants, in mountains, in the spider, etcetera. The fact that a river's high waters are of limited duration, briefly rise and fall, may be reflected in Enki's inconstancy; his eventual, near fatal, illness alludes perhaps to the near drying up of the rivers in an arid summer.

Another myth pitting Enki and Ninhursaga against each other, "Enki and Ninmah,"[162] calls her Ninmah, "August lady." It tells how in the beginning of time the gods had to toil to gain their livelihood, how they appealed to Enki's mother Nammu (perhaps, as suggested earlier, a deification of the riverbed), and how she then asked him on their behalf to create a worker to relieve them. Enki thought of the engendering clay of the deep (Apsu) which had sired him and told his mother to have two womb goddesses pinch off this clay for her. When she had put limbs on it, she was to give birth to it, assisted by Ninmah and eight other goddesses. Nammu thus gave birth to mankind to relieve the gods of their toil. At the feast celebrating Nammu's delivery both Enki and Ninmah drank too much and began to quarrel. Ninmah boasted that she could change man's form at will from good to bad. Enki dared her to try, wagering that he could find a position and livelihood for even the worst she could do. So

Ninmah began to make misshapen creatures: a giant, a person unable to control his urine, a barren woman, a being with neither male nor female organs, and so forth; but in each case Enki was able to find a place in society for the freak and to ensure it a living.

After she gave up Enki challenged her to take similar care of what he could create. He fashioned a creature beset by all the debilities of illness and old age, unable to move and to take nourishment. Ninmah, unable to cope with it, and horrified at what Enki has brought into being upbraided him passionately. Enki answered in conciliatory words and the story, which unfortunately is lost in a lacuna here, seems to have ended on a note of restored harmony.

Enki put his ingenuity to more constructive use in a myth that might be called "The Eridu Genesis."[163] This myth, the beginning of which is missing, described the creation of man by the four great gods: An, Enlil, Ninhursaga (here called Nintur), and Enki. After Nintur had decided to turn man from his primitive nomadic camping grounds toward city life the period began when animals flourished on earth and kingship came down from heaven. The earliest cities were built, were named, had the measuring cups, emblems of a redistributional economic system, allotted to them, and were divided between the gods. Irrigation agriculture was developed and man thrived and multiplied. However, the noise made by man in his teeming settlements began to vex Enlil sorely, and, driven beyond endurance, he persuaded the other gods to wipe out man in a great flood. Enki, thinking quickly, found a way to warn his favorite, one Ziusudra. He told him to build a boat in which to survive the flood with his family and representatives of the animals. Ziusudra wisely followed Enki's instructions and after the flood had abated Enki was able to persuade the other gods not only to spare Ziusudra but to give him eternal life as a reward for having saved all living things from destruction.

A less formidable opponent of Enki than Ninhursaga or Enlil — but on the whole more successful — is his granddaughter, the goddess Inanna. In a myth called "Inanna and the Powers of Office,"[164] she gets the better of him when she visits him in Eridu, absconding with an assortment of powers of office which he has given her while in a mellow mood, after drinking deep at the party in honor of her visit. When he wakes the next morning it is too late to get them back, try though he will.

Another time — in the myth "Enki and World Order"[165] — she complains to him out of envy and bad humor that other goddesses have offices while she alone has none. Enki goodnaturedly points out to her how many offices she does hold, then softens and gives her such motley powers as he happens to have left. Unfortunately, the text at this point is too damaged for anything more than a guess as to what she receives and what she does with it. In both cases there is no contest of wits. Inanna wins by taking advantage of a moment when Enki's guard is down or when he wants to avoid trouble. Inanna understands her own limitations and her grand-father's superior ingenuity very well; when her heedless impetuosity lands her in serious trouble, as it does in the myth "Inanna's Descent,"[166] it is to Enki's tricky mind that she looks for salvation.

"Enki and World Order," to which we have just referred, celebrates Enki as the source and center of human cultural pursuits no less than of the natural order. It begins with a long laudatory address to Enki which is followed by two successive self-praises by the god, celebrating his powers. Eventually, after a broken passage, the text moves on to tell how Enki blessed one after the other of the then known great cultural centers: Sumer (which here stands for the city of Nippur), Ur, Meluhha (Ethiopia), and Tilmun, giving to each their individual character.

After this Enki turns to organizing the world and to instituting its crafts and economies. He arranges for the sea, for the rivers, for clouds, and for rain. Then he institutes economies such as agriculture and herding, begins crafts such as house-building and weaving, and fixes boundaries by setting up boundary stones. For each such cosmic feature or human activity Enki appoints an appropriate deity to take charge of it: the goddess Nanshe for the sea, Ishkur for the clouds, Enkimdu and the grain goddess Ezinu for agricultural pursuits, Dumuzi-Amaushumgalanna for herding, and so forth. The end of the myth is taken up by Inanna's stormy complaint about having been overlooked in the allocation of powers.

Another myth with Enki as central figure is "Enki Builds E-engurra"[167] which tells in hymnic style how Enki built a house for himself in Eridu, then traveled up the Euphrates to his father Enlil's temple Ekur in Nippur, where he prepared a feast for Enlil and the other gods to celebrate the event.

A myth in which Enki was challenged by Ninurta is better dealt with in connection with that god, and so is an Akkadian myth about the thunder-bird Anzu (Imdugud) in which Enki advised Ninurta about how to over-come the bird. Two major Akkadian myths in which Enki plays a promi-nent role, "The Story of Atrahasis" and the Babylonian creation epic, Enûma elish, are likewise best considered later.

A short, but characteristic, myth in which he figures is the Akkadian "Myth of Adapa."[168] It tells — using Enki's Akkadian name Ea — how he had a very competent human servant, Adapa, who ran his house. One day when Adapa was out fishing the south wind capsized his boat and in his anger Adapa broke its wing with a powerful spell. When the south wind ceased to blow An noticed it and was informed of what had happened. He summoned Adapa to appear before him in heaven and answer for what he had done. Things looked very bleak for Adapa, but Ea, who did not want to lose his capable servant, advised him how to make friends in

heaven. He was to dress in mourning, and when he came to the gate of
An's palace and when the gods Dumuzi and Gishzida, who guarded it,
asked why he was so attired, he was to say that it was because two gods had
vanished from the earth, Dumuzi and Gishzida. Ea also told him not to eat
and drink anything offered to him, for it would be food and drink of
death.

When Adapa arrived at An's gate he did as Ea told him, and the
gatekeepers were so pleased at being still mourned on earth that they put
in a good word for Adapa with An. As a result An treated him as a guest
rather than a culprit. Moreover, since good manners demanded that food
and drink be offered to a guest, Adapa was given heavenly food and
drink, which is food of life and water of life and would have made Adapa
immortal. Adapa, however, declined both, and when asked why, told of
Ea's instructions. At this An laughed heartily for he had not wanted to
make Adapa immortal any more than Ea had, but good manners had
seemed to leave him no choice.

In concluding a sketch of Enki one must note that the ruler metaphor
only applies to him in a modified degree. Its essence, overwhelming
power does not truly fit him. It is not his nature to overwhelm; rather, he
persuades, tricks, or evades to gain his ends. He is the cleverest of the
gods, the one who can plan and organize and think of ways out when no
one else can. He is the counsellor and adviser, the expert and the trouble-
shooter, or manipulator, of the ruler; not the ruler himself. He or-
ganizes and runs the world, but at the behest of An and Enlil, not for
himself; he saves mankind and the animals from extinction in the flood,
but does not challenge Enlil's continued rule. His aim is a workable
compromise, avoiding extremes. Generally friendly to man, he does not
go to extremes for him: when Ninmah makes freaks he moderates the
evil, finds ways for them to support themselves, but does not try to stop
her — and he himself does worse than she. Similarly, while he saves man
in the flood stories, he does not try to prevent the flood itself. He is a
trimmer, a moderator, but not a wielder of ultimate power.

Divine Interplay = "The Story of Atrahasīs"

The interplay of the personalities of the four most powerful deities in
the ancient Mesopotamian cosmos is presented vividly in a great Akkadian myth of beginnings called "The Story of Atrahasīs."[169] It may therefore be appropriate to consider that story at this point, in order to sum up
what we have said of the four most powerful gods. The story is in large
measure preserved in a copy of Old Babylonian date, but it is doubtful
whether it dates back further, into the third millennium. It is also ques-
tionable whether its sources are all Sumero-Akkadian or in part West

Semitic. Nevertheless, the background against which it moves and its major theme, pitting man against nature and its divine forces, fit in with the spirit of earlier periods in Mesopotamia remarkably well. There is no serious reason why we should not take it up, a little prematurely, at this point; it speaks with the voice of the third (in some odd ways even the fourth) millennium B.C. It begins:

> When Ilu (i.e., Enlil) was the boss
> they were burdened with toil,
>   lugged the workbasket;
> the gods' workbasket . . . was big,
>   so that the toil was heavy,
>   great the straits.

Before man had been created, the gods had had to work themselves, dig canals and shoulder all the other hard tasks of irrigation agriculture. The three highest gods, Anu, Enlil, and Enki had divided the universe between them by lot, much as sons divide a paternal estate, and thus Anu, their father and king, got heaven, the warrior Enlil, their counsellor, got earth, and Enki, the clever one, received the underground waters and the sea.

Enlil, having received the earth as his share, was in charge of the gods who toiled endlessly away day and night, year after year, digging out the Euphrates and the Tigris.

Eventually they tired of their condition and began grumbling. They spoke of appealing to their sheriff, Enlil's son Ninurta, and even about fetching Enlil himself, the highest authority. One of their number, however, advised against these relatively peaceful proposals: they would only lead to more of the same. He advocated a show of violence, an immediate attack upon Enlil's house. The gods listened to him. They burned their tools and surrounded Enlil's dwelling. It was the middle of the night when Enlil's doorkeeper heard them. He quickly locked the gate and sent Enlil's vizier Nusku to wake him up. Enlil, hearing what was afoot, became thoroughly alarmed, and Nusku had to remind him that the gods were, after all, his own children and so not to be feared. He also suggested that Anu and Enki be called in for consultation.

This was done. Anu and Enki arrived and Enlil indignantly reported what had happened. At Anu's suggestion Nusku was then sent to the protesting gods to ask who the instigator of the attack was, but the gods assured him that the decision had taken shape collectively because of the heavy toil that was killing them. Moreover, under no circumstances would they go back to work.

When Enlil heard this he burst into tears and at once offered his resignation. He would retire to heaven and stay with Anu. At this point the diplomatic Enki intervened and proposed a compromise. The work of the strikers, he argued, was in fact much too heavy. Now, here with them sat the birth goddess. Let her fashion man to bear the yoke so that the gods could be free.

Nintur, the birth goddess, was willing if Enki would help, which he readily agreed to do. At his suggestion the gods then killed one of their number — apparently the ringleader of the rebellion — one We-e, who "had the idea," and Enki instituted ablution rites on the first, seventh, and fifteenth of every month to expiate them for the killing. With the slain god's flesh and blood Nintur mixed the clay from which man was to be fashioned. The gods gratefully gave Nintur the name Bêlit-ili, "Mistress of the gods," and she and Enki retired to the "house of destiny" where the new beings were to receive their forms and fortunes.

Here the clay was trodden by special womb deities and Nintur recited the proper incantations at Enki's prompting. Then she pinched off fourteen pieces of clay. She placed seven on the right and seven on the left, with a brick between them. From these pieces seven pairs of womb deities each fashioned one male and one female embryo.

After nine months the time of birth-giving arrived and Nintur "with a beaming, joyful face put on headdress and performed the midwifery." She also gave rules for the celebration of births in the future: the mother of the child was to remain in confinement, but the midwife could share in the merrymaking of the family. Furthermore, a brick was to be laid down for nine days in honor of Nintur. She ended with rules for a later nine days of merrymaking when normal marital relations could be resumed by the parents.

This solution to the difficulties of the gods worked almost too well. New picks and spades were made to replace those that were burned, the work on rivers and canals went forward, and food was grown for humans and gods alike. As a result man multiplied so rapidly that after 1,200 years the din of the ever-increasing human population had grown to such proportions that Enlil could get no sleep: "the land was bellowing like a bull." Enlil, thoroughly vexed, had the gods agree to send a plague, hoping thereby to diminish the number of humans and thus the noise.

Now, there lived in those days a very wise man, Atrahasīs, who was a servant of Enki. He appealed to his clever master for help with stopping the plague, and Enki advised him to consult with the elders and have heralds proclaim that people must make less noise and that everybody must shift their daily worship and offerings from their various personal gods to the god of the plague, Namtar. At the overwhelming show of offerings and attention Namtar became too abashed to harm the people further and he stayed his hand.

However, after another 1,200 years man had again multiplied and so had his noise. This time Enlil made the gods agree to a drought; Adad, the god of rain, was to hold the rains back. Again Atrahasīs appealed to Enki and again he was advised to concentrate worship and offering on the god immediately responsible. Adad felt embarrassed, just as had Namtar, and released his rain.

But once more, apparently, the people and their noise grew till they kept Enlil sleepless. This time — as far as one can surmise from a broken text — the gods decided upon a general embargo of all nature's gifts. Anu and Adad were to guard heaven, Enlil the earth, and Enki the waters, to see that no means of nourishment reached the human race.

This device, which could not be defended against by any concentration of worship, proved deadly:

> They cut off nourishment from the people,
> scant became the vegetables in their bellies.
>
> Up above Adad made rare his rain;
> down below the (yearly) flood was dammed,
>   could not rise up into the (river) sources.
>
> The field cut down on its yield,
> Nidaba (the grain goddess) turned tail.
>
> The black acres whitened,
> the broad plain brought forth salt.
>
> Earth's womb rebelled,
> no plant came forth, grain pushed not through.
> Infirmity befell people,
> the womb was tied up,
>   could not speed the child out right.
>
> . . . .
> When the second year arrived,
> they heaped up stores.
>
> When the third year arrived,
> the looks of the people had changed out
>   of hunger.
>
> When the fourth year arrived,
> their long strides (?) grew short,
> their broad shoulders had narrowed,
> people walked in the street, hunched.
>
> When the fifth year arrived,
> a daughter (from her house)
>   would be seeing her mother come home,
>   (lit. "go in" — i.e., to the mother's house)
> (yet) the mother was not opening her door
>   to the daughter.
> The daughter was watching the scales
>   of the mother.
> The mother was watching the scales
>   of the daughter.

When the sixth year arrived,
they served up a daughter for a meal,
served up a son for a daily ration.
One house set upon the other.
Their faces were covered
    as with dead malt;
the people hung on to life, having ceased breathing.

Ultimately, the plan seems to have been foiled by Enki, who — accidentally, he maintained — let large quantities of fish through to feed starving mankind.

By this time Enlil had lost all patience and thoroughly riled by the amused smiles of the gods at the way he was outmaneuvered by Enki, he determined on the complete annihilation of man. He bound all his fellow gods by oath to bring on a flood.

At first Enlil wanted Nintur and Enki to create the flood as they had created man, but Enki demurred; the flood was Enlil's responsibility. Then, although bound by oath not to reveal the god's plan, Enki managed to warn Atrahasīs by pretending to speak, not to him, but to the reedhut in which he was lying. Atrahasīs built a huge boat, explaining to the town elders that he was leaving because of the bad blood between his personal god, Enki, and Enlil, in whose domain the town of Shuruppak lay. Having loaded the boat with animals of all kinds and brought his family on board, he saw the weather changing. Sick with foreknowledge of doom, he secured the hatch, and the flood came raging over the land, drowning all in its path.

The gods were horrified at the destruction and heartbroken at the wholesale slaughter of humans. Soon, moreover, with no offerings to sustain them, they began to feel the pains of hunger cramps. Seven days and seven nights the flood lasted, then the storms abated and the ship of Atrahasīs became grounded. Thankfully he prepared a sacrifice, and the hungry gods, sniffing the delicious smell, gathered around it like flies.

Only Enlil remained unmoved. When he saw the ship he became furious and angrily asked how man could possibly have survived, at which Anu said the obvious thing: who but Enki could have engineered it?

Enki, undaunted, defended himself. He blamed Enlil for his indiscriminate punishment of innocent and guilty alike and — the text is broken at this point — presumably suggested other ways to deal with the noise problem. At this Enlil calmed down and proposed that Enki and Nintur confer together about what might be done to prevent further intolerable crises.

Their deliberations resulted in a scheme for birth control. They introduced the type of the barren woman, created a demon, Pashittu, who kills children at birth, and established several categories of priestesses for whom childbearing was taboo.

After another damaged passage the myth ends on a note of praise of Enlil and his powers:

> As praise to you let the Igigi(-gods)
> hear this song and heed your great feat,
> I sang of the flood to all people, Hearken!

The modern reader may well feel that Enlil, easily frightened, ready to weep and threaten to resign, insensitive to others, frustrated at every turn by the clever Enki, cuts rather a poor figure. Not so! The ultimate power of Enlil, the flood, stuns ancient imagination and compels respect. The myth is about the flood.

All the same it is clear that the myth views absolute power as selfish, ruthless, and unsubtle. But what is is. Man's existence is precarious, his usefulness to the gods will not protect him unless he takes care not to become a nuisance to them, however innocently. There are, he should know, limits set for his self-expression.

Nanna/Suen = Princeliness

As we have seen, the four highest ancient Mesopotamian gods, An, Enlil, Ninhursaga, and Enki, the gods who together made the great existential decisions, were the powers in the principal cosmic elements: the skies above, the storms ruling the atmosphere, the rocky ground, and the flowing fresh waters. Their roles found expression in the positions they held in the family of the gods. The highest authority of all was An, the father of the gods. Next in rank came Enlil, his son, commanding the respect and obedience due to the older brother in the family. With him ranked Ninhursaga as older sister. Only Enki, who was included in the group very late (at the beginning of the second millennium), had no innate authority; he was a younger son, and dependent on his wits.

The Moon God

The powers in lesser cosmic elements — the moon, the thunderstorm, the sun, the morning and evening star — are seen as grandchildren and great-grandchildren of An, not matching their elders in authority. The oldest of these younger generations of gods was the moon god, Nanna or Suen — a name later contracted to Sîn — the firstborn son of Enlil. Nanna seems to refer to him specifically as the full moon, S ú - e n, as the crescent, and yet a third name, A š - i m₄ - b a b b a r, as the new light. The majestic sight of the full moon moving slowly over the night skies makes it easy to understand that, alone of his generation, Nanna was regularly given the name of "father"; he is typically "Father Nanna." The numinous awe he could inspire comes through in a Sumerian address which greets him in these words:

> O you, who, perfect in lordliness,
>   wear a right crown,
> awesome visage, noble brow, pure shape
>   full of loveliness!
> Your grandeur lies imposed on all lands!
>   Your glory falls over the clear skies!
> Your great nimbus is fraught with holy dread.[170]

Nanna's cosmic functions were essentially to light up the night, to measure time, and to provide fertility. The first two of these are obvious functions for a power informing the moon, which is naturally seen and addressed as:

> . . . lamp appearing in the clear skies,
> Sîn, ever renewing himself, illuminating
>   darkness,
> bringing about light for the myriad people[171]

or as:

> Nanna, great lord,
> light shining in the clear skies,
> wearing on (his) head a prince's headdress,
> right god bringing forth day and night,
> establishing the month,
> bringing the year to completion;
> who has entree to Ekur,
> who has in hand the right decision-making
> at his father's place, (he) who begot him,
> beloved son of Ninlil,
> Ash-im-babbar.[172]

Corresponding to the phases of the moon, festivals called e š e š (i.e., "all-temple" or "general" festivals) were celebrated on the first, seventh, and fifteenth of the month during the Third Dynasty of Ur. Special offerings were made on the day the moon was invisible and thought to be dead: u d - n ú - a, "the day of lying down," the day Nanna went to the netherworld to judge and make administrative decisions there with the chthonic deities, Enki[173] and Ninki. A hymn to him says

> When you have measured the days of a month
>   when you have reached this day,
> . . . .
> When you have made manifest to the people
>   your "day of lying down" of a completed
>   month,
> you grandly judge, o lord, law cases
>   in the netherworld, make decisions superbly.

> Enki and Ninki, the great lords, the great princes,
>> its lords making (its) administrative decisions,
> wait upon what issues from your mouth,
>> as to a father . . . they . . . to you.
> Just verdicts you put in all mouths,
> make the proper thing apparent,
> the honest hearts you please, the administrative decisions
>> you make honestly. . . .[174]

Eventually, his work in the netherworld done, the god reappears in the skies as the new moon:

> On the broad firmament of heaven . . .
>> you spread light, the darkness you illumine;
> upon your rising wait the Anunnaki gods
>> with libations and petitions;
> upon your splendidly rising new light,
>> full of loveliness, a goodly sight,
> waits for you in joy the great lady of Kiur,
>> Mother Ninlil.[175]

Relations with the King

The monthly lunar festivals were, it seems, intimately connected with the king and his house. During the Third Dynasty of Ur the offerings on the day the moon was invisible seem to have been in charge of the reigning queen,[176] and in Umma, and perhaps elsewhere, the e š e š festivals were a responsibility of the temples of the deified deceased rulers of the dynasty.

A cause for considerable anxiety was, as might be expected, the occasional occurrence of an eclipse blotting out, or partly darkening, the bright smiling face of the moon. In the first millennium B.C. such an event was the occasion for the great gods to inquire of Suen how the evil portended by the eclipse might be avoided;[177] a seemingly earlier conception,[178] preserved in the so-called "Eclipse Myth," took a more serious view of the event. In that view the eclipse was due to an attack by evil demons on Nanna after they had seduced his two children, Inanna and Ishkur, to their side. In the ensuing crisis Enlil was able to alert Enki, who sent his son Marduk to aid Nanna — presumably with satisfactory results. The text ends with a magic ritual involving the breaking of a thread and ritual ablutions of the king, who

> like the new-light, Suen, holds in his hands
>> the life of the land,
> like the new new-light wears on his head
>> holy dread.

The passage underlines again the close connection between the moon god and the ruling king. The king here quite clearly substitutes for the god and achieves the purification of the god by the lustrations he undergoes.

Lustrations to keep the bright moon free of defilement appear indeed to have been a fairly general feature of the cult and to have taken place not only at eclipses but annually at New Year (z a g - m u (. a k)), which in Ur probably fell at the beginning of the month M a s h d a g u, and at the "Great Festival" (E z e n - m a h) in the ninth month which took its name from it. When King Ibbi-Suen of the Third Dynasty of Ur brought home a costly and exotic gold jar from a campaign in Elam he dedicated it to Nanna:

> so that at Ezen-mah and New Year, at the lustrations
> of Nanna, oil may not be wanting in the place where
> the (rite of) "mouth-opening" is performed
> on Nanna's copper bath pitcher.[179]

This bath pitcher on which the reinvigorating rite called "mouth-opening" was performed in order to make it effective when it was used in the lustration rites, we know from other sources. It stood in Nanna's bedroom on top of the ziggurat of his temple Ekishnugal in Ur and was too sacred to be seen by profane eyes.[180] It owed its purity and purifying powers to Enki, lord of the Apsu.[181]

God of the Cowherders

Ur, chief city of Nanna, was located on the lower Euphrates on the edge of the marshes in a country belonging partly to the orchardmen along the riverbanks, and partly to the cattlemen who grazed their herds in the marshes. It is not surprising, therefore, to find the varying forms of the god seen and comprehended in terms of the experience of orchardmen and marsh-dwelling cattle breeders. Seeing the god as a "fruit self-grown" [182] was probably the orchardman's way, while apprehending the horns of the crescent as those of a "frisky calf of heaven" [183] came naturally to the cattleman. It is likely that we owe to the latter the description of the crescent as a "boat" or "barge" [184] of heaven, since its shape does suggest that of the long, graceful boats which were — and are to this day — the chief means of getting around in the marshes. In time, however, as the human form came to dominate, these immediately experienced older forms tended to adapt themselves, so that the "bull" slowly gave way to the "cowherd" and the "boat" to the "boatman."

To the cowherder and the marshes belongs also the figure of Ningal, the wife of Nanna. Her name Ningal, "The great lady," does not in itself tell much about her, but she was the daughter of Ningikuga, "The lady of the pure reed" (n i n - g i . k u g . a (k)), who was wife to Enki, the god of the watery deep.[185] One may assume, therefore, that like her mother she was a reed goddess. This seems confirmed by another name that she shared with the human high priestess who incarnated her on earth, *Zirru*, "Reed-fence." [186] Conceivably the herder in the marshes, seeing the moon rise nightly out of the reeds to set again in them by morning, may have thought of it as the moon leaving and returning to his house and his wife.

Perhaps because the relation of the moon to the tides had been observed or perhaps because, as god of the cowherders, his worshipers looked to him to provide the spring floods on which they depended, the moon god Nanna/Suen was also a god of fertility. In fact he reminds us of that other herdsman's god of fertility, Dumuzi. In the case of Nanna/Suen, however, the texts show a curious looking beyond the god to an ultimate power. In some respects Nanna/Suen is himself the source of the abundance he brings, in others, the real source is his father, Enlil of Nippur, who grants him things out of love. The fertility that Nanna himself provides is the more narrowly circumscribed one of the cowherder: rise of the waters, growth of the reeds, increase of the herds, abundance of milk, cream, and cheese. The fecundity derived from Enlil is more general.

As in the case of Dumuzi we have myths and songs dealing with Nanna as wooer. An Akkadian myth[187] tells how he was particularly fond of boating, invented various aids for hunting, and, having set his heart on Ningal, proposed to her, united with her, and married her without asking her father's consent.

The impetuosity characteristic of him and Ningal here is discernible also in a Sumerian song about them.[188] The beginning is lost, but it seems to open with an address by Ningal of which only the last lines are preserved. They tell of her longing to be in the arms of her beloved. She is answered by Nanna who invites her out into the marshes. He considerately tells her to cut reeds for leggings to protect herself, and offers to gather birds' eggs for her to eat, after which she can wash her hands in the waters of the swamp. Later on Nanna says he will milk his cows, prepare the milk, and carry it for her to her mother's house — but oh! if only he could visit her without her mother Ningikuga being there! Ningal answers that she will come to him and

> O my Nanna, your (lover's) plaint is sweet,
>   it is the plaint of my heart.

In the Dumuzi cult the love songs led up to the marriage of the god, which was celebrated in a rite of sacred marriage. In this rite the king assumed the identity of the god while a high priestess seems to have embodied the goddess. Such a rite appears also to have formed part of the

Nanna cult. We know that the high priestess of Nanna in Ur, chosen from the royal family, was considered to be the human spouse of the god.[189] She was, as one such high priestess described herself, "the loins suitable as to holiness for the office of high priestess." [190] Her title, *zirru*, is a name for Ningal, so she may well have been a ritual embodiment of the goddess. One may guess that the sacred marriage was celebrated at the Akiti festival of Nanna in the twelfth month, when offerings connected with "setting up the bed" are recorded.[191]

The abundance brought by Dumuzi was often represented as the god's bridal gifts or as gifts of cream, milk, and so forth, in response to a request from his bride Inanna.[192] A song giving dialogue between Nanna and Ningal presents a very similar case.[193] In it Nanna sends a love message to Ningal with a traveler, telling her of all the delicious dairy products he has and very clearly wishing her to join him. She sends word back, however, for him to wait. When he has filled the rivers with the early flood, has made grain grow in the field, and caused fishes to be in the marshes, old and new reeds in the canebrake, stags in the forest, plants in the desert, honey and wine in the orchards, cress in the garden, and long life in the palace — only then, she says, will she come to live with him in his lofty dwelling on top of the ziggurat in Ur:

> In your house on high, in your beloved house,
>   I will come to live,
> O Nanna, up above in your cedar perfumed mountain,
>   I will come to live,
> O lord Nanna, in your citadel
>   I will come to live,
> Where cows have multiplied, calves have multiplied
>   I will come to live,
> O Nanna, in your mansion of Ur
>   I will come to live,
> O lord! In its bed I for my part
>   will lie down too!

Of the other kind of text, in which Nanna is not the ultimate source of fertility but obtains a large measure of his blessings as gifts from his father Enlil, the largest and most central myth is called "Nanna's Journey to Nippur." [194] It tells how Nanna decides to go to Nippur to visit his father and loads his boat with all kinds of wood and animals. On the journey upriver from Ur he passes several major cities, at each of which the tutelary goddess comes out to greet and bless him. Eventually he reaches Nippur where he tells the doorkeeper of Enlil's temple to open: he has come to feed the herds and flocks, to fill baskets with birds' eggs, to look after the reeds of the marshes, bring wild pigs and various fishes. He is also going to get myriad ewes with lamb, letting the rams in among them, myriad goats with kid, letting the bucks in among them, and myriad cows with calf, letting the breed bulls in among them. The gatekeeper joyfully opens the gate and Enlil, delighting in his son, prepares a treat for him. He calls for cakes such as Nanna loves, bread, and he has beer poured for him — all agricultural rather than herding delicacies — and in addition he gives him general prosperity to take back with him to Ur: carp-flood in the rivers, grain in the fields, fishes in the rivers, reeds in the marshes, plants in the high desert, harts in the forests, and long life in the palace.

The myth of Nanna's journey to Nippur is closely connected with the spring rite of the n i s a ĝ-boat (its name means "the first fruits boat") which took gifts of the first dairy products of the year from Ur to Nippur.[195] The meaning of this ritual act, we would suggest, was religious celebration and sanction of the exchange of products of the different economies of the cattlemen in the southern marshes and of the farmers in the north.

"Nanna's Journey to Nippur" is not the only treatment of this topic. In a well-known hymn to Nanna[196] he is hailed as lord of Ur and its temple, Ekishnugal, as he drifts across the skies in his boat, refreshing himself with beer and keeping an eye on his numberless herds of cows — here obviously the stars — while his father Enlil in Nippur looks joyfully on and sings his praises. Enki, from his temple in Ur, does the same. The hymn ends with the happy awareness that water is even now welling up in the river canals and marshes, an event which the hymn attributes to Nanna. A similar song[197] pictures Nanna as a herdsman with numerous cows — again, probably, the stars — telling how he takes off their fetters, milks them, pours the milk into his churn, and carries it in; then, when his work is done, how he puts the fetters back on, drives the cows to pasture, and watches over them as herdsman. His mother Ninlil asks him to come to Ekur when the night has passed. There he is dearly beloved and can ask whatever he wishes of Enlil. Nanna/Suen obeys, pours milk in the churn, arranges for the washing of hands before eating, and announces that his father Enlil is to eat the best of his pure products. The song ends with Ninlil's renewed praise of him.

Ninurta = Warlike Prowess

Nanna belongs to the same generation as another son of Enlil, Ninurta, god of the thunderstorm and spring flood. Since the moist air and thunderstorms of spring soften the soil and make ploughing possible, it is understandable that Ninurta is also god of the plough. His name may in fact contain an old cultural loan word for that instrument, (u r t a < *ḫurta < *ḫurt), and may mean "Lord Plough." Unlike Nanna, whose milieu was that of the cowherder, Ninurta is predominantly a god of the farmer; among the farmers in the north, in Nippur, and in the east, in Girsu, he tends to displace Nanna as firstborn son of Enlil.

The Thunderbird

His external form was originally the thundercloud, mythopoeically experienced as an enormous bird floating on outstretched wings in the sky. Since the roar of the thunder could rightly issue only from a lion's mouth the bird was early given a lion's head. The name of the god was, as so often, that of the phenomenon in which he was the power, in this case Imdugud, "heavy rain." Since i m - d u g u d can also denote "sling-stone" or "ball of clay," [198] the reference is perhaps — if only by popular etymology — to the hailstorm. A curious survival of this nonhuman form of the god is preserved for us in the "Lugalbanda Epic" [199] in which the hero meets the god in his bird shape in the eastern mountains. Although a bird, Imdugud is as much the "son of Enlil" as later human forms, Ninurta and Ningirsu. Just as Ninurta in the epic L u g a l - e constructs the near mountain ranges to serve as protective walls, locking them before the country, so Enlil has made Imdugud lock the mountains like "a great doorleaf" before the country; and just as Ninurta makes unalterable decisions, so does Imdugud.

The growing feeling that only the human form was suitable for visualiz-ing a god led to difficulties in the case of Imdugud. In the Diyala Region as early as the Second Early Dynastic period representations on seals show the bird god growing a human lower body or in the case of a representa-tion in the round showing the god entirely in human shape and relegating the bird shape to serve as an emblem on the base of the statue. The humanizing process was a slow and uneven one. In Girsu, as late as Enannatum in the outgoing Third Early Dynastic period, a mace head dedicated to the humanized god "Lord of Girsu" (i.e., Ningirsu) still shows the donor, Baragkiba, in a pose of adoration before the thunder-bird. Still later, when Gudea saw his lord Ningirsu in a dream, the god appeared with Imdugud's wings, and his lower parts ended in a flood.[200] Finally, in Assyrian times in the first millennium, a relief of Ashurnasir-pal's that graced Ninurta's temple in Nimrud shows the god in human form, but still winged. Significantly he is throwing thunderbolts at his own older form, a variant of the lion-headed bird, a winged bird-lion.[201]

This protracted contest between anthropomorphic and nonan-thropomorphic shapes was one of growing bitterness. The unworthy nonhuman form, so difficult to annihilate, became more and more of a problem. It was relegated to the status of a mere emblem or symbol of the god. Yet still when the god went to war with the army or when oaths were sworn by touching him in law cases, it was in the old nonhuman form, the "emblem," that he was encountered. At last the dislike of the nonhuman form and the difficulty of expunging it made it a foe, a captured enemy. The bird form, Imdugud, became an enemy of the human form, Ningirsu(k) or Ninurta, captured by him in a fight in the mountains,[202] much as the human form of the god of the fresh waters, Enki/Ea, captured his own nonhuman form, Apsu, the fresh waters underground.

The Warrior King

The humanization of the outer form of the thunderstorm god accompanied the socialization of his inner form. Thunder and lightning are violent phenomena. In the thunder the ancients not only heard the roar of the lion or the bellow of the bull, but also at times the rumble of the war chariot, while the lightning became the flash of arrows in the sun. Thus Ninurta/Ningirsu, having captured his bird form in a battle in the mountains, hitched it before his war chariot and drove it across the skies, rain pouring — as is shown on Old Babylonian cylinder seals — out of its mouth.[203] As victorious charioteer, the human form of the god became a war leader, a king. At this time kingship as such was only emerging. It did, however, furnish the metaphorization and key to the social significance of the power in the thunderstorm which became, like the emergent king, a defender against outer foes and a righter of internal wrongs. In the following third and second millennia these were the aspects of Ninurta that predominated in hymns and prayers. His role as bringer of rain, floods, and fertility receded into the background.[204]

Rain God Myths

In the myths about Ninurta his character as a force of nature remains alive. The myth called A n - g i m d í m - m a, "Who counts as much as An," [205] is basically an incantation to appease the thunderstorms that threaten Nippur. It describes the thundercloud warrior, Ninurta, returning from battle in his war chariot, still all sound and fury. Enlil, disturbed, sends his vizier, Nusku, to meet Ninurta and tell him to quiet down so as not to disturb his father with his clamor. Ninurta puts away his weapons, stables his team, and enters Ekur where his appearance hushes the Anunnaki. His mother, Ninlil, greets him with affectionate words which he answers with a long swaggering speech extolling his warlike powers. Eventually the god Ninkarnunna, Ninurta's barber, steps in to pacify his master and eases him quietly into his temple, Eshumesha.

The longest and best known Ninurta myth, L u g a l - e u d m e - l á m - b i n i r - ǧ á l, "King, storm, the glory of which is noble," [206] likewise deals with the god as a force of nature, but humanizes him and shows him as a young king and warrior. The natural events underlying the myth are apparently the appearance of the thunderstorms in the spring and their spending themselves over the mountains, where their waters and those of the melting snow swell the Tigris and its tributaries, thus causing the yearly flood. The myth presents the raging of the thunderstorms over the mountains as a battle between Ninurta and a rival king, Azag, whose name, like that of Ninurta's older nonhuman form Imdugud, means "sling-stone" and probably as suggested earlier, refers to hailstones. He seems thus to be but the older lion-bird form of the god made into his enemy as winged bird-lion, the very one shown on the Assyrian relief mentioned earlier. After the victory over Azag, Ninurta reorganizes his newly won territories. The myth humanizes the power behind the yearly flood into a young king undertaking major irrigation works.

> At that time the waters of the earth coming from below
>   did not come pouring over the fields,
> (nay!) as ice long accumulating they rose in
>   the mountains on the other side.
> The gods of the country who were stationed there,
> who carried pickaxes and baskets
> and whose assigned tasks were thus,
> poured it, according to what they had first
>   chopped off (from it), on a man's field.
> The Tigris, for which a great fate (was decreed?),
>   did not rise in flood,
> its outlet did not take it straight into the sea,
>   did not carry sweet water.
> At the quay no man dipped(?) a water pail,
> in dire famine nothing was produced,
> the canals no man cleared,
>   dredged not the silt from them,
> on the fertile field water was not poured,
>   there was no making of dikes.
> In land after land there was no planting in furrows,
>   the grain was broadcast.[207]

To remedy all of this Ninurta built a stone wall, the near ranges, which would protect the land and would serve also as a dike to keep the waters of the Tigris from going east into the mountains.

> The lord directed (his) great intelligence to it,
> Ninurta, the son of Enlil, wrought magnificently.
> He made a heap of stones in the mountains —
> like drifting rain clouds they came
>   (floating) on outstretched wings —
> set bar before the country as (with) a great wall.

Well sweeps he set up on it in myriad places.
That warrior was shrewd, watered(?) the cities
    equally.
The mighty waters followed along the stone.
Now these waters do not rise from the earth
    into the eternal mountains.
What had been scattered he gathered,
what in the mountains had been consumed
    by swamps
he gathered and threw it into the Tigris,
had the carp-flood pour over the fields.[208]

At the abundance produced by these irrigation works: barley, orchard
fruits, and piles of produce, the kings and gods of the country rejoiced
and praised Ninurta to his father Enlil. His mother Ninlil, overcome with
longing for him, decided to visit him; and Ninurta, overjoyed to see her,
made her a gift of the vast stone pile he had made. First, though, he
provided it with vegetation, wildlife, and minerals, and called its name,
h u r s a ǧ. Thus Ninlil became Ninhursaga, "Lady of the foothills." The
myth ends with a detailed account of how Ninurta sat in judgment over
the various kinds of stones (they had formed the army of Azag), praising
some of them who had behaved properly and giving them office in his
new administration, but cursing with heavy penalties those who had been
viciously hostile to him. In this manner the stones got their characteristics.
Flint, for instance, was chastised by a sentence that it should break when
the far softer horn was pressed against it — as in fact it does.

Power in The Flood

The myth, L u ǧ a l - e, in its present form can be dated, on inner
criteria, to the time of Gudea or shortly afterward. It is typical of the
slowness with which humanization took place and the ease with which its
stages existed side by side that the highly humanized picture presented in
L u ǧ a l - e is contemporaneous with Gudea's dream in which, as we have
mentioned, the god seemed to be "according to his wings the Imdugud
bird, according to his lower parts a flood."[209] Even more striking is the
way the god appears in Gudea's prayer to him, which we quoted earlier to
illustrate the application of the ruler metaphor; we return to it now to
indicate the extent to which nonhuman metaphors are still alive in it, for
Ningirsu is simply the reddish floodwaters as they come roaring down the
mountain tributaries. They are semen ejected by the eastern highlands
(the k u r - g a l), into the foothills (the h u r s a ǧ) and they are reddish
because they were ejected in a deflowering and so are tinted by blood:

O my master Ningirsu, lord, seminal waters
    reddened in the deflowering;

able lord, seminal waters emitted by the
  "great mountain" (Enlil). . . .[210]

Their force as they come rushing is the god's violent essence:

Your heart, rising as (rise the waves in)
    mid-ocean,
crashing down as (crash) the breakers,
roaring like waters pouring out (through a
    breach in a dike),
destroying cities like the flood wave.[211]

With L u g a l - e we must mention — for its intrinsic rather than its
literary interest — a Sumerian myth of which we have only the middle
part.[212] When it begins Ninurta has apparently conquered the young
Imdugud bird, following instructions from Enki. The Imdugud bird held
in its claws the powers of office needed for controlling the Apsû, and
Ninurta had hoped to acquire them by vanquishing the bird. As his
weapon struck it, however, the bird opened its claws from pain and the
powers of office returned of their own accord to Enki and the Apsû. The
situation fits so exactly with what we are told in the Akkadian myth of
"Ninurta and the Anzu Bird" [213] that we may assume that both reflect the
same mythological background. In the Akkadian story the Anzu bird stole
the tablets of fate from Enlil and flew to the mountains. In the Sumerian
story we assume the powers were stolen from Enki. In both, Ninurta
(through Enki's advice), is able to overcome the bird in a battle in the
mountains, but what we know of the Akkadian story stops here. In the
Sumerian, Ninurta, disappointed in his hopes, was flown back to the Apsû
by the bird. There Enki received him kindly, praised him, and assigned
him the bird as his captive. None of this, however, satisfied Ninurta's
ambitious heart. He went to his post in the Apsû and there he darkened
and yellowed a wave, making its heart rebellious and setting its face
against the world. Though Ninurta had told nobody of his plans, somehow the crafty Enki was aware of what was going on, and when this
terrifying flood wave came sweeping against the Apsû temple, he sent his
vizier to Ninurta. Ninurta, however, refused to budge, and would not
come out. Enki then resorted to a ruse. He created the turtle, placed it at
the entrance to the Apsû and deceitfully called to Ninurta that his post
had been given to the turtle. Ninurta came out, the turtle managed to slip
behind him, quickly dug a pit, and threw Ninurta in. He became the butt
of Enki's sarcasm and scorn:

You chased my powers in the mountains,
    found them here,
you set your face against me, to kill me!

> Bragging upstarts I put down or let rise
>   (at will);
> how could you set your face against me?
> What position of yours have I taken from you? . . .
> Where has your might gone, where is your valor?
> He used to destroy great mountains —
>   now it is verily: "Alas!"[214]

The story as we have it ends with Ninurta's mother being told what has happened and lamenting Enki's cruelty. Presumably it went on to tell how she eventually obtained her son's release.

Once more, it will be seen, we are dealing with the theme of the hydraulic cycle and the spring thunderstorm in the mountains: first, the escape of the waters in cloud form (the thunderbird Imdugud/Anzu) evaporating from the Apsû; next, the vanquishing of the thunderbird, the rains, in the mountains; then the floodwaters, fed by the rains, pouring down the rivers to Apsû in Eridu and to the lagoons of the marshes — represented in the myth as Ninurta's return to Apsû with the thunderbird and his creation of the yellowish dark flood wave. Lastly, the subsiding of the flood and the lowering of the water table as the summer lengthens corresponds to Ninurta's being cast into the pit. The myth's hero is Enki, who successfully recovers control of the waters, first from the thunder-showers, Imdugud, then from the flood, Ninurta.

The view of this myth (heavily biased in Enki's favor) is not, however, the only view of the natural processes involved to be found in the texts. Ninurta's journey to Apsû and Eridu, the passing of the flood down the rivers, was seen by his own worshipers not as an attempt to depose Enki but as the performing of a high office through which to insure fertility and abundance. The cult of the god comprised a journey to Eridu from Girsu, where he was called Ningirsu,[215] and from Nippur, where his name was Ninurta. In both cases the god was presumably conveyed as cult statue or possibly as cult emblem. A processional hymn from Nippur celebrating this ritual journey states its purpose succinctly:

> To make the (administrative) decisions for abundance,
> to make myriad places sprout profusely,
> to make grass and herbs, verdure, sprout profusely
>   in the wide desert,
> to make the buffalo milk and cream
>   heavy in pen and fold
> and rejoice the shepherd,
> did the warrior Ninurta decide to go to Eridu;
> to make the Tigris and the Euphrates roar,
> to make the Apsû tremble(?), the deep shiver,

to provide(?) HI-SUHUR and SUHUR-MAŠ fishes
   in the marsh,
old and new reeds, first cream,
   all kinds of things in the canebrake,
to cause the beasts to multiply,
   the living things in the desert,
to . . . stags and wild sheep in the forests,
. . . .
and to see that the rituals of Shumer not perish,
   the schedules for all lands not be changed. . . .[216]

In this text Enki hardly seems to exist, everything is accomplished by Ninurta with the approval of An and his father Enlil.

Utu = Righteousness

To the generation after Suen and Ninurta belong Nanna/Suen's three children: Utu, Ishkur, and Inanna. Utu is the sun god, the power in light, the foe of darkness and deeds of darkness. On the social plane he therefore becomes a power for justice and equity.

As he is presented in hymns and prayers of supplication the aspect of him as a power in nature, bringing the day and shedding light in darkness, is unmistakeable, and the mythopoeic imagination provided a team of swift mules (originally storms) and a chariot and driver for Utu's daily journey across heaven.[217] But on the whole Utu's social role as guardian of justice is his most important function. He is the judge of gods and men, presiding in the morning in courts such as the one we know from the Bathhouse Ritual, where demons and other evildoers are sued by their human victims.

At night he judges disputes among the dead of the netherworld.[218] He is the last appeal of the wronged who can obtain no justice from their fellow men, and their cry of despair to him, i - U t u! was feared as possessing supernatural power. In one story about Gilgamesh[219] this cry made the earth open up so that Gilgamesh's cherished playthings fell into the netherworld. It is no wonder, therefore that the term for it took on overtones of "malcontent," and that the kings of the Third Dynasty of Ur and of the Isin Dynasty were determined to stamp it out as a social evil.

Ishkur = The Rainstorm

Utu's brother, Ishkur — in Akkadian, Adad — was a god of rain and thundershowers like Ninurta. We even possess a text in which, as with Ninurta in A n - g i m d i m - m a, his clamorous approach to Nippur disturbs Enlil and he is asked to turn away.[220]

Whereas Ninurta was clearly the rain god of the farmers, however, Ishkur seems to belong specifically to the herdsmen: he is "King of abundance," "King of verdure," and "King making grass and herbs grow long" [221] — that is to say, he is the rains that bring verdure and pasture in the desert. Like other personifications of the life-giving spring rain, Ishkur shows in his mythology reflections of ancient man's distress at the early ceasing of the rains: a myth preserved in a copy of the Agade period has him held captive in the mountains.[222]

Ishkur's early, nonhuman, forms were those of the bull and the lion — their roars were heard in the thunder — and, humanized, he appeared like Ninurta as a warrior driving his thundering chariot across the skies, throwing his large and small sling-stones — hailstones and raindrops — down from it. The chariot was drawn by seven storms and his vizier, "lightning," walked before it.[223] It is no wonder that Ishkur's sheen lies over the land "like a cloth"[224] and that his martial clamor disturbs and frightens the other gods.

Besides the tradition in which Ishkur is the son of the moon god Nanna/Suen, there was apparently another which made him son of the god of heaven, An, and twin brother of Enki. In many ways that seems a more natural family grouping, but there is no way of telling this alternative tradition's age or where it was at home.[225]

Inanna = Infinite Variety

The Power in the Storehouse

Sister of Utu and Ishkur and in some respects the most intriguing of all the figures in the pantheon is a third child of Nanna, the goddess Inanna (in Akkadian, Ishtar). We have already described her as the beloved and the bride of Dumuzi-Amaushumgalanna. We suggested then that she was in origin the numen of the date storehouse who married Amaushumgalanna of the date harvest at the time the harvest was stored; also that her range was early extended to that of the storehouse generally, including wool, meat, and grain.

In part this may reflect a process of gradual unification of the fertility cults of the dual economies of Uruk, date-growing and husbandry, blending a date god and storehouse goddess (Amaushumgalanna and Inanna) with a different shepherd's god and goddess (Dumuzi and Inanna — the latter conceivably a rain goddess). Actually Inanna has a good many more aspects than those which characterize her in her relations with Dumuzi, so many different ones in fact that one is inclined to wonder whether several, originally different deities have not here coalesced in one, the many-faceted goddess Inanna.

The Power in Rains

Still quite clear in the materials, is the aspect of Inanna as goddess of thunderstorms and rain, very close in character to her brother, Ishkur, and to Ninurta. As does Ninurta, she controls the lion-headed thunderbird, Imdugud. We hear of her letting it fly out of the house,[226] and in the story "Enmerkar and the Lord of Aratta" it is called "the curb of Inanna put as bar in the mouth of all the world." [227] In that story her method of forcing Aratta to submit to Uruk is to withhold rain and expose it to drought. The lion, typically an image or emblem of thunder gods such as Ishkur and Ninurta, occurs also with her. Her chariot is drawn by seven lions, she rides a lion, or she is herself the lion.[228] The other thunder animal, the bull, is lent to her, albeit reluctantly by An when she wants the "Bull of Heaven" to kill Gilgamesh.[229] Her character as the power in the thunderstorm is stated directly in the opening lines of a major hymn to her[230] in which she is called "Inanna, the great dread storm of heaven." In an address to her, Enheduanna, the daughter of Sargon of Akkad, says:

> O destroyer of mountains,
>   you lent the storm wings!
> O beloved one of Enlil,
> you came flying into the country,
> attended to the instructions of An.
> O my lady, at your roar you made
>   the countries bow low.[231]

And elsewhere in the same composition we hear that:

> With the charging storm you charge,
> with the howling storm you howl,
> with Ishkur you roar,
> with all evil winds you rage! [232]

Inanna describes herself as rain goddess more gently in a hymn where she says:

> I step onto the heavens, and the rain
>   rains down;
> I step onto the earth, and grass and herbs
>   sprout up.[233]

But when she gets angry her outbursts are not merely tempestuous, they are truly the tempest itself, with its thunder shaking heaven and earth and its lightening burning and destroying. Here is her wrath at the untimely death of Urnammu:

> Inanna, the dread storm, the oldest child of Suen,
>   what did she do?

> She was making heaven tremble, the earth shake,
> Inanna was destroying the cow pens, burning the sheepfolds,
> (crying:) "Let me berate An, the king of the gods!" [234]

This aspect of Inanna as a goddess of rain makes it more understandable that a persistent tradition linked her with the god of heaven, An, as his spouse, even to the point of identifying her with Antum;[235] for, as we have seen earlier, An (Akkadian Antum) was the sky seen as female and referred to the overcast sky, the clouds of which were "breasts of the sky" from which flowed the rain. Antum and Inanna represent the same phenomenon of nature, the power in the rain clouds. To the tradition of Inanna as a rain goddess belongs also the Eclipse myth, with which we have dealt earlier.[236] There, Inanna joins Ishkur and the storms in their attack on their father, the moon god, because she aspires to marry An and become queen of heaven. (Actually, "queen of heaven" is one interpretation of her name.) The same view of her also informs the late myth called the "Elevation of Inanna."[237] Here the gods propose to An that he marry Inanna "with whom you have fallen in love," and this he readily does. He also confers on her his name and all his powers, then Enlil gives her his powers, and lastly Enki gives his to her. As queen of the universe she thus comes to unite in her person all its highest powers.

Goddess of War

In the process of humanization, gods of rain and thunderstorms tended — as we have seen with Ishkur and Ninurta — to be envisaged as warriors riding their chariots into battle. Correspondingly we find that Inanna's warlike character and skill with weapons is celebrated from early myths, like the one telling of her battle against the mountain Ebih[238] (modern Jebel Hamrin), to late compositions, such as the "Elevation of Inanna," and to the royal inscriptions of Assyrian kings. In fact, battle was to the Sumerians "the dance of Inanna"[239] and she herself proudly tells us in a hymn that:

> When I stand in the front (line) of battle
>   I am the leader of all the lands,
> when I stand at the opening of the battle,
>   I am the quiver ready to hand,
> When I stand in the midst of the battle,
>   I am the heart of the battle,
>   the arm of the warriors,
> when I begin moving at the end of the battle,
>   I am an evilly rising flood,
> when I follow in the wake of the battle,
>   I am the woman (exhorting the stragglers):
>   "Get going! Close (with the enemy)!"[240]

She celebrates her power as goddess of thunderstorms and wars in the proud lines

> My father gave me the heavens,
>   gave me the earth,
> I am Inanna!
> Kingship he gave me,
> queenship he gave me,
> waging of battle he gave me,
>   the attack he gave me,
> the floodstorm he gave me,
>   the hurricane he gave me!
> The heavens he set as a crown on my head,
> the earth he set as sandals on my feet,
> a holy robe he wrapped around my body,
> a holy sceptre he placed in my hand.
> The gods are sparrows — I am a falcon;
> the Anunnaki trundle along — I am a splendid
>   wild cow;
> I am father Enlil's splendid wild cow,
> his splendid wild cow leading the way![241]

Morning and Evening Stars

Besides being a rain goddess and goddess of war, Inanna is also the goddess of the morning and evening star. A remarkable hymn from the time of Iddin-Dagan of Isin[242] hails her as she rises in the sky in the evening. It tells how every month at the new moon she holds court for the gods to hear their petitions, how music is played for her and war games staged by her guardsmen attendants, ending in a mock parade of prisoners and a perhaps not so mock shedding of blood. The hymn then returns to her in her character as the evening star, which marks the end of the day's work for men and animals. All may go to rest while she, shining in the sky, judges the cases of just and unjust.

In the morning (as the morning star) she signals the awakening of man and beast. Copious offerings are brought her and the personal gods of mankind approach her with their gifts of food and drink.

The final cantos of the hymn, discussed above in chapter 2, are taken up by a description of the yearly rite of the sacred marriage in which the king, here Iddin-Dagan, takes on the identity of Amaushumgalanna, her divine bridegroom.

The canto that hails the goddess as she rises in the evening sky may be quoted:

> The great queen of heaven, Inanna,
>   I will hail!

The only one, come forth on high,
   I will hail!
The great queen of heaven, Inanna,
   I will hail!

The pure torch that flares in the sky,
the heavenly light, shining bright like the day,
the great queen of heaven, Inanna,
   I will hail.
The holy one, the awesome queen of the Anunnaki,
the one revered in heaven and earth,
   crowned with great horns,
the oldest child of Suen, Inanna,
   I will hail!

Of her majesty, of her greatness,
   of her exceeding dignity
of her brilliant coming forth
   in the evening sky
of her flaring in the sky — a pure torch —
of her standing in the sky
   like the sun and the moon,
known by all lands from south to north,
of the greatness of the holy one of heaven
to the lady I will sing.[243]

The Harlot

Evening, after work but before rest, is the time for play and dancing.
The hymn touches on this in passing as people go to sleep:

The dancer of the country,
   the celebrant of the festival,
the young hero, opens his heart (in bed)
   to his spouse.[244]

This dancing in the evening is stressed more as something in which the
goddess has a benevolent interest in a passage in the Lugalbanda Epic that
tells how Inanna, rising as the evening star, sends her rays into the cave
where young Lugalbanda lies ill. The poet introduces her and her kind
offices saying:

So as to set the poor folk going at their dances,
   having (with her light)
   made the dancing green more pleasant,
and to make the spots to bed down in
   more pleasant for the harlot
   setting out for the alehouse,
did Inanna, the daughter of Suen,

like a dancer (proudly) raise her head
   over the land.[245]

This passage, as will be noted, includes a further typical feature of the
evening: the harlot setting out to pick up customers among the people
returning from work in the fields; and perhaps because it was a common
sight to see the harlot appear with the evening star there was a bond
between them. Inanna is the protectress of the harlot as well as of the
alehouse out of which she works. Moreover, the evening star is itself a
harlot soliciting in the skies, and its power informs Inanna's sisters below,
making them incarnations of the goddess, their pickups, her bridegroom
Dumuzi. A hymn addresses Inanna in these words:

O harlot, you set out for the alehouse,
O Inanna, you are bent on going into your (usual) window
   (namely, to solicit) for a lover —
O Inanna, mistress of myriad offices,
   no god rivals you!
Ninegalla, here is your dwelling place,
   let me tell of your greatness!
As the herds make the dust (they kick up)
   settle in layers,
as oxen and sheep return to pen and fold,
you, my lady, dress like one of no repute
   in a single garment,
the beads (the sign) of a harlot
   you put around your neck.
It is you that hail men from the alehouse!
It is you, tripping along into the embrace
   of your bridegroom Dumuzi!
Inanna, your seven bridal attendants are
   bedding you![246]

Ishtar

Interestingly enough, the aspects of the goddess that we have mentioned — rain goddess, goddess of war, and goddess of the morning and
evening star — form a unit, also in the Akkadian and general Semitic
deity Ishtar with whom Inanna was identified. Ishtar — her name goes
back through the form *Eshtar* to **'Attar* — corresponds to the West Semitic
god of the morning star, 'Attar, who was also a rain deity but of semiarid
regions where agriculture was possible only with the use of irrigation.
Accordingly, in West Semitic mythology when 'Attar tried to take the
place of the dead Ba'al, the rain god of the regions of rain agriculture, he
did not prove big enough to fill Ba'al's throne.[247] His female counterpart,
Astarte (older 'Attart), goddess of the evening star, was a war goddess and

also goddess of sexual love.[248] Whether this coincidence of functions may be taken to indicate that Inanna's character as goddess of rains, war, and the morning and evening star is of Semitic origin and were borrowed from the Akkadian Ishtar with whom she was identified in historical times, or whether — as seems more reasonable — the fact that she had similar characteristics was what prompted the identification with Ishtar cannot be definitively determined with our present knowledge.

Variety and Contradictions

So far, then, we have considered Inanna as numen of the storehouse, as rain goddess, as goddess of war, as goddess of the morning and evening star, and as goddess of harlots. And yet we are far from exhausting her nature. She seems to have a hand in almost everything and is rightly termed N i n - m e - š á r - r a, "Lady of a myriad offices."[249] She is in charge of the lighting of fires, but also of the putting out of fires; of causing tears, and also of rejoicing; of enmity and of fair dealings; and so forth.[250] Also:

> To pester, insult, deride, desecrate — and to
>   venerate — is your domain, Inanna.
> Downheartedness, calamity, heartache — and
>   joy and good cheer — is your domain,
>   Inanna.
> Trembling, affright, terror — dazzling and
>   glory — is your domain, Inanna.[251]

and so on.

It is remarkable that in this medley of contradictory traits, the humanizing process of myths and tales, should have been able to find an inner unity and to present their infinite variety as but facets of one believable divine personality. Yet to a very considerable extent that is the case. What could not be absorbed or was felt to be peripheral seems to have become offices that the goddess held, rather than traits of her character.

Myths

In the epics and myths Inanna is a beautiful, rather willful young aristocrat. We see her as a charming, slightly difficult younger sister, as a grown daughter (a shade too quick, perhaps, to see her own advantage), and a worry to her elders because of her proclivity to act on her own impulses when they could have told her it would end in disaster. We see her as sweetheart, as a happy bride, and as a sorrowing young widow. We see her, in fact, in all the roles a woman may fill except the two which call for maturity and a sense of responsibility. She is never depicted as a wife and helpmate or as a mother.

As younger sister she appears in a story[252] in which her brother Utu, the sun god, has found a suitable husband for her, the shepherd god Dumuzi, only to discover that Inanna could never dream of marrying a shepherd; it has to be a farmer, and so a farmer it is. As a dutiful daughter she goes in another tale to visit her grandfather, Enki, in Eridu.[253] Enki, overjoyed to see his granddaughter, gives a party for her during which he drinks more deeply than he should and in his expansive mood presents her with one high office after another. The next morning he wakes up sober, only to find Inanna gone and the offices with her. She gets herself into more serious trouble when she takes it into her head to wrest the rule of the land of the dead from her powerful older sister, Ereshkigal.[254] As we have already described, she goes alone to the netherworld but proves no match for the queen of the dead and the powers below. Her elders have the difficult task of extricating her and bringing her back to life — which her clever grandfather Enki succeeds in doing. When she comes back to the world Dumuzi does not display sufficient suffering over her loss to please her, and with the quick flaring anger of a child she hands him over as her substitute to the deputies from the netherworld. With rather more reason she tries to kill Gilgamesh when he has spurned her,[255] forcing her grandfather, An, to lend her the fearful bull of heaven by wildly threatening to break open the gates to the netherworld and let the dead out among the living if he refuses.

The restraint and demureness that were considered good manners in a young girl did not come easy to Inanna. She was perfectly capable of slipping away for a tryst in the canebrake.[256] Her young man pleads:

> Our two heads are but two, our feet but four;
> . . . .
>
> O my sister, if I embraced you in the canebrake,
>   if I kissed you there,
> what spying eye would see you?
> Maiden Inanna, if I embraced you in the
>   canebrake if I kissed you there,
> what spying eye would see you?
>
> That lone (spying) bird in the sky? Let me kill it!
> That lone (spying) fish in the marsh? Let me
>   kill it!
> If you wish I will lie with you —
>   as in the days of yore — if you wish,
>   divine one?
> Inanna, if you wish I will lie with you —
>   as in the days of yore —
>   if you wish, divine one?

And Inanna answers:

> I, the queen, the divine one,
>> sitting with a lad, as in the days of yore,
>> am a truant!
> Me whom she seeks of the lad,
>> seeks, as in the days of yore,
>> me, my mother will not find!

With Inanna everything had to be right away. She threw things imperiously against the gate of the netherworld and threatened to break it down if the doorkeeper did not quickly let her in.[257] Smitten with the handsomeness of the hero Gilgamesh, she at once brazenly proposed to him.[258] Gilgamesh, it must be admitted, showed even worse manners by pointing out that she was not to be relied upon: calling her a shoe that would pinch the foot that wore it, a brazier that would go out when it was cold and there was need for it, a back door that let in cold blasts, and to drive home his point enumerated no less than six others (besides Dumuzi) she had loved and who had come to grief at her hand.

And in this there is something characteristic of Inanna. She destroys those she loves or, at any rate, they come to grief. In the story of her descent to the netherworld and in Gilgamesh's chiding of her she is made directly responsible. In other stories such is not the case and she is in no way to blame yet those she loves perish: her young husband is killed by attackers as he tends sheep in the desert, or he drowns in the flooded river and Inanna goes to the desert to mourn over his body. An aura of death and disaster surrounds her.

In Inanna, then, an unusually interesting and complex character has come into being — so vividly that the natural background is gradually less felt. The numen of the storehouse, inevitably losing its young husband, the stores, is less and less sensed in Inanna's loss of husbands or lovers. The power of a real thunderstorm is less and less felt behind Inanna's tempestuous temper. The evening star rising when the harlots appear as if it were one of them, the ruttish powers of fecundation of the herds cease to explain Inanna's wantonness and freedom with her favors. And her quick bolting with the "offices" from Eridu seems so characteristic that one inquires no further into the whys and wherefores of Inanna's being the power in and behind the motley collection of a hundred or so activities which the myth so laboriously specifies. She is become truly all woman and of infinite variety.

5

Second Millennium Metaphors. The Gods as Parents: Rise of Personal Religion

Statue of a worshiper found at ancient Eshnunna (modern Tell Asmar) by the Iraq expedition of the Oriental Institute of the University of Chicago. The statue dates from the early third millennium B.C.

Personal Religion

Terms that are rich in emotional content, terms for things that go deep in us, are rarely clear-cut — nor can they well be, for what they seek to express is subjective and will differ subtly from person to person.

Personal religion in the title of this chapter is just such a term: it will almost necessarily mean different things to different people and one can only try to explain what it is intended to mean here. We use it to designate a particular, easily recognized, religious attitude in which the religious individual sees himself as standing in close personal relationship to the divine, expecting help and guidance in his personal life and personal affairs, expecting divine anger and punishment if he sins, but also profoundly trusting to divine compassion, forgiveness, and love for him if he sincerely repents. In sum: the individual matters to God, God cares about him personally and deeply.

A few characteristic examples will show this attitude more clearly than any description. They are from the religious literature of Israel, Egypt, and Mesopotamia, and date to the first millennium B.C. (the Egyptian example is a little earlier). We begin with some lines from Psalm 25 : 4–7.

> Shew me thy ways, O Lord; teach me thy paths.
> Lead me in thy truth, and teach me:
>   for thou art the God of my salvation;
>   on thee do I wait all the day.
> Remember, O Lord, thy tender mercies
>   and thy lovingkindnesses;
>   for they have been ever of old.
> Remember not the sins of my youth,
>   nor my transgressions:
>   according to thy mercy remember thou me
>   for thy goodness' sake, O Lord.

Here are the essential elements of the attitude with which we are concerned: guidance ("Lead me in thy truth, and teach me"), expectance of divine anger and punishment for sin ("Remember not the sins of my youth, nor my transgressions"), and trust in divine compassion ("for thy goodness' sake, O Lord").

These elements are present rather more fervently in Psalm 38.

> O Lord, rebuke me not in thy wrath:
>   neither chasten me in thy hot displeasure.
> For thine arrows stick fast in me,
>   and thy hand presseth me sore.
> There is no soundness in my flesh
>   because of thine anger;
>   neither is there any rest in my bones
>   because of my sin.

For mine inequities are gone over mine head:
  as an heavy burden they are too heavy
  for me.
My wounds stink and are corrupt
  because of my foolishness.
I am troubled; I am bowed down greatly;
  I go mourning all the day long.
For my loins are filled with a loathsome disease:
  and there is no soundness in my flesh.

. . . .

Forsake me not, O Lord:
  O my God, be not far from me.
Make haste to help me, O Lord, my salvation.

As an example from Egypt we quote a prayer to Re-Har-akhti:

Come to me, O Re-Har-akhti,
  that thou mayest look after me!
Thou art he who does, and there is no one who
  does without thee,
unless it be that thou actest with him.

. . . .

Do not punish me for my many sins,
for I am one who does not know himself,
I am a man without sense.
I spend the day following after my own mouth,
like a cow after grass. . . .
  Come to me . . . thou who
  protectest millions
and rescuest hundreds of thousands,
  the protector of the one who cries out to him![259]

And as examples from Mesopotamia, first some lines from a prayer to Ishtar,

I have cried to thee, (I) thy suffering, wearied,
  distressed servant.
See me, O my lady, accept my prayers!
Faithfully look upon me and hear my supplication!
Say "A pity!" about me, and let thy mood be eased.
"A pity!" about my wretched body
  that is full of disorders and troubles,
"A pity!" about my sore heart
  that is full of tears and sobbings,
"A pity!" about my wretched, disordered,
  and troubled portents,
"A pity!" about my house, kept sleepless,
  which mourns bitterly,

"A pity!" about my moods,
 which are steadily of tears and sobbings.[260]

and later on the prayer:

What have I done, O my god and my goddess?
As one not fearing my god and my goddess
 I am treated!
Sickness, headache, loss and destruction
 have befallen me,
Terrors, (people) averting (their) faces (from me),
 swelling with anger (at me) have befallen me.
Wrath, rage, and resentment of gods and men.

I have seen, my lady (but) days of gloom,
 months of depression, years of grief;
I have seen, my lady, slaughter, disorders, riots;
death and distress hold me in thrall.

My sanctuary is silenced, silenced my chapel,
stillness lies poured over my house,
 my gate, my fields,
the face of my god is turned elsewhere,
my family is scattered, my pale torn asunder.[261]

In another prayer[262] the sufferer has sought help from god and goddess:

I kept seeking but no one took my hand,
I wept, but they came not to my side,
I lamented — no one heard me —
I am afflicted, covered over, cannot see.
"O my merciful god, turn unto me" I entreat thee,
I kiss the foot of my goddess; before thee I
 crawl![263]
. . . .
O Lord, throw not over thy servant.
He lies cast into the waters of a morass,
seize thou his hand!
Turn the sins I committed into good!
Let the wind carry away
 the crimes I perpetrated!
Many are my iniquities,
 slip them off (me) like a garment!
O my God! The crimes are seven times seven,
absolve my crimes![264]

"Many are my iniquities, slip them off (me) like a garment." The line is characteristic of the attitude we have tried to exemplify through biblical, Egyptian, and Mesopotamian expressions of it. We may now consider more closely what that attitude directly expresses and what it implies about human relationship to the divine.

The aspect that first strikes one very vividly is of course the ostensible humbling of self, the self-abasement of the penitent. Fervently, he admits to being wrong, weeps, implores, and crawls; he stresses how unprepossessing he is, how his wounds stink and are corrupt. And it is only natural that this feature of the attitude has focused attention upon itself and that psalms such as those with which we are dealing have been grouped under the heading, "penitential psalms."

But though this self-abasement and humility is arresting, it would be unwise to stop with it and not penetrate to its underlying presuppositions. Clearly, it would be pointless were it not for an underlying conviction in the penitent that God still cares deeply and personally about him and his fortunes. And the more we attend to this unspoken presumption, the more our first impression yields to something rather different, something which is not humility but unconscious human self-importance and, considering that the attitude is an attitude to the Divine, self-importance almost without limits.

It seems, in fact, that one can go back to the various expressions of humility and self-abasement, and reread them with attention to what they imply, and subtly sense that in these psalms the penitent and his personal affairs are not only thought to matter, but matter supremely. They swell to fill the whole picture. The penitent becomes so centrally important in the universe that he can monopolize God's attention, can involve God deeply and emotionally in anger, compassion, love for him, and before this onslaught of unlimited ego, the figure of God appears to shrink: no longer the awesome creator and ruler of the All, he dwindles to "the God of *my* salvation." As in love that is *only* need-love the beloved ceases to be a person in his own right and is seen only as a means of gratifying desires in the lover, so here God is in danger of becoming a mere instrument for relieving personal needs in one individual.

To make what we are trying to say a little clearer we may perhaps set the personal attitude to God in the penitential psalms and its implications about the way he cares about the individual over against the very different attitude of Psalm 8 : 3–9:

> When I consider thy heavens,
>   the work of thy fingers,
>   the moon and the stars, which thou hast ordained;
> What is man, that thou art mindful of him?
>   and the son of man, that thou visitest him?
> For thou hast made him a little lower than the angels,
>   and hast crowned him with glory and honor.
> Thou madest him to have dominion

over the works of thy hands;
  thou hast put all things under his feet:
All sheep and oxen, yea, and the beasts of the field;
The fowl of the air, and the fish of the sea,
  and whatsoever passeth through the paths of the seas.
  O Lord our Lord, how excellent is thy name in all the earth!

Here, clearly, there is more real humility (the individual and his personal
concerns have disappeared into the totality of mankind and it is even a
cause for wonder that God would be mindful of man as such) and rightly
so, for there is no diminution of the image of God here; he appears in his
full majesty as creator and upholder of the whole cosmos.

More enlightening still is comparison with passages such as Exodus 20 :
18–19:

And all the people saw the thunderings, and the lightnings, and the noise of
the trumpet, and the mountain smoking: and when the people saw it, they
removed, and stood afar off. And they said unto Moses, speak thou with us,
and we will hear: but let not God speak with us, lest we die

or Isaiah 6 : 5:

Then said I, Woe is me! for I am undone; because I am a man of unclean lips,
and I dwell in the midst of a people of unclean lips: for mine eyes have seen
the King, the Lord of hosts.

The sense of the holiness of God, of the awe surrounding him, that too
vanished in the little personal individual world of the penitential psalms.

We have chosen to illustrate mainly by biblical passages, but it is proper
to point to at least one Mesopotamian example to show that there, too, the
majesty and awe of the divine was strongly felt and vividly expressed. This
is the hymn to Enlil as organizer of the universe and provider of all:

Enlil, by your skillful planning in intricate designs —
their inner workings a blur of threads
  not to be unraveled,
thread entwined in thread, not to be traced by the eye —
you excel in your task of divine providence.

You are your own counselor, adviser, and manager,
who (else) could comprehend what you do?

Your tasks are tasks that are not apparent,
your guise (that of) a god, invisible to the eye.

You are lord: An, and king: Enlil (in one),
judge and decisionmaker for (both) heaven and earth,
you know no rescinder of your great decrees,
  they being as respected as is An.[265]

With these examples we have touched, it would seem, a paradoxical core in the attitude of personal religion: its tacit bridging of the cosmic world and the personal world of the individual. How — one may ask — could such a union of contradictions in one attitude come to be; all that is highest, most awesome, and terrifying approached with such easy and close familiarity: "Make haste to help me, O Lord, my salvation" or "Come to me Re-Har-akhti, that thou mayest look after me" or "I have cried to thee, (I) thy suffering, wearied, distressed servant. See me, O my lady, accept my prayers!"

Historical Evidence

To find the answer let us consider first the historical evidence for the attitude with which we are concerned to see where and when it originated and in what circumstances and context.

The earliest examples of our attitude appear in Mesopotamia toward the beginning of the second millennium B.C. and remain unparalleled for half a millennium. Its first occurrence outside Mesopotamia is with the Hittites in the Prayer of Kantuzilis[266] circa 1350. In Egypt it appears one hundred years later, around 1230 B.C.,[267] after the Amarna age with its international intellectual climate in which Mesopotamian writings and ideas spread far and wide throughout the Near East. Since the Egyptian examples appear suddenly as a new element in popular religiosity unconnected with established Egyptian religion, it would seem likely that they reflect influence from outside — specifically from Mesopotamia — and when we come down to the first millennium when Israel's religious thinking took form, Mesopotamian influence and ideas are so pervasive that the attitude of personal religion may be considered to have been part of the general cultural environment.

We must look, therefore, to Mesopotamia for origins, and as we follow the broad stream of personal religion there backward in time, we see it narrowing like a stream followed toward its source. The source toward which it narrows is one specific aspect or concept of Mesopotamian religion, the so-called personal god. While in later times we can find the attitude of "personal religion" directed toward almost any figure of the pantheon, in our earliest examples it is limited to appeals by a person to his "personal" god or goddess only — the only exception, seemingly, is an appeal to a goddess of healing.[268]

The Mesopotamian genres in which the attitude of personal religion first appears are the "Penitential Psalms" and the "Letters to Gods."[269] As an early example of the first of these one might cite the composition called "A Man and His God"[270] in which a man complains to his personal god that the god neglects him so that he has no luck with anything, all goes awry for him:

> I am a young man, I am knowledgeable; but what I know
>   does not come right with me.
> What I truthfully say turns into falsehood,
> The wrongdoer hoodwinks me:
>   I lay hold of the handle of the sickle for him,
>   (i.e., do innocently his dirty work for him).
> My arm all unknowing sullies me in your eyes,
>   and you bestow on me the most burning of miseries.[271]

His god — his powers of clear and fast thinking — fails him when friends deceive him or impute falsehood to him.

> My friend speaks to me words not reliable,
> my companion imputes falseness
>   to words I truthfully speak,
> the wrongdoer says shaming things to me,
> but you, my god, do not answer them back,
> you take away my wits![272]

His god has clearly lost interest in him: "How long will you not ask for me, not seek / out my whereabouts?"[273] It is, he is sure, his fault, but who can live an altogether blameless life: "Men of experience say a word true and fair: / 'A child without faults? Never did its / mother give birth to it!' "[274] So he wishes the god would at least tell him what he has done wrong, so that he may confess!

> O my God, . . . when you have let my eyes
>   recognize my faults,
> in the gate of the assembly (i.e., "publicly")
>   those of them that have been forgotten,
>   and those of them that are (still) mentioned,
>   I shall tell,
> I, young man, shall publicly avow my faults
>   before you.[275]

From the genre of "Letters to Gods" we may quote two passages from one of the longest and most elaborate letters.[276] The letter is to Enki, the personal god of the writer, a scribe by the name of Suen-šamuh. He complains that his case has not been looked into and judged; that he is suffering for trespasses he has not committed; that he is abandoned ". . . like a cart of a caravan, the yoke of which / is broken, I am left standing in / the road"[277] and he suffers:

> I lie down on a bed of wails and woes,
>   grief cuts me (to the quick);
> my comely frame droops toward the ground,
>   I grovel at (people's) feet.[278]

Nothing comes out right for him:

> I, a literate person, have been changed
>   from one who knew things into a clod,
> my hand has been stayed from writing,
>   my mouth has had (its power to) discourse lessened,
> I am no oldster, (yet) I have become hard of hearing,
>   my eyesight dim![279]

Much more is wrong but still he has not lost hope:

> Today let me take my trespasses to you,
>   snatch me from my foes,
> and when you have seen where I fell,
>   take pity on me,
> When you have turned my dark stretches
>   (of road) into daylight
> let me pass through your gate,
>   which releases from sin and wrongdoings,
>   let me sing your praises,
> let me confess, (roaring) like a bull,
>   my trespasses to you,
>   and let me tell of your greatness.[280]

The attitude is not restricted to Sumerian works; it appears in Akkadian compositions as well. A fragment of a penitential psalm which, to judge by the writing, dates to the early Isin-Larsa period sounds the unmistakeable note:

> I can not, with the (helping) hand of an heir,
>   hold up my head!
> How long will it be that I shall not eat my fill?
> A good dress of my own I do not possess,
> cannot anoint my (mere skin and) bone with oil,
> misery has come like weeds into my heart![281]

There are other, larger compositions which could be quoted but a single passage from a long appeal to Ishtar in which the officiating priest intercedes for the penitent will suffice:

> Ishtar, who but you can clear a path for him?
> Hear his entreaties!
> He has turned to you and seeks you.
> Your servant who has sinned, have mercy on him!
> He has bowed down and loudly implored you.
> For the wrongs he committed he shouts a psalm of penance.
> In full he counts up the benefactions of Ishtar,
> what he remembers — and what he had forgotten.
> . . . .
> He has sinned, all his conduct he lays open.
> The weariness with which he wearied himself he recounts!

"I have done wrong — the wrongs I committed
Ishtar had made good for me, I weep ardently!
I had no qualms, Ishtar. . . ."[282]

It will therefore repay us to consider more closely and in some detail this specific religious concept of the personal god.

The Personal God

Luck

We may begin by noting the luck aspect of the personal god. The personal god was, *ab ovo*, intimately connected and concerned with one individual's fortunes. So much so that one might almost say that the god was a personification of the power for personal success in that individual.

It is not uncommon — most people have experienced something similar at times — that sudden, unexpected luck and good fortune is felt as "uncanny," as if a supernatural power had suddenly taken a hand in one's affairs. It is a very simple and unsophisticated reaction, perfectly expressed in the title of an autobiography some years ago by a man who thought life had been kind to him: *Somebody Up There Likes Me.*

The ancient Mesopotamian felt very much that way, and both in Sumerian and in Akkadian there is only one term to describe luck and good fortune: "to acquire a god."[283] If we turn to the omen literature we find that a favorable portent may indicate that "that house will acquire a god, that house will endure,"[284] while, conversely, a bad portent may indicate that "that house will grow poor, will not acquire a god."[285] The writer of an Old Babylonian letter is afraid of being driven out of the house where he lives, and says "if he comes back empty-handed he will throw me out and I shall not have a chance of coming back"[286] — literally: "I shall not acquire a god who will bring me back." In another letter[287] a girl writes to a playmate of hers who has made a good marriage and bettered herself by becoming the wife of "His Honor, the chief of the tribesmen." The girl who writes the letter is not — it would appear — altogether free of jealousy. She says:

> To Elmeshum say, thus says Sirum: "May Shamash and Marduk . . . for my sake long keep you alive! Here is how you show your sisterly feelings! Oh sure, we grew up together from children, but since your good fortune (literally, since you acquired a god) you have not thought of me three penny's worth. And yesterday when you came, I took an *abarahhu* cane, and you were not happy until you had got it away from me, saying: 'From yonder I shall send you a good walking stick and handle(?).' And you did not send it. . . . Now I am sending a man to you. . . . send me a hundred grasshoppers and food to the value of one-sixth of a shekel of silver and in that let me see your sisterly feelings."

Power to Succeed

The examples mentioned so far show "luck" and "success" as things happening to a person. More often, however, the acquired god calls for a degree of cooperation. The god is not only luck, he is what it takes to succeed. A proverb expresses it neatly: "When you plan ahead your god is yours, when you do not plan ahead your god is not yours.[288] Here the god is clearly a power for effective thinking, planning, and inspiration, and this is the central element in the concept. A portent presages, for instance, that "at the command of his god and goddess he will build the house he is yearning for,"[289] that is, he will have the impulse and the power to realize his dreams about a house of his own. When Gudea of Lagash was to build the temple of the god of his capital Girsu, he dreamt that he saw light coming forth on the horizon. That light, he was told by the goddess Nanshe who interpreted the dream for him, symbolized his personal god Ningishzida, and the dream meant that Ningishzida was able to be present anywhere in the world,[290] or — in our terms — that Gudea's personal effectiveness and influence would be felt all over the world as he procured building materials from Ethiopia, the Amanus range on the Mediterranean coast, and similar far-off places.

As the personal god is here the personal effectiveness and success in a man, so we see that Ningishzida, the god, and Gudea, the man, work hand in hand in the building of Ningirsu's temple: "Ningishzida built it on firm base (deep down), Gudea, ruler of Lagash, filled in the foundation terrace"[291] and such teaming up of a man and his god we can follow back to the beginnings of the third millennium B.C. when Ur-Nanshe of Lagash tells about building the temple in Girsu: "Shul-utula, the (personal) god of the king, carried the holy basket (with bricks and mortar), Ur-Nanshe, king of Lagash, son of Gunidu, son of Gurshar built the temple of Girsu."[292]

Just as the personal god is the power for personal effectiveness and accomplishment, so he gives pride in accomplishment and self-assurance. To return to Gudea and his personal god, Ningishzida, we hear that Gudea is "the one whom his god, Ningishzida made appear proudly (lit., head held high) in the assembly"[293] and when Gudea had built the temple for the city goddess, Baba, he placed a statue of his own god, Ningishzida, in one of the chapels, and tells us why. Ningishzida (that is, the power that made Gudea effective and successful as ruler and restorer of temples) was to "restore the Temple of Baba, to cause abundance to appear for it, to make firm the foundations of the throne of Lagash, to put a rightful sceptre in the hands of Gudea, ruler of Lagash, and to make long the days of his life."[294]

Responsibility

As the power that inspired actions and made them succeed, the personal god became largely responsible for them. And — though divinely inspired — such actions were not necessarily good. As early as the third millennium we have an example of this in a curse by Eannatum. He had presented a stone mortar to the goddess Nanshe and wished upon anyone who harmed it in the future that "before the face of Nanshe his personal god shall not walk, nor shall he walk."[295] Somewhat later we have a text lamenting a raid by Lugalzagesi, ruler of Umma, into the territory of Uruinimgina of Girsu and Lagash. It assures that:

> The man of Umma, after he had sacked Lagash, having committed a sin against (the god of Lagash) Ningirsu, having laid hands upon it (i.e., the field of Ningirsu), went on harvesting from it. There was no sin on the part of Uruinimgina, king of Girsu. Let Nidaba, the personal deity of Lugalzagesi, ruler of Umma, carry that sin on her shoulders.[296]

Lastly, there is an Old Babylonian private letter from around 1700 B.C. The writer is angry that the man to whom he writes has chosen to settle down where he did. He says: "Have you no qualms about settling down there? May the name of your god and whosoever encouraged you (in this) and caused you and your brother to settle down there, perish."[297]

Identifiability

We have seen, then, from the passages quoted so far that the personal god was a supernatural power that would inspire a man to action and generally lend success to what he was doing. We should also note that our earliest examples from the third millennium make it clear that the ancient Mesopotamians were never in doubt as to the identity of any personal god and could identify him or her as a known figure of the pantheon: such and such a person had such and such a god as his personal god. The indefinite "somebody" of *Somebody Up There Likes Me* was already specified. Furthermore, any god, even the great cosmic powers, might take on the role of personal god for an individual, so that we find Sîn, god of the moon, Shamash, god of the sun and justice, Adad, god of the thunderstorm, and Nergal, the ruler of the netherworld, in this capacity, to mention only a few.

Parent

A last aspect of the belief in the individual's personal god in Mesopotamia that should claim our attention is the inner form or image under which he was envisaged. Just as the center of the concept of the personal god, the caring and concern for an individual, stands apart in Mesopotamian religious literature as something quite special, so the "inner form," "image," or — to be precise — "metaphor" under which the personal god was seen is also quite unique: it is the image of the parent — divine father or mother — an image for the gods in their relation to man which we meet nowhere else. Normally, the image of the god in relation to his worshiper is quite a different one, that of master and slave. Even the most powerful king was a slave in relation to the god of his city and country; only in relation to his own personal god was he, to quote a standard phrase, "the man, son of his god."[298]

In considering this concept more closely we may distinguish some of the various strands that make it up. First, its physical aspect: the father as engenderer of the child; the mother as giving birth to it. Second, the provider aspect: the father as provider for his family. Third, the protector and intercessor aspect. Fourth, the claim parents have upon their children for honor and obedience.

We may consider, then, the physical aspects. A common way of referring to the personal god is as "the god who 'created' or 'engendered' me" or "the divine mother, who gave birth to me."[299] To see more precisely what these terms imply we must realize that the personal god dwelt in the man's body. If "his god removed himself from his body,"[300] the body was open for evil demons of disease to take over and "possess" the man.

As a divine power dwelling in the man and causing him to succeed, the god would naturally be present and active in the most decisive and necessary achievement of fulfilment for the ancient Mesopotamian, that of engendering a son. Without children, without sons, there could be no personal adequacy, no success in life. Thus it was the personal god and goddess, incarnate in the father and mother, who engendered the child and brought it into being. Accordingly, the ancient Sumerian ruler Lugalzagesi, whose personal deity, as we have mentioned, was the goddess Nidaba speaks of himself as "child born of Nidaba;"[301] similarly, Urbaba, whose god was Nin-á-gal, calls himself "child engendered by Nin-á-gal."[302] In a self-laudatory hymn, Urnammu, the founder of the Third Dynasty of Ur, says of himself: "I am a brother of the great Gilgamesh, I am the offspring of Ninsûna;"[303] while his successor Shulgi, whose personal god and goddess likewise were Lugalbanda and Ninsûna, is addressed as "thou child born by Ninsûna."[304] Shulgi also calls that most famous child of Lugalbanda and Ninsûna, the legendary hero Gilgamesh, his "brother and comrade."[305] Still another hymn[306] tells how Ninsûna takes the little Shulgi with her to her divine throne, fondles him at her breast and addresses him as,

> Shulgi, you sacred seed to which I gave birth,
> you holy semen of Lugalbanda;

> on my holy lap I raised you,
> at my holy breast I determined the destiny
>   for you,
> you are the best that fell to my portion.

Also very specific is a passage in the cylinders of Gudea. That ruler had as personal god Ningishzida and as personal goddess Ninsûna, who was in her nature a cow goddess, her name meaning "Lady of the wild cows." In the passage Gudea is addressed as follows:

> You who — your god being the lord Ningishzida,
>   scion of An,
> your divine mother Ninsûna, a mother bearing
>   good offspring
> and loving the offspring —
> were born of a good cow in woman-fashion.[307]

Many more examples could be quoted.

From a look at the various Mesopotamian dynasties known to us, we learn that father and son invariably had the same personal god and goddess. The god passed therefore from the body of the father into the body of the son as generation followed generation. This explains a passage that has given Assyriologists much trouble. An ancient commentary[308] explains the term "daughter of his god" as meaning "his sister." Since the god who resided in a man's body had earlier been present in his father's body and had there engendered both him and his sister he is "the son of his god" and his sister is "the daughter of his god." This belief underlies also the standard Old Assyrian term for the personal god, "god of the fathers,"[309] as in "Ashur, the god of your fathers," "Ilbrat, the god of our father(s)," or "Ilabrat, the god of your father(s)," with which one may compare Exodus 3 : 15: "The Lord God of your fathers, the God of Abraham, the God of Isaac, and the God of Jacob."

The word "father" suggests not only an engenderer but also a provider for the family, and this aspect is prominent in the concept of the personal god, as is natural since the god is power for effective, successful achievement. Since this element runs through so many of the passages we have already quoted and still have to quote, we shall restrict ourself to one pithy statement from "A Man and His God": "Without the (personal) god man eats no bread."[310] It could hardly be said more succinctly.

As the father is provider, so he is also protector and intercessor with higher powers. In fact the Akkadian term for "fatherhood" (*abbûtu*) tends to become specified because of this typical role of the father to meaning "intercession." In the highly complex social and political world of the ancient Mesopotamian pantheon "ability to protect" often meant "connections" and influential friends. And so we find statements such as that of the ruler, Entemena: "May his personal god, Shul-utula, forever stand before Ningirsu in Eninnu (praying) for his (i.e., Entemena's) life,"[311] a formula occurring in many shorter varients in inscription after inscription. The personal god's role as protector is often stressed. Man lives in the "(protective) shadow" of his god.[312] In the omen texts a good sign denotes that "the lasting (protective) shadow of the (personal) god will be upon the man,"[313] while bad signs indicate that "the weak will leave the protective shadow of the strong, and the strong the shadow of his god."[314] An amusing illustration of the duty of the personal god to protect his "child" and use his influence with more powerful gods is this Old Babylonian letter in which a man charges his personal god with neglect:

> To the god, my father, speak!
>   Thus says Apil-adad thy servant:
> Why have you neglected me (so)?
> Who is going to give you one
>   who can take my place?
> Write to the god Marduk, who is fond of you,
> that he may break my bondage;
> then shall I see your face
>   and kiss your feet!
> Consider also my family, grown-ups and little ones;
> have mercy on me for their sake,
>   and let your help reach me![315]

Lastly, there is the point that the personal god has as much claim as a human parent to be honored, obeyed, and provided for by his son. We shall quote only two passages. A proverb expresses the need to praise one's god: "When you see the profit from worshiping the god, praise the god and bless the king."[316] Another passage is even more explicit:

> Daily, worship your god
> with offerings, prayers and appropriate incense.
> Bend your heart to your god;
> That befits the office of personal god,
> prayers, supplication,
>   pressing (the hand to) the nose (as greeting)
> shall you offer up every morning,
> then your power will be great,
> and you will, through the god
>   have enormous success.[317]

Implications

We now return to our original question about the attitude of "personal religion" which meets us in the penitential psalms of the first and second millennia B.C. We traced this attitude to the beginnings of the second millennium in Mesopotamia and found it to be at home in and limited to the specific relationship of a man to his personal god. Having examined this concept of personal god in some detail, we may now consider whether it helps us to understand a little better the paradoxical character of personal religion, with its conspicuous humility curiously based on an almost limitless presumption of self-importance, its drawing the greatest cosmic powers into the little personal world of the individual, and its approach to the highest, the most awesome, and the terrifying in such an easy and familiar manner.

In some ways the psychological possibilities of the attitude are more easily understood in its original context. The certainty of concern for the individual and his fortunes is given with the origin of the concept of the personal god in a personification of the power which causes luck and success in the individual. This is at the very root of the conception of personal god. Its negative counterpart is the feeling that lack of success and misfortune is due to the power having left the person; that it is angry, so it punishes.

Furthermore, the inner "form" or "metaphor" of the parent, of "father" or "mother" under which the personal god came to be seen, does more: it serves as psychologically possible bridge to the great and terrifying awesome cosmic powers. For it is within human experience that even the highest, greatest, and most terrifying personages in society have a mild, human, and approachable side in their relations to their children. Children, in their immediacy, their certainty of being loved, can over-come — being entirely unaware of it — the terror and awe of power and status precisely because they seek and see only the personal in the relation. Thus the possibility that even the cosmic powers could be personal gods, could have an unfrightening, loving, ever-forgiving side toward their little human children, is psychologically conceivable.

But if we can thus, by following personal religion back to its original setting, see more clearly how its attitude could be psychologically possible, this does not change or remove the original and basic paradox with all its inherent contradictions. As the attitude began to permeate religion generally, as it could be assumed not only toward one's personal god, but toward any god, even the one and only God, it was inevitable that its paradoxical nature should become apparent. There is a stage in childhood when parents are all-powerful and divine to the child. The child (to grow up) has eventually to adjust to the disturbing realization that parents are after all only other human beings with human limitations. But in this case such adjustment was excluded. The divine parents were, and had to remain, divine. Thus experience could not but drive its cruel wedge ever more deeply between the dispassionate, terrifying, cosmic aspect of the divine which governed the way things really are and really happen, and the personal, concerned, angry, forgiving, loving aspect in which I, the individual, matter so profoundly that love for me must sway the universe off its course to help and sustain me.

This is the problem of the righteous sufferer. It forces itself upon religious consciousness in Mesopotamia about the middle of the second millennium and is dealt with in two remarkable works, *Ludlul bêl nêmeqi* ("Let me praise the expert")[318] and the Babylonian Theodicy.[319] In the first of these we hear about a man, pious and righteous, who nevertheless falls on evil days:

> *Alu*-disease has clothed itself in my body
>   like a garment;
> sleep in a net enmeshes me;
> my eyes stare but see not,
> my ears are open, but hear not;
> weakness has seized all my body.[320]

The unfeeling, cosmic aspect of the divine is taking its course with no regard for him at all:

> No god came to my aid, or grasped my hand,
> my goddess did not pity me,
>   walked not at my side[321]

and the incomprehensibility of the ways of the universe, of its failure to take account of him, is so great that he can only escape in doubt about himself and his own powers of judgment.

> What seems good to oneself,
>   is a crime before the god.
> What to one's heart seems bad,
>   is good before one's god.
> Who may comprehend the minds of gods
>   in heaven's depth?
> The thoughts of (those) divine deep waters,
>   who could fathom them?
> How could mankind, beclouded,
>   comprehend the ways of gods?[322]

The Theodicy comes to similar conclusion. It is a discussion by two friends about the patent injustice of what goes on in the world. Good loses out; evil triumphs:

> The divine mind is remote
>   like the inmost of the heavens,
> knowledge of it is arduous,
>   people are uninformed.[323]

The contradictions are indeed insoluble as long as the attitude of personal religion is allowed to reduce existence, the infinite universe, to the narrow compass of a personal world, and expect it to center in an individual and his personal needs.

A significant step toward a solution was only made later, in the middle of the first millennium, by the religious genius of Israel: the treatment of the problem in the Book of Job. Here, in God's speech, the imbalance is redressed. The personal, egocentric view of the sufferer — however righteous — is rejected. The self-importance which demands that the universe adjust to his needs, his righteousness, is cast aside, and the full stature of God as the majestic creator and ruler of the universe is reinstated. The distance between the cosmic and the personal, between God in his infinite greatness and mere individual man, is so great and so decisive that an individual has no rights, not even to justice:

> Then Job answered the Lord and said, I know that thou canst do everything, and that no thought can be withholden from thee. Who is he that hideth counsel without knowledge? Therefore have I uttered that I understood not; things too wonderful for me, which I knew not. Hear, I beseech thee, and I will speak. I will demand of thee, and declare thou unto me. I have heard of thee by hearing of the ear: but now mine eyes seeth thee. Wherefore I abhor myself, and repent in dust and ashes.[324]

A last question remains — that of the power and vitality of personal religion. In Mesopotamia it seems to have remained an individual attitude and not decisively to have come to dominate public religion and shape the relation of the nation to national gods. There are indications, however, that this was a direction which Mesopotamian religious development might have taken, for in the famous "Lament for the Fall of Ur" which would seem to date very close to 2000 B.C. there is a final prayer suggesting that human suffering and repentance, individually and collectively, might sway the heart of a great god to compassion and redress of national misfortune. It reads:

> From the days of old when (first) the land was founded
> O Nanna, have worshipful men, laying hold of your feet
> brought to you their tears over the ruined temple,
>   their chanting (allowed) before you,
> So, with the dark-headed people cast away from you,
>   let them (yet) make obeisance to you,
> with the city laid in ruins,
>   let it yet tearfully implore you,
> (and), O Nanna! with your restoring the city
>   let it rise into view again before you
> and not set, as set the bright stars,
>   but let it walk in your sight!

The personal god of a human has brought you a greeting gift,
    a (human) supplicant is beseeching you,
O Nanna, you, having mercy on the country!
O Lord Ash-im-babbar, you having
    according to what your heart prompts
absolved, O Nanna, the sins of that man,
the man who beseeches you,
    may you bring your heart to relent toward him,
and having looked truly
    upon the supplicant for them who stand here,
O Nanna, whose penetrating gaze searches the bowels,
may their hearts, that have suffered (so much) evil
    appear pure to you,
may the hearts of those who are in the land
    appear good to you,
and, O Nanna! in your city again restored,
    they will offer up praise unto you.[325]

But in the following periods — though we hear of human misdeeds calling forth divine punishment on a national scale and about national gods temporarily angry with their people and leaving them — we find little talk of nationwide repentance and self-abasement as a means of regaining divine favor.

As far as we can see, it is only Israel that decisively extended the attitude of personal religion from the personal to the national realm. The relationship of Yahweh to Israel — his anger, his compassion, his forgiveness, and his renewed anger and punishment of the sinful people — is in all essentials the same as that of the relation between god and individual in the attitude of personal religion. With this understanding of national life and fortunes as lived under ultimate moral responsibility, Israel created a concept of history as purposive — one which in basic essentials still governs conceptions of meaningful historical existence.

6
Second Millennium Metaphors. World Origins and World Order: The Creation Epic

A four-faced god found at ancient Neribtum (modern Ishchaly) by a shepherd in
1929 and shortly afterward purchased by the Oriental Institute of the University
of Chicago. The statue dates from the Old Babylonian period at around 1700
B.C., is about 7 inches (17.3 cm) high, and is cast in bronze. The figure may be
interpreted as Marduk treading victoriously on Ti'āmat, represented as a goat. It
is difficult to be certain of this, however, and there is the possibility that the
statue is of another god similar in character to Marduk.

Enûma elish

The New England transcendentalist Margaret Fuller was, we are told, given to exclaiming: "I accept the universe!" Carlyle, when he heard about it, wryly commented: "Gad! She'd better."

In a sense, of course, the dour Scot was right; man has little choice in the matter. He finds himself in the universe, has nowhere else to go, and so must somehow come to terms with it. In another sense, though, that was not really the question. The question — unspoken, admittedly — was and is whether man *can* thus come to terms — terms acceptable not only to his mind but also to his heart.

The ancient Mesopotamian epic of creation, Enûma elish,[326] is a very early and in many respects a very remarkable attempt at coming to terms with, at understanding, and at accepting the universe.

The copies we have date mostly from the first half of the first millennium B.C. The language in which they are written, however, seems somewhat older than Akkadian of that date, and suggests that the epic was composed earlier, say, sometime during the middle of the latter half of the second millennium B.C.

The central figure is Marduk, chief god of Babylon; however, in the early part of the first millennium when Assyria rose to become the dominant power in the world, an Assyrian scribe apparently replaced Marduk with his own god, Ashur, and made a few changes to let the story fit its new hero. In this form we find it in a copy from Assyria found in the original capital, Assur.

The materials on which the story is built seem varied in both time and place of origins. For instance, there are Sumerian elements such as the tradition underlying the theogony that serves as introduction and that is known to us in more detail — and with more inner logic — from the genealogy of An given in the great god list A n = *Anum*.[327] Vague echoes of the Sumerian Ninurta myth, L u g a l - e, in which Ninurta builds the mountain range in the east and arranges for irrigation after his victory may be behind the account of Marduk's creation of the universe, while his trial of Kingu and his giving the defeated gods offices in his administration may be reminiscent of Ninurta's judging his captive enemies, the stones.[328]

The motif of the dance and play of gods preventing the older powers from sleeping may be Akkadian. It reminds of how mankind kept Enlil awake with its din in the Old Babylonian Atrahasis[329] story. That story also has the motif of the creation of man from the blood of a slain god, as with Kingu in Enûma elish. The motif of gaining world rule through parricide which in muted form underlies the Apsû and Ti'āmat episodes may likewise be Akkadian. It occurs over and over again in the stark myth

of the "Dynasty of Dunnum" [330] which spread to Phoenicia and Greece —
where it underlies Hesiod's *Theogony*. A variant form of it also reached the
Hittites. The motif of a battle between a storm god and the sea, which
underlies the battle between Marduk and Ti'āmat finally, is known from
Ugarit on the Mediterranean coast where it occurs in the myth of Ba'al
and Yam. Perhaps it was brought east with the Amorites of the First
Dynasty of Babylon.[331]

The Story

Theogony

The epic falls roughly into two sections: a short one dealing with the
origins of the basic powers in the universe, and a long one telling how step
by step the present world order was established. It begins with a description of how things were in the beginning, before the first gods were born.

> When heaven above was not (yet even) mentioned,
> firm-set earth below called by no name;
> (when) but primeval Apsû, their begetter,
> and the matrix, Ti'āmat — she who gave birth
>   to them all —
> were mingling their waters in one;
> when no bog had formed,
>   (and) no island could be found;
> when no god whosoever had appeared,
> had been named by name,
>   had been determined as to (his) lot:
> then were gods formed within them.

The description presents the beginnings of the world as a watery chaos
in which the powers of the fresh waters underground, Apsû, and the
powers in the salt waters of the sea, Ti'āmat, mingled. There was nothing
else, no other form. Even the idea of a sky above had not been entertained
by anyone, nor was there an earth below, not even a single island or a
swampy bog, and there were, as yet, no gods.

Then in the midst of these waters two gods, Lahmu and Lahāmu, came
into being. The text clearly wants it understood that they were engendered by Apsû and born of Ti'āmat; and their names suggest that they
represent silt which had formed in the primeval ocean.[332] In their turn
they engendered Anshar and Kishar, the horizon, the circular rim of
heaven and the corresponding circular rim of earth. Anshar and Kishar
gave birth to Anu — the Akkadian form of An, the god of heaven — and
Anu engendered Nudimmud, who is more familiar to us under his other
names, Enki and Ea. He is, as we have seen, the god of running waters,
rivers, and marshes.

> Lahmu and Lahāmu appeared and they were named;
> incrẹasing through the ages, they grew tall,
> Anshar and Kishar then were formed,
>   surpassing them,
> they lived for many days, adding year onto year.
> Their heir was Anu, equal to his fathers,
> Anshar made his firstborn Anu
>   to his own likeness,
> and Anu engendered *his* likeness Nudimmud.
> Nudimmud excelled among the gods his fathers,
> with ears wide open, wise, mighty in strength,
> mightier than his father's father, Anshar.
> He had no equal among the gods his brethren.

The story told here is known to us, as we have mentioned, in a more original and complete form in the great Mesopotamian list of gods called A n = *Anum* and can be supplemented from older Sumerian myths.[333] This allows us to see its original meaning. The speculations by which the ancient Mesopotamian sought to penetrate the mystery of origins were based, apparently, on observations of how new land came into being. Mesopotamia is alluvial, formed by silt brought down by the rivers. It is the situation at the mouth of the rivers where the sweet waters, Apsû, flow into the salt waters of the sea, Ti'āmat, and deposit their load of silt, Lahmu and Lahāmu, to form new land that has been projected backward to the beginnings. This original silt was deposited along the edge of the primeval ocean to form first the horizon Anshar and Kishar, then as it grew more and more toward the center, two large discs An and Ki, heaven and earth, which were eventually forced apart by their son, the storm god Enlil. He was the father of Nudimmud-Ea.

Our epic, Enûma elish, modifies the story in two ways: first, it omits from the genealogy the wife of heaven, Ki, her child, Enlil, and Enlil's consort, Ninlil, going directly from Anu, that is An, god of heaven, to Nudimmud, father of the hero of the epic, Marduk; second, the epic spiritualizes the original story. Instead of dealing with the major elements of the cosmos — the underground water table, the sea, the horizon, silt, heaven and earth, etcetera — as one with the powers in them, the epic tells *only* of the "gods" of these things. It presents a *theogony*, moving, as it were, in an inchoate world of potentialities only. The creation of the corresponding actualities, the *cosmogony*, we are told about at a much later point in the story.

Theomachy as Private War: Anarchy

Just as his observation about the physical origins of his country guided the ancient Mesopotamian in his speculations about the origins of the universe, so do his memory and his experience of its political organization seem to have governed his thinking about the origins of order in that universe.

Politics in Mesopotamia in the Old Babylonian period, various and unstable, abounded in tribal and urban political forms. It ranged from near anarchy to democratic or semidemocratic forms based on general assemblies to monarchies. Its continually shifting power combinations and frequent attempts at achieving supremacy now by one, now by another, undoubtedly afforded many an object lesson in how to win power when common danger imposed unity and in how to preserve such power by wise and benevolent rule after the immediate danger was past.

In the epic, world order is seen as the outcome of just such a successful drive toward supremacy. Its beginnings lie in a theomachy, a prolonged conflict between representatives of two opposed principles: the forces of motion and activity (the gods), and the forces of inertia and rest (the older generation of powers). In this conflict stages of progressively greater concentration and permanence of power arise one out of the other: virtual anarchy and private war give way to primitive democracy with an ad hoc war leader, the king, chosen in a general assembly when common danger imposes unanimity and concerted action, and this in turn resolves into permanent monarchy with its promise of administrative benefits far beyond merely temporary safety of life and property.

To return to our story: with the birth of the gods, a new principle — *movement, activity* — has come into the world. The new powers, the gods, contrast sharply with the older ones who stand for rest and inactivity. In the manner typical of myth, this contrast is given form in a dramatic situation; the gods come together to dance.

> The divine brethren met together
> and nimbly stepping toward one another,
>   they roiled Ti'āmat,
> roiled Ti'āmat's belly.
> By dancing they had the heart
>   of heaven's foundation worried.
> Apsû could not subdue their clamor,
> and Ti'āmat kept silent before them.
> Though their doings were noisome to her,
> and their ways not good, she indulged them.

At this point the conflict is out in the open and the first power to react to the challenge of the gods and their provocative new ways is Apsû. The servant of Apsû, Mummu, whom we meet here for the first time,[334] is, according to his name, *mummu* ("mold," "matrix"), a hypostasis of "form." Most likely he represents will to the only form then in existence, the archetypal watery form.

Then Apsû, the begetter of the great gods,
called his vizier Mummu, saying to him,
"Mummu, my vizier, who gladdens my heart,
come let us go to Ti'āmat."
They went and sat down before Ti'āmat,
consulted about the matter of the gods,
    their firstborns.
Apsû opened his mouth
saying to pure Ti'āmat:
"Their ways have become noisome to me!
I am allowed no rest by day;
    by night no sleep.
Let me abolish, yea, let me smash to bits
    their ways
that peace may reign (again) and we may sleep."

But Apsû was speaking to the loving and long-suffering heart of a mother, and Ti'āmat would have none of it.

Ti'amat, when she heard this,
became upset, cried out against her husband,
cried out, hurt, the only one indignant.
She took the evilness (thereof) to heart:
"How could we destroy
    what we (ourselves) have brought into being?
Though their ways be noisome,
    let us bear it in good part!"

Her reluctance might have stayed Apsû's hand had it not been for Mummu who spoke up to urge again the destruction of the troublemakers and to hold up to Apsû the enticing prospect of uninterrupted sleep:

"Abolish, O my father, the disorderly ways,
that you have rest by day,
    and sleep by night."
Apsû rejoiced in him,
    and his countenance brightened,
because he plotted evil
    against the gods, his sons,
he flung his arms around Mummu's neck,
was sliding him onto his knees
    and was kissing him.

News of these plottings quickly reached the gods. At first they ran about in wild confusion, and even after they quieted down they could only sit speechless with fear. Only the wise Ea kept his wits about him enough to think of a counterstroke:

He of supreme intelligence, skillful, capable,
Ea, comprehending everything,
    sought a strategem against them.
He formed, yea, he fixed against him
    the configuration of the All,
skillfully made his overpowering sacred spell.
He recited it so that he quieted down
    in the waters,
poured slumber over him,
    so that he soundly slept.

While Apsû, succumbing to the magic, lay asleep, Ea took from him his crown and cloak of fiery rays, killed him, and established his own abode above him. Mummu, stunned and dazed by the same spell, was locked up and a string was passed through his nose to hold him securely.

The meaning of all this is perhaps not so immediately clear to us as it probably was to contemporary listeners. Yet we can grope for an understanding if we attend closely to what is said. Ea employs a spell, that is, a magically authoritative command, for the ancients viewed authority as a power inherent in commands, a power in them to be obeyed, to realize themself, to come true. In this case the power in Ea's command was great enough to force into being the situation expressed in it and hinted at when it is called "the configuration of the All." It is the cosmic design that still obtains: Apsû sank into an eternal sleep — that sleep which holds the sweet waters underground motionless and still. Directly above them was established Ea's abode, the temple in Eridu built on the waters of a lagoon. He sat there controlling Mummu, "the original watery form," thus allowing forms other than the liquid one to come into being, creating the possibility of the present world with its multiplicity of forms.

Let us note that this first victory of the gods was gained by a single god acting on his own initiative, not through the concerted efforts of the whole divine community. The myth moves on a primitive level of social organization, of virtual anarchy, in which dangers to the community are met by individual action by one of the more powerful of its members — Apsû no less than Ea. War is still a private undertaking.

Ad Hoc King for Safety

In the dwelling which Ea built over Apsû and where he settled with his spouse, Damkina, his firstborn, Marduk (the real hero of the myth) was born. The poet rapturously describes his looks:

Robust was his build,
    flashing the glance of his eyes,

    full-grown he came forth,
        mightiest from the first.
    Anu, his grandfather, saw him,
    rejoiced, and brightened,
        gladness filled his heart.
    The like of his (own) godhead,
        he fastened unto him.
    Tall he was, exceedingly,
        surpassing them in all things.
    Subtle beyond conceit his measures were,
    incomprehensible, perturbing to behold.
    Four were his eyes, and four his ears,
    fire blazed forth when he moved his lips.

Anu, young Marduk's grandfather, was inordinately fond of his grand-
child as grandfathers will be and so he devised toys for the little Marduk:

    Anu begot, engendered, the four winds,
    gave them into his hand (saying), "Let my
        grandson play!"
    He fashioned dust, had the south-storm carry it,
    caused a wave to be, roiling Ti'āmat.
    Roiled was Ti'āmat, day and night the gods were astir,
    suffering restlessness with each storm.
    Having plotted evil in their hearts,
    they said to their mother Ti'āmat:
    "When they killed Apsû, your husband,
    you did not march at his side, you sat still.
    (Now someone) has created four fearsome winds,
    your belly is roiled, so we cannot sleep.
    Apsû, your husband, was not in your heart,
    nor Mummu, who was bound! You kept apart!
    You are no mother, you stir roiled around,
    and we, who cannot go to sleep, us you do not love!"

These objecting gods were a group of deities who for some reason or
other were siding with Ti'āmat, and their petulant complaint proved
effective: Ti'āmat was thoroughly stirred up and set about creating a
formidable army. To spearhead it she gave birth to a frightening group of
monsters:

    Angry, scheming, resting not day or night,
    they were bent on fighting,
        raged and prowled like lions,
    gathered in council, they devised the strategy.
    Mother Hubur — molding everything —
    added irresistible weapons, bore monster serpents,

sharp-toothed, with fang unsparing,
filled their bodies with poison for blood.
Fierce dragons she clothed in terrors,
crowned them with glories
   and made them like gods,
so that whoever looked upon them
   should perish with fear,
and they, should they rear up their bodies,
   would not turn back their breasts.

To lead her army Ti'āmat chose her second husband, Kingu, gave him full authority, and entrusted him with the "tablets of the decrees" on which the decisions made by the assembly of the gods were entered. They symbolized supreme power over the universe. The attack upon the younger gods was ready.

News of what was going on came first, as usual, to the alert and well-informed Ea, who realized how much more serious was this threat than Apsû's. This time he did not know what to do:

Ea heard of this matter,
lapsed into dark silence, wordless sat.
Then, having deeply pondered
   and his inner turmoil quieted,
himself pursued the path to his father Anshar,
went in before Anshar, his father who begot him.
To him he recounted all Ti'āmat had plotted.

Anshar, hearing the news, was as perturbed as was Ea; he smote his thigh and bit his lip. His first thought was to send Ea to Ti'āmat to order her to desist, but Ea was cowed by her and turned back. Then Anu was sent and given broader authority: if she did not obey him Anu was to command her in the name of all the gods. But Anu, too, failed. Ti'āmat thrust her hand against him and made him turn tail. Now the gods faced their darkest hour, they sat silent without hope:

Anshar fell silent, staring at the ground,
gnashing his teeth, shaking his head at Ea,
(while) the Igigi, and all the Anunnaki,
   ranged in assembly,
their lips closed, wordless sat.

At long last, Anshar bethought himself of young Marduk and sent for him. Marduk had no hesitation about confronting Ti'āmat, but he made one condition: if he was to champion the gods they must delegate to him their authority, he must have supreme command:

(My) Lord! Gods of the decrees! Great gods!
If I am to be your champion,

vanquish Ti'āmat, and save you,
then assemble and proclaim what I decree supreme.
Sit down together joyfully in U b - š u - u k k i n n a;
let me as your representative, by word of mouth
   determine destiny,
so that whatever I devise shall not be altered,
my spoken order not revoked, not countermanded.

Anshar agreed, and a messenger was sent to Lahmu and Lahāmu to tell them about the emergency and call them to assembly. Horrified, they hastened to respond to the call. The gods met in the courtyard U b - š u - u k k i n n a, greet each other affectionately, sat down to a banquet, and talked and talked:

They chatted and sat down to the feast;
breadstuff they ate, and drank dark beer.
The sweet drink dispelled their fears,
they sang for joy, drinking strong wine.
Carefree they grew, exceedingly,
   their mood elated,
for Marduk, their campion,
   they decreed (his) status.

They made a princely dais for him,
and he sat down, facing his fathers,
   to (receive) rulership:
"You are of consequence among the great gods,
your decree is unsurpassed, your command is Anu.
Marduk, you are of consequence among the great gods,
your decree is unequalled, your command is Anu.
From this day onward shall your orders
   not be countermanded,
to elevate and to abase —
   this be within your power.
What you have spoken shall come true,
   your word shall not prove vain.
Among the gods, none shall encroach
   upon your rights.
Upkeep is the due of the seats of the gods,
so let the management of their sanctuaries
   rest secure with you.

What the gods here convey is kingship:

We gave you kingship,
   power over all and everything.
Take your seat in the council,
   and may your word prevail.

> May your weapon not yield,
>   may it smite your foes.
> Grant breath of life, O Lord,
>   to whomever is trusted by you,
> but if a god embraces evil, shed his life.

Marduk thus is given decisive civic power to promote and demote without interference by any other god, and corresponding responsibility to see that the god's temples are properly taken care of; and he is given military power, "kingship," overall command, victorious weapons, and the power to pardon or to kill captive enemies.

To test whether Marduk actually has the power they have given him, the gods set up a constellation and ask him first to order it destroyed, then that it become intact.

> They placed a constellation in their midst
> and said to Marduk, their firstborn:
> "O Lord, your decree be truly foremost
>   among gods.
> Command destruction and construction,
>   and may both come true.
> May your spoken word destroy the constellation,
> then speak again and may it be intact."
> He spoke, and at his word
>   the constellation was destroyed.
> He spoke again,
>   and the constellation was (re)constructed.
> The gods, his fathers,
>   seeing (the power of) his word,
> rejoiced, paid homage: "Marduk is king."

Satisfied, the gods give him the royal insignia, arm him, and speed him to battle:

> They gave him sceptre, throne,
>   and royal robe besides,
> gave him an irresistible weapon
>   overwhelming the foe:
> "Go cut Ti'āmat's throat!
> And let the winds bring her blood hither
>   as tidings of joy!"
> The gods, his fathers,
>   determined the status of the lord:
> Make him take the road of "Safety and Obedience."

The formula is programmatical and emphasizes that Marduk holds an emergency authority, yielded by the gods under pressure of threat of attack. They only obey to obtain security.

Armed with bow and arrows, a mace, and a net to enclose Ti'āmat, Marduk set lightning before him, filled himself with blazing flame, and mounted his storm-chariot, followed by various stormwinds he had created. Thus — the image of a thunderstorm — he issued forth to meet Ti'āmat:

> He made a bow, designed it as his weapon,
> let the arrow ride firmly on the bowstring.
> Grasping (his) mace in his right hand,
>   he lifted it,
> hung bow and quiver at his side,
> set the lightning before him,
> and made his body burn with searing flame.
> He made a net wherein to encircle Ti'āmat,
> bade the four winds hold on,
>   that none of her escape.
> The south wind, north wind,
>   east wind, west wind,
> gifts from his (grand-) father Anu,
>   he brought up to the edges of the net.

As the armies faced each other, Marduk, scanning the enemy forces, discovered that their leader Kingu was confused, his actions contradictory, while his helpers eyes had clouded over with terror as they gazed on Marduk. Only Ti'āmat stood her ground, first seeking to distract Marduk with flattery about his rapid rise to prominence:

> On her lips she held blandishments —
>   they were lies:
> "Thou are honored, O Lord, in that the gods
>   have taken (their) stand with thee,
> they gathered to their place,
>   and (now) they are (here) with thee"

But Marduk is not taken in, he sternly charges her with falsehood:

> The lord lifted the floodstorm,
>   his great weapon,
> at Ti'amat (who tried) ingratiating herself
>   thus he let fly:
> "Why wear your sweetness
>   (as cloak) on the surface,
> though your heart plots
>   (when to) signal the skirmish?
> The sons have withdrawn,
>   their fathers acted wrongfully,
> and you, who gave birth to them,
>   hate (your) offspring.

> You have named Kingu as your spouse,
> installed him to make the decisions of the lordship —
>   (an honor) of which he is undeserving.
> Against Anshar, king of the gods,
>   you seek evil,
> and have proved your evil (intent)
>   against the gods, my fathers:
> Verily your forces are ranged,
>   they are girt with weapons (of) your (making).
> Set to! Let me and you do battle!"

The younger gods have had to withdraw, their fathers were in their eyes acting unjustly toward them when Apsû sought to destroy them; and now she, their mother, hates them and is bent on attacking them, as is abundantly clear from her standing here in the midst of an army fully armed by her.

At Marduk's challenge Ti'āmat, seized with a terrible rage, lets out a roar, and starts trembling with anger as she attacks:

> Ti'āmat and the champion of the gods, Marduk,
>   engaged,
> were tangled in single combat,
>   joined in battle.
> The lord spread his net, encompassing her;
> the tempest, following after,
>   he loosed in her face.
> Ti'āmat opened her mouth as far as she could;
> he drove in the tempest
>   lest she close her lips.
> The fierce winds filled her belly,
> her insides congested and (retching)
>   she opened wide her mouth:
> he let fly an arrow, it split her belly,
> cut through her inward parts
>   and gashed the heart.
> He held her fast, extinguished her life.

With Ti'āmat slain, her followers turned to flee, but were caught in Marduk's net, disarmed, and made prisoners. Kingu was bound and Marduk took the "tablets of the decrees" from him, sealing them for safekeeping.

King Continued in Office for Benefits: The Cosmos

Having established Anshar's victory over his enemies Marduk returned to Ti'āmat, broke her skull with his mace, cut her arteries, and ordered the north wind to bring her blood back (one imagines the reference is to rains) as a joyous victory message. Then he rested, contemplating the carcass of his enemy and planning clever things to do with it. His first ingenious contrivance was the cosmos.

He first split Ti'āmat in two and made heaven of one half, providing for bolts and guards so that her waters could not escape. Traversing the newly made heaven looking for a building plot, he came upon the spot where he directly confronted Ea's dwelling, Apsû, below. Here, after first carefully measuring the shape of Apsû, he built an exact duplicate of it, his own great estate, Esharra. The text tells us that the name means "the sky." Marduk next made constellations, organized the calendar, fixed the polestar, and instructed the moon and the sun:

> He bade the moon come forth;
>   entrusted night (to him);
> assigned to him adornment of the night
>   to measure time;
> and every month, unfailingly,
>   he marked off by a crown.
> "When the new moon is rising
>   over the land
> shine you with horns, six days to measure;
> the seventh day, as half (your) crown (appear)
> and (then) let periods of fifteen days be counterparts,
>   two halves each month.
> As, afterward, the sun gains on you
>   on heavens foundations,
> wane step by step,
>   reverse your growth!"

The phenomena of winds and storms Marduk reserved for himself. Below, he heaped a mountain over Ti'āmat's head, pierced her eyes to form the sources of the Euphrates and the Tigris (the Akkadians have but one word for "eye" and "source," *înu*, and presumably considered them in some way the same thing), and heaped similar mountains over her dugs, which he pierced to make the rivers from the eastern mountains that flow into the Tigris. Her tail he bent up into the sky to make the Milky Way, and her crotch he used to support the sky.

When heaven and earth had thus been fashioned, Marduk returned triumphantly home, where he presented the "tablets of the decrees" to his grandfather, Anu, and paraded the captive gods before his fathers. The monsters Ti'āmat had created he disarmed and bound. Their fearsome looks were such that he made statues of them to set up in his paternal home — in the gate of Ea's house Apsû — to serve as a memorial for all time.

The gods, his fathers, were understandably delighted. Anshar went to meet him, and Marduk, as king (that is, warleader), formally announced to him the state of peace and security achieved. After he had received the greetings of the gods and their greeting gifts, Marduk bathed, washed off the dust and grime of battle, dressed in full regalia, and took his seat on the throne of the throne room to formally receive the homage of the gods. His spear, named for his mandate "Security and Obedience," was set appropriately at his side. Now his parents, Ea and Damkina, reminded the gods that Marduk was no longer merely their beloved son, but king; and the assembled gods then named him L u g a l - d i m m e r - a n - k i - a, "King of the gods of heaven and earth," reaffirming their allegiance. The formula they now used was, however, not the one they used before. A great change had been wrought. With Ti'āmat dead the dire need for protection and security was no longer an incentive to obedience; however, with Marduk's creation of the universe, a powerful new one had come into being: hope to benefit from his administrative competence and ingenuity. And so the gods in reaffirming their allegiance to him as king employed a new formula: "Benefits and Obedience."

> When they gave Marduk the kingship
> they pronounced to him the formula
>   of "Benefits and Obedience":
> "From this day forward you shall be
>   the provider for our sanctuaries,
> and whatever you order let us carry out."

Permanent Capital for Benefits: Man

Marduk's first demand upon the gods was that they build him a city and a house to serve as a permanent royal administrative center and a place for them to stay when they gathered for an assembly: a signpost to permanence. Its name was to be Babylon. The gods, his fathers, listened to Marduk and asked questions: who would assist him in administering what he had created and carry out his wishes? They suggested that they themselves move to Babylon, have their daily offerings brought there, in order to be more available to help.

In the meantime, Marduk magnanimously pardoned those gods who had sided with Ti'āmat, released them and assigned the building work to them. Released from the shadow of death, they prostrated themselves before him, hailed him as their king and savior, and promised to build the house he wanted. Their willingness to undertake the hard task moved Marduk's heart to think of his second ingenious contrivance. To ease things for them, a great new benefit, he decided to create man.

> Arteries I will knot
>   and bring bones into being.

> I will create *Lullu*, "man" be his name,
> I will form *Lullu*, man.
> Let *him* be burdened with the toil of the gods,
>   that they may freely breathe.
> Next I will skillfully dispose
>   of the ways of the gods;
> verily, they are clustered together like a ball,
>   let them be divided in two.

On the advice of his father, Ea, he called an assembly, at which he had Kingu indicted as the instigator of the attack on the gods and the one who had stirred up Ti'āmat. Kingu was then taken before Ea and killed, and Ea fashioned man from his blood:

> They bound him, held him before Ea,
> inflicted the penalty on him,
>   severed his arteries;
> and from his blood he formed mankind,
> imposed toil on man, set the gods free.

The task was truly a marvel:

> That work was not meet
>   for (human) understanding.
> (Acting) on Marduk's ingenious suggestion
>   Ea created.

With man there to do the menial work the gods were free for the various lighter administrative tasks throughout the universe, and so Marduk divided them into two groups: one to help Anu in the administration of heaven, one to look after things on earth. He gave all of them their instructions and assigned their portions.

The grateful gods showed their appreciation with action: they took, for the last time, spade in hand to build Babylon and its temple:

> The Anunnaku wielded the hoe,
> for one year they made its bricks;
> when the second year arrived,
> they raised the summit of Esaǧila
>   (over and) opposite Apsû,
> and built the upper (counterpart
>   to the) ziggurat of the Apsû.
> For Anu, Enlil, Ea, and him,
>   they established seats,
> in grandeur he sat down before them,
> (the) horns (of) his (crown) looking (up)
>   toward the roots of Esharra (the heavens).

King Made Permanent: Monarchy

When all was finished, Marduk invited the gods to a feast in the new house, and after they had eaten and drunk, disposed of administrative business, and distributed the celestial and terrestrial offices, the great gods went into session and permanently appointed the "seven gods of destinies," or better, "of the decrees" to formulate in final form the decrees of the assembly. Marduk placed his bow and net before the gods and Anu was so delighted with the bow that he adopted it as his daughter and gave it a seat with the gods, its brothers, in the assembly. Next Anu seated Marduk on the royal throne. The gods prostrated themselves before him and bound themselves by oath by touching their throats with oil and water. They then formally gave Marduk the kingship as a permanent office, appointing him permanent lord of the gods of heaven and earth. Even this seemed not enough to Anshar, who proceeded to give him a new name, Asalluhe, and enjoined the gods to reverence him. Marduk's office and its duties he outlined as follows:

> Surpassing be his lordship,
>   may he have no rival,
> may he perform the shepherdship
>   over the dark-headed people,
> and may they speak of his ways,
>   that they be not forgotten
>   to the end of time.
> Let him establish large food portions
>   for his fathers,
> let him see to their upkeep,
>   take care of their sanctuaries,
> let him cause incense to be smelt,
>   have their cellas rejoice.
>
> Corresponding to what he has done in heaven,
>   be done on earth!
> Let him assign dark-headed people
>   to his worship,
> let the subjects be mindful, their god invoked.
>
> Let them heed *his* word, as if it were that
>   of their tutelary goddess.
> Let food portions be brought
>   to their (the people's) gods and goddesses,
> may they not be forgotten,
>   let them (i.e., the people) remember their gods,
> let them (the people) make their countries outstanding,
>   build their throne-daises,
>
> And let individual personal gods be given
>   as share to the dark-headed people.

As for us, as many as we are called by name,
  he is our tutelary god.

The story ends with Anshar exhorting the assembled gods to name Marduk's fifty names, which they do, each name indicative of a power or a deed that characterizes him.

Structural Analysis

Major Structural Line: The Political Theme

The story told in Enûma elish is unusually complex and detailed. It may, therefore, not be amiss to trace its major structural lines in order to gain a clearer understanding of the ends it has in view and the paths it follows to attain them.

The story's final goal is certainly Marduk's attaining to the position of permanent king of the universe, thereby creating the monarchical form of government. A major step toward making that possible was his vanquishing Ti'amat in a decisive victory of the powers for energy and movement, the gods, over the older powers who stood for inertia and rest.

Not only the story itself, as one now reads it, but also the ancient mise en point contained in its concluding lines (which sum it up as "the song about Marduk, who vanquished Ti'āmat and assumed kingship") speaks in favor of seeing in these events the gist of what Enûma elish is about.

To indicate through what ups and downs the story leads on to these goals we have listed in the accompanying diagram the chief events of the tale in order along a horizontal axis and indicated by upward or downward movement along a vertical axis whether a given event furthers or hampers ultimate achievement of the goals. The resulting curve begins with the birth of the gods and the contrast between their nature and that of the older powers which is fundamental to the conflict. In its further course the curve shows four major peaks, each representing a "trigger" event which leads on to a separate episode.

The two first such trigger events, in which the exuberant energy of youth — which is of the very essence of the gods — finds expression in dance and in play, constitute irritants exasperating the older powers who are deprived of their rest. First Apsû, then Ti'āmat are roused to seek the annihilation of their tormentors, only to be themselves defeated and killed. This section of the story is presumably covered in the summary by the clause "who vanquished Ti'āmat," since the overcoming of Ti'āmat is its high point.

Actually, the two episodes that make it up are somewhat different in character and may be seen as representative of two aspects of the political form of primitive democracy: (1) inability to set it in motion and achieve concerted action, either because of failure to reach agreement or because

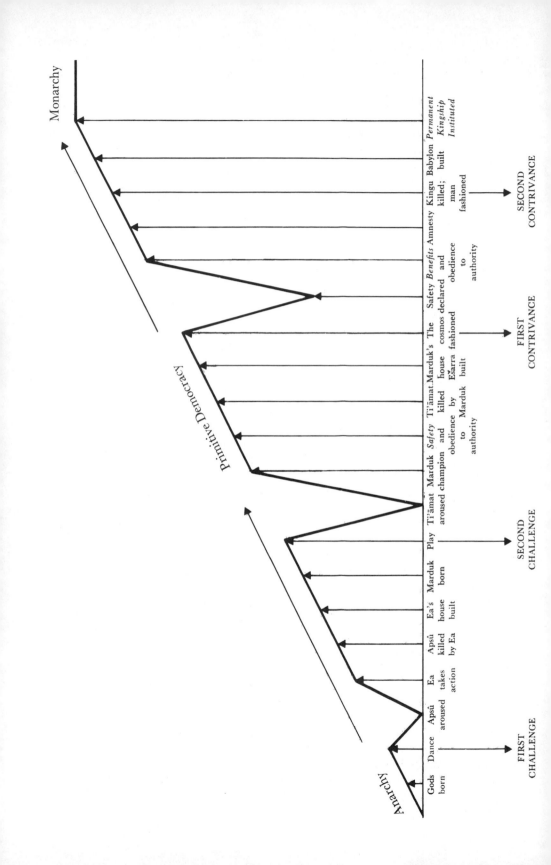

of a paralyzing fear, both of which leave things at a level of virtual anarchy, and, (2) the successful functioning of its machinery to impose unanimity in times of clear and present danger.

The first of the two episodes, in which Apsû is the attacker, represents failure. Apsû is unable to get Ti'āmat to join him and proceeds on his own. Ea, when the news reaches the gods, is confronted with bewildered, stymied gods incapable of any initiative and likewise acts on his own.

The second episode, in which Ti'āmat is the chief antagonist, is notably different. It has as its background the full and functioning apparatus of primitive democracy with general assemblies in time of crises and election of ad hoc leaders. When a group of Ti'āmat's children have roused her against the gods, an assembly of wide scope is called, which includes descendants of the younger powers, the gods. Kingu is made leader of the host and given attendant offices and insignia. Correspondingly, when word of the danger reaches the gods, and appeals to the power inherent in the commands of members of the family of Anshar individually and collectively have failed, Anshar calls, at Marduk's request, a larger assembly to confer leadership — kingship — on Marduk in the defensive war the gods face. The ad hoc nature of the office and its basis in the momentary threat to the gods is expressed in the formula, "Safety and Obedience."

The trigger events that introduce episodes later in the story are of a different cast from those of the first part; they are not irritants but incentives. The later part of the story would seem to be covered in the summary at the end of the composition by the clause "and assumed kingship." It tells how Marduk — after his victory over Ti'āmat has removed the threat that was the factual basis for his authority — is yet able through his outstanding intelligence and leadership to win first a continuation in office, then a permanent, true monarchy, by reason of the unheard of benefits his rule conferred.

The first of these "ingenious contrivances," *niklātu* as the text has it, is Marduk's creation of the present universe out of Ti'āmat's body. As the lifting of the threat to the gods becomes progressively clearer with patent signs of victory, with Marduk conscientiously handing over power to his elders, Ea and Anu, and with his formal declaration of a state of peace to Anshar, the diminished need for his protection is replaced by the lure of highly tempting promises of advantages held out by his creation of the cosmos. Accordingly, the assembled gods continue him in power. His parents renounce their authority over him, and the new basis for his authority is openly expressed in the new formula with which the gods hail him king: "Benefits and Obedience" replacing the earlier "Safety and Obedience."

The next step toward the goal of permanence is adumbrated by Marduk when he proposes the building of a permanent capital, Babylon, in response to which his fathers spontaneously offer to move there as members of his administration for the new universe, and even the captive gods to whom he has extended amnesty gratefully declare their willingness to undertake the titanic building task.

One more trigger event, one more "contrivance" of Marduk, follows and finally brings about permanence and monarchy: the creation of man. That this requires the killing of a god is a difficulty overcome by using due process of law in convicting and executing Kingu for instigating the war, and the freed gods show their trust in Marduk by truthfully denouncing Kingu in the assembly called to judge him. With the creation of man, all the gods, including those Marduk has just freed, become once and for all relieved of menial toil and are given administrative positions in the universe. Thus complete reconciliation is established.

As their last menial task the gods build Babylon as permanent meeting place at the center of the universe and gather there to establish permanent organs of government. First the committee of the "seven gods of decrees" — that is, the seven gods who give the decrees of the assembly their final, binding formulation — is made permanent. Then Marduk is installed with oaths of allegiance as permanent king. True monarchy has finally been achieved.

Minor Structural Line: The Parricide Theme

The progression from initial anarchy to primitive democracy to monarchy may be considered the major structural line in Enûma elish. It is its political theme. However, beside this political theme and interwoven with it runs in Enûma elish's first half also another, minor one which has family authority rather than political authority as its subject, the parricide theme. The pattern of the parricide theme, which governs both the Apsû and the Ti'āmat episodes, has a parent provoked beyond endurance by expressions of youthful exuberance — dancing or playing — by his or her offspring. An open conflict of generations follows and ends in parricide, after which the slayer founds his own house upon the body of the dead parent.

As a motif considered in itself, this is perhaps most naturally interpreted as a symbolization of emotions centering around the transfer of authority in the family from parent to son at the death of the parent. The parricide element may well represent more or less repressed wishes in the younger generation; while the son's founding his house on his parent's body might be a somewhat drastic projection of the situation after the son has taken over as head of the house, with the parents laid to rest in the family vault beneath it.

As used in Enûma elish the motif seems, however, more equivocally handled. On the one hand, the author clearly seeks to play it down and soften it; on the other, he is just as clearly at some pains to point it up by emphasizing sympathetically the parental character of the victims, particularly the motherliness of Ti'āmat. As an effort to soften the motif, one may consider that the author has the warring parents and sons separated by many generations so that the parricide becomes the slaying of remote first ancestors rather than the direct killing of a father and mother. The author also seems intent on justifying the killings as far as possible. The dancing and play at which the older powers take umbrage were clearly not intended to be provocations. The onus of initiating hostility is consistently placed on the parents, so that the sons act entirely in self defense. Marduk pithily expresses this in his accusing answer to Ti'āmat:

> The sons have withdrawn,
>   their fathers acted wrongfully,
> and you, who gave birth to them,
>   hate (your) offspring.

But while the aspect of parricide is thus mitigated both by making the parents remote ancestors and putting them plainly in the wrong, part of this effect is countered — deliberately, it would seem — by the stress on Ti'āmat's motherliness and by presenting her repeatedly in a sympathetic light. Her mother's heart is much in evidence, for instance, when she refuses to side with Apsû:

> Ti'āmat, when she heard this,
> became upset, cried out against her husband,
> cried out, hurt, the only one indignant.
> *She* took the evilness (thereof) to heart:
> "How could we destroy
>   what we (ourselves) have brought into being?
> Though their ways be noisome,
>   let us bear it in good part!"

Similarly, when she is finally roused to fatal action, it is by appealing to her motherly instincts of protection — not from lack of patience or forbearance on her part — that she is brought around:

> "You are no mother, you stir roiled around,
> and we, who cannot go to sleep, us you do not love!
> Our water is stagnant, our springs run dry!"

So odd is this sympathetic treatment of the archenemy, Ti'āmat, that one can hardly escape feeling that the author is here in the grip of conflicting emotions: love, fear, and a sense of guilt that requires palliation.

In the second half of the story, which is concerned with Marduk's

efforts to achieve permanent kingship, the parricide theme dies out.
There is a killing of one of the older powers, Kingu, but kinship with
Kingu is nowhere stressed, he remains curiously wooden and lifeless.
There is also a house building, Esaḡila and Babylon, but it is not upon
Kingu's body, and the house is to serve not just Marduk but all gods,
including those who were on the side of Ti'āmat. In contrast to the theme
of parricide is the stress laid upon Marduk's exemplary relations with his
parents, grandfather, and great-grandfather, and the peaceable and willing ways in which they confer upon him the authority he wishes.

It still remains to ask what the purpose of introducing the parricide
theme into the story can have been and what relation it has to the political
theme of the evolution of monarchy.

In seeking an answer we may perhaps begin by considering other
statements of the conferring of kingship on Marduk, specifically, the very
early such statement that begins the Code of Hammurabi:

> When august Anu, king of the Anunnaki (gods),
> and Enlil, lord of heaven and earth,
> who issue the decrees for the nation,
> decreed for Marduk, the firstborn of Enki,
> (exercise of) the Enlil functions for the
>   totality of people
> and made him great among the Igigi (gods),
> called Babylon's lofty name,
> made it supreme in the four regions (of the
>   world),
> and established permanently in its midst a
>   lasting kingship,
> the foundations of which are as solidly
>   laid as (those of) heaven and earth,
> at that time. . . .[335]

Here one easily recognizes the age-old Sumerian tradition of an assembly of the gods meeting under the presidium of Anu and Enlil in Nippur
to confer or take away from one of its members and his city, and city ruler,
the kingship of Southern Mesopotamia, of Sumer and Akkad. There is,
though, one very noteworthy difference from earlier language. As late as
the generation following the fall of the Third Dynasty of Ur (and perhaps
later), the Sumerian political pattern for the world of the gods remained a
primitive democracy and the kingship that the assembly of the gods
conferred was still the ad hoc office with the limited terms of that pattern.
This, though true monarchy had by then long-dominated the human
scene. We may recall the words of Enlil after the fall of Ur:

> There is no revoking a verdict,
>   a decree of the assembly.

A command of An and Enlil is not known
  ever to have been changed.
Ur was verily granted kingship —
  a lasting term it was not granted.
From days of yore when the country was first settled,
  to where it has not progressed
Who ever saw a term of royal office completed?[336]

New in the statement from the Code of Hammurabi is therefore the qualification "lasting" used to characterize the kingship established in Babylon, since that is exactly — even to using the same word — what Enlil denied about kingship as it was granted to Ur. We thus have here, foreshadowed and in embryo as it were, the political theme of Enûma elish with its transition from the temporary kingship of primitive democracy to the permanent kingship of primitive monarchy achieved by Marduk.

Also of interest about the kingship as envisaged in the Code of Hammurabi is its cosmic scope. It is granted by An, king of the gods, and Enlil, lord of heaven and earth, and it is Enlil's functions as they apply to the rule of all mankind that are given to Marduk. Correspondingly, Marduk's city becomes supreme in the world. This cosmic aspect is traditional. It flows from the character of the gods as national and cosmic powers in one. It is the heaven and earth above the united Sumer and Akkad over which Enlil is lord. The political and cosmic horizon goes no farther.

In the Code of Hammurabi the occasion for Marduk's investiture is a historical one, the victory of Hammurabi over Rîm-Sîn, in his thirtieth year of reign, which brought Southern Babylonia, ancient Sumer, under his sway and united the country as it had last been under the Third Dynasty of Ur. Marduk's becoming king is thus here a recent historical event. Not so in Enûma elish: there Marduk's kingship has been from the beginning and dates back to mythical time. In view of this difference and the fact that the unification under Hammurabi proved anything but "lasting" (the South splitting off less than twenty years later under his son, Samsuiluna), it appears unlikely that in that short time its recent origin could have been forgotten and that an author could have projected it back to mythical time. We must clearly look elsewhere for what underlies the picture presented in Enûma elish.

A clue seems to be furnished by Enûma elish itself through its choice of the sea, Ti'āmat — in later, contracted form Tâmtum — as Marduk's main antagonist. This choice must seem odd, for the sea, the Persian Gulf, lay far to the south behind vast marshes and could have played little part in the average Babylonian's experience of the world. Some quite specific conditioning circumstance would therefore need to have been involved, and just such a one is the fact that, historically, Marduk's and Babylon's main antagonist from shortly after the death of Hammurabi to well into the Cassite period was precisely the "Land of Ti'āmat" (*māt tâmtim*), the "Sealand," which covered precisely the territory of ancient Sumer.[337] It was finally conquered by Ulamburiash, who thus reunited Southern and Northern Babylonia, Sumer and Akkad more lastingly than before.

If Ti'āmat represents the Sealand, and Marduk's victory over her its conquest and unification with Babylon and the North under Ulamburiash — however dimly remembered as momentous happenings of a remote past — many things about Enûma elish become more understandable. The almost complete absence of any reference to Enlil and Nippur in the story, for instance, has long been a crux, since traditionally cosmic kingship was granted by An and Enlil acting for the gods meeting in Enlil's city, Nippur. If Ti'āmat is the Sealand, however, Enlil's absence becomes understandable, for Nippur was part of it. Thus Nippur and Enlil would have been on the side of Ti'āmat, with Enlil one of the captive gods and not a fit source of authority.

More important, however, is the insight we gain into the parricide theme. In warring with the Sealand, Babylon warred with the territory of ancient Sumer and all its renowned and venerable ancient cities and their gods. It waged an upstart's war with its own parent civilization. And that this was a live issue, that the Sealand was keenly aware of being heir to and continuer of Sumerian civilization, is clear from the fact that its kings, especially those of the latter half of the dynasty, sport elaborate Sumerianized names.[338] Understandably, therefore, Babylon might have felt — consciously or unconsciously — its victory to be in some sense parricidal. Understandably also it might have sought justification for its hostility in its being the victim of attack, and in seeing itself as representing youth and youthful vigor pitted against age and stagnant tradition.

Above all, however, the concern with reconciliation and unity in the tale becomes meaningful: the often sympathetic presentation of Ti'āmat, the amnesty granted the gods siding with her, and the rapid drawing of them into the new administration all fit in as reflecting a sense of unity and kinship with the former enemy, which presumably was conscious policy after the unification.

In Enûma elish the kingship, Marduk's and Babylon's rule over all of Babylonia, existed from the beginnings. It is accordingly unlikely that very precise memories of its historical origins could have persisted when the epic was written. What did persist, it would seem, were emotional echoes and smouldering residues of pride and guilt.

Objectives and Ends

We now return to the question posed at the beginning of this chapter about the acceptability of the universe, ·directing it specifically to the universe that meets us in Enûma elish. For Enûma elish, as we have seen, operates on more than one level. It is a mythopoeic adumbration of Babylon's and Marduk's rise to rulership over a united Babylonia, but projected back to mythical times and made universal. It is also an account of how the universe is ruled; how monarchy evolved and gained acceptance as a unifier of the many divine wills in the universe. It is a story of world origins and world ordering. World origins, it holds, are essentially accidental: gods were born out of a mingling of the primeval waters and they engendered other gods. The active nature of the gods led to conflict with the older powers who stood for inertia, repose, and, in subtle ways, for the dead hand of a powerful old cultural tradition. World ordering is essentially the outcome of youthful leadership: conscious, creative intelligence in a born ruler, Marduk. He created the present universe, overcame old fears and hatreds by magnanimously granting amnesty to the gods he captured in battle, provided the gods with leisure (based on the slave labor of man), and assigned them offices in his administration. Thus was the world established as a state, a well-run paternalistic monarchy with permanent king, capital, parliament, and royal palace in Babylon.

As a view of world order this is in many ways impressive. It sees the universe as grounded in divine power and divine will: even those wills traditionally felt as older, more authoritative, or hostile, are unified under the leadership of a single ruler who governs through consultation, persuasion, and conviction. It is religiously of great profundity, leading in its picture of Marduk toward the aspects of awe and majesty. Moreover, it is intellectually admirable in providing a unifying concept of existence: political order pervades both nature and society. Finally, it is humanly satisfying: ultimate power is not estranged from mankind, but resides in gods in human form who act understandably. The universe is now moral and meaningful and expression of a creative intelligence with valid purpose: order and peace and prosperity.

Second Millennium Metaphors. "And Death the Journey's End": The Gilgamesh Epic

The face of Huwawa, whom Gilgamesh and Enkidu killed. The face is of unknown provenance and is now in the British Museum. It dates from around 700 to 500 B.C. and is about 3 inches (7.5 cm) high.

Problems, Hero, Versions

We viewed Enûma elish as a remarkable attempt to understand and accept the universe, to come to terms with the human condition. The author of Enûma elish was able to do so wholeheartedly, but his was by no means the only possible attitude, as may be illustrated from the only slightly older epic of Gilgamesh,[339] which also comes to terms with the human condition, but not easily and perhaps not altogether convincingly. Unlike Enûma elish its concern is not with the gods and the rule of the universe but with man; its problem is man's mortality, the fact that we must all eventually die.

Gilgamesh, as far as one can judge, was a historical figure, the ruler of the city of Uruk (the biblical Erekh) around 2600 B.C. It stands to reason that stories about him would have been current long after his death, but they only become graspable to us around 2100 B.C. when they were taken up by the court poets of the Third Dynasty of Ur. The kings of that dynasty counted Gilgamesh as their ancestor. We possess a number of short epical compositions in Sumerian, the originals of which must date to that revival of interest, but the Gilgamesh Epic proper, with which we are here concerned dates from around 1600 B.C., at the end of the Old Babylonian period, and was composed in Akkadian. Strictly speaking, we should perhaps not say the "epic" but the "contours of the epic," since what we have of Old Babylonian date are fragments, and may represent only separate songs of a loosely-connected Gilgamesh cycle.[340] These fragments do, however, cover all the essential — largely internally dependent — episodes that make up the tale in its later version. This version, made probably toward the end of the second millennium by one Sîn-liqi-unninnī, is preserved for the most part in copies from around 600 B.C. from the famous library of Ashurbanipal in Nineveh. It contains much that is extraneous to the tale, and it lacks the freshness and vigor of the Old Babylonian fragments. In our retelling of the story here we shall therefore quote the older fragments whenever possible.

The Story

The story begins in the high style of "romantic epic," by introducing the hero to us. As the *Odyssey* begins with a characterization of Odysseus:

Tell me, Muse, of that man, so ready at need,
who wandered far and wide, . . .
and many were the men whose towns he saw
and whose minds he learnt,

> yea, and many the woes he suffered in his
>   heart upon the deep,
> striving to win his own life and the return
>   of his company . . .[341]

so the Gilgamesh Epic opens with lines calculated to whet the listener's
interest in its hero as a man who has had strange and stirring experiences
and who has seen far-off regions:

> He who saw all, throughout the length of
>   the land
> came to know the seas, experienced all things. . . .

But there is a special note to the Gilgamesh Epic introduction not found in
the *Odyssey*, a stress on something beyond mere unusual, individual
experience, a focus rather on lasting tangible achievements, typified by
the walls of Uruk, still extant,[342] still a cause for wonder when the introduction was written:

> He built the town wall of Uruk, (city) of sheepfolds,
> of the sacred precinct Eanna, the holy storehouse.
> Look at its wall
>   with its frieze like bronze!
> Gaze at its bastions, which none can equal!
> Take the stone stairs that are from times of old,
> approach Eanna, the seat of Ishtar,
> the like of which no later king — no man —
>   will ever make.
> Go up on the wall of Uruk, walk around,
> examine the terrace, look closely at the brickwork:
> Is not the base of its brickwork of baked brick?
> Have not seven masters laid its foundations?

From our first meeting with the young Gilgamesh he is characterized by
tremendous vigor and energy. As ruler of Uruk he throws himself into his
task with zeal. He maintains a constant military alert, calls his companions
away from their games, and harasses the young men of the town to the
point where it gets black before their eyes and they faint from weariness,
and he leaves them no time for their families and sweethearts.

The people of Uruk are understandably not very happy at this, and
they begin to pester the gods with complaints and entreaties to do something about it. The gods divine with remarkable insight what is at the root
of the trouble: Gilgamesh's superior energy and strength set him apart
and make him lonely. He needs a friend, someone who measures up to
him and can give him companionship on his own extraordinary level of
potential and aspiration. So they call the creator Aruru and ask her to
create a counterpart of Gilgamesh:

> You, Aruru, created the wild bull (Gilgamesh)
> now created his image,
>   in stormy heart let it equal Gilgamesh,
> let them vie with each other,
>   and Uruk have peace.

Aruru forms a mental image of the god of heaven as a model, washes her hands, pinches off clay, throws it down in the desert, and thus creates Enkidu.

Enkidu is, as it were, man in a state of nature. He is enormously strong, goes naked, and hair covers all of his body; his locks are long like a woman's and grow as luxuriantly as grain. He knows nothing about the country and people but roams with the gazelles in the desert, eating grass and slaking his thirst in the evening with the animals at the drinking places. As their friend he helps protect them by filling in pits dug to catch them and destroying traps set for them. This brings him into contact with man. A trapper in the neighborhood finds his livelihood severely threatened by Enkidu's actions, but since Enkidu is so big and strong, there is nothing he can do. Dejected, he goes home to his father and tells about the newcomer and how he prevents him from carrying on his trade. The trapper's father advises him to go to Gilgamesh in Uruk and ask for a harlot who will go along and try to seduce Enkidu away from his animals. The trapper makes his way to Uruk and appeals to Gilgamesh. Gilgamesh listens to his story and tells him to take along a harlot to use her wiles on Enkidu.

So the trapper finds a harlot and together they walk out into the desert, until, on the third day they reach the watering place where Enkidu likes to come with the animals, and here they sit down to wait. One day passes, then a second, and on the third Enkidu and the animals appear and go down to drink. The trapper points Enkidu out to the harlot and urges her to take off her clothes and try to attract Enkidu's attention. In this she is eminently successful. For six days and seven nights Enkidu enjoys himself with her, oblivious to everything else. When at last satisfied, after the seventh night, he wants to go back to his animals. But they shy away. He runs after them, only to find that he no longer has his old power and speed and can no longer keep up with them.

In part, of course, that may be simply because he is by then a bit tired; but almost certainly the author of the story saw more in it. Something magical and decisive has happened. The easy, natural sympathy that exists between children and animals had been Enkidu's as long as he was a child, sexually innocent. Once he has known a woman he has made his choice, from then on he belongs to the human race, and the animals fear him and cannot silently communicate with him as they could before. Slowly, Enkidu comprehends some of this. "He grew up," says the author, "and his understanding broadened."

So Enkidu gives up trying to catch up with the animals and returns to the harlot, who is very kind to him, saying:

> I look at you Enkidu,
>   you are like a god!
> Why do you roam
> the desert with animals?
> Come, let me lead you
> into Uruk of the wide streets,
> to the holy temple, the dwelling of Anu,
> Enkidu, rise, let me take you
> to Eanna, the dwelling of Anu,
> where Gilgamesh is administering the rites.
> You could do them too, instead of him,
>   installing yourself!

This speech pleases Enkidu, and he takes her suggestions very much to heart. She then undresses, clothes him in the first of her garments, herself in the second, and, holding him by the hand, leads him through the desert until they come to a shepherd's camp where they are kindly and hospitably received. Here Enkidu has his first meeting with civilization and its complications. The shepherds set food and drink before him, something he has never seen before.

> He was wont to suck
> the milk of the wild beasts only;
> they set bread before him.
> He squirmed, he looked,
> and he stared.
> Enkidu knew not
> how to eat bread,
> had not been taught
> how to drink beer.
> The harlot opened her mouth
> and said to Enkidu:
> "Eat the bread, Enkidu,
> it is the staff of life!
> Drink the beer
>   it is the custom of the land!"
> Enkidu ate bread,
> until he was full up,
> drank beer —
> seven kegs —
> he relaxed, cheered up,
> his insides felt good,
> his face glowed.
> He washed with water

his hairy body,
rubbed himself with oil,
and became a man.
He put on a garment,
was like a young noble.
He took his weapon
and fought off the lions,
and the shepherds slept at night.

For some days Enkidu stays with the shepherds. One day, however, as he is sitting with the harlot, he sees a man hurrying by and asks the harlot to bring the man to him that he may hear why he has come. The man explains that he is bringing wedding cake to Uruk, where Gilgamesh is about to be married.[343] This upsets Enkidu; he grows pale, and immediately sets out for Uruk with the harlot. Their arrival creates a stir. The people gather around them gaping at Enkidu, noting his tremendous strength and stature. He is slightly shorter than Gilgamesh but equally as strong.

As they admire him, Gilgamesh approaches with his nuptial procession, going to the house of his father-in-law for his wedding, but as he nears the door Enkidu bars the way and does not let him in to his bride. The two seize each other, fighting like young bulls, destroying the threshhold and shaking the walls. Eventually, Enkidu gains the upper hand, and Gilgamesh sinks down on one knee; but as the defeated Gilgamesh subsides and turns his back, Enkidu speaks to him — not gloatingly as a victor, but full of admiration and respect:

Matchless your mother
bore you,
the wild cow of the corral
Ninsûna,
raised above men is your head,
kingship over the people
Enlil assigned to you!

Enkidu's magnanimity wins Gilgamesh's heart, and out of their battle grows a lasting friendship. Gilgamesh takes Enkidu by the hand, leads him home to his mother, and she accepts Enkidu as a son, a brother for Gilgamesh.

Thus all problems are solved. Enkidu is happy in Uruk, Gilgamesh has found a friend but — as so often — the happiness does not last. In his new life Enkidu is going soft. The hardness of his muscles is disappearing; he feels flabby, out of condition, no longer fit as in the old days in the desert. Gilgamesh comes upon him one day weeping and instantly divines what to do. What they both need is a good strenuous expedition with lots of hardship and high adventure. They ought, he proposes, to set out to-

gether to kill a terrible monster called Huwawa, who lives far away in the
cedar forest in the west.

Much as Enkidu may deplore the loss of his old hardihood, this way of
regaining it seems rather more than he bargained for. For while Gilgamesh has only heard of Huwawa, Enkidu has actually seen him in the
days he was roaming the desert, and he has acquired a healthy respect for
him:

> Huwawa, his roar is a floodstorm,
> his mouth very fire,
> his breath death.
> Why do you want
> to do this?
> An irresistible onrush
> is the trampling of Huwawa!

But Gilgamesh is not to be dissuaded. He chides Enkidu for lack of
courage and shames him into going along. They have mighty weapons
forged for them, take leave of the elders of the town, who give them much
paternal advice about how to travel, and say goodbye to Gilgamesh's
mother.

Their trip is told in great detail, and we especially hear of Gilgamesh's
dreams, all of which are terrifying warnings of disaster. But Enkidu is
headstrong and with unconscious impiety interprets every one of them to
mean that they will overcome Huwawa.[344] The section of the story that
deals with their actual encounter with Huwawa is unfortunately badly
preserved in all the versions we have, but it seems clear that in one way or
other Huwawa loses out, begs for his life, which Gilgamesh is inclined to
spare, and is eventually killed at Enkidu's insistence. The most complete
account of the episode we have is earlier than the epic, a Sumerian tale
which probably was among the sources that the author of the epic had at
his disposal.[345] It tells how Gilgamesh at first succumbs to the terror
encompassing Huwawa and is unable to move. From that perilous situation he saves himself by pretending to Huwawa that he has not come to
fight him but to get to know the mountains where he lives and to offer him
his older sister as wife and his younger sister as handmaiden. Huwawa is
taken in, divesting himself of his armor of rays of terror. Thus defense-
less, he is set upon by Gilgamesh, who smites and subdues him. Huwawa
pleads for his life and Gilgamesh — as a gentleman — is inclined to spare
him, until Enkidu, with a peasant's distrust, speaks thus:

> "The tallest who has no judgment
> Namtar (death) swallows up,
>   Namtar who acknowledges no (excuses).
> Letting the captured bird go home,
> the captured lad return to his mother's lap,

you will never make it back
  to your (own) city and mother who bore you."

Huwawa, furious at this interference, cuttingly asks whether Enkidu, "a hireling who, to the detriment of the food supply, walks behind his companions," is thus to put him in the wrong, at which Enkidu, stung by the insult, cuts off Huwawa's head.

When Gilgamesh and Enkidu return to Uruk — we are now back with the epic — Gilgamesh washes the grime of battle and travel off his body and dresses in fresh clothes. Thus arrayed he is so attractive that the goddess of Uruk herself, Ishtar, becomes enamored of him and proposes marriage: If he will become her husband she will give him a chariot of gold and lapis lazuli, kings will kneel before him, his goats will have triplets, his sheep twins. Gilgamesh though, will have none of it and seems to rather panic at the thought. Instead of quietly and calmly refusing, he heaps insults upon her: she is an unfinished door which does not keep out wind and drafts, pitch that dirties the one who carries it, a water skin which leaks on the one who carries it, a shoe that pinches the foot of its owner, and so on. Worse yet, all her previous lovers have come to a bad end. There was Dumuzi, or Tammuz, the love of her youth, for whom she instituted laments year after year. There was the varicolored bird she loved, only to break its wing so that it now runs round in the forests and cries *"kappee! kappee!"* ("my wing! my wing!"). There was the lion, for which she dug pits, and the war-horse, for which she destined whip and spurs. There was the shepherd whom she loved and then turned into a wolf so that his own dogs set upon him, and there was her father's gardener, Ishullānu, who came to grief at her hand when he refused her advances.

At this catalogue of her shortcomings, Ishtar — never very patient — rushes to her father, Anu, the god of heaven, tells him that Gilgamesh has insulted her, and begs him to let her have the "bull of heaven" to kill him. Anu is not eager to comply, suggesting that probably Ishtar herself has invited the scolding, but Ishtar is so incensed that she threatens to break the gates of the netherworld and let the dead up to eat the living if Anu does not let her have her way. Anu points out that the bull of heaven is such a destructive animal that, if let loose, there will be seven years of famine. But Ishtar assures him that she has stored enough grain and hay for man and beast for seven years, and in the end, Anu gives in to her.

As Ishtar takes the bull of heaven down to Uruk it shows itself a terrible threat. Its first snort blows a hole in the ground into which fall a hundred men, its second traps two hundred more. But Gilgamesh and Enkidu prove old hands at handling cattle. Enkidu gets behind the bull and twists its tail — an old cowboy trick — while Gilgamesh like a matador plunges his sword into the neck of the bull.

The death of the bull of heaven shocks Ishtar. She mounts the city wall, treads a mourning measure, and curses Gilgamesh. At this Enkidu tears off a hind leg of the bull and hurls it up at her, shouting: "You! Could I but get at you I would make you like unto it." Ishtar and her women set up a wail over the shank of the bull, while Gilgamesh calls together the craftsmen so that they can admire the size of the bull's horns before he presents them as a votive offering to his father, the god Lugalbanda. Then he and Enkidu wash themselves in the Euphrates and return to Uruk in triumph. The entire population of the city come out to gaze at them and Gilgamesh exultantly sings out to the maids of the palace: "Who is noblest of youths? / Who, most renowned of swains? and they answer: "Gilgamesh is noblest of youths! / Enkidu most renowned of swains!"

At this point in the story the two friends stand at the pinnacle of power and fame. They have killed the terrible Huwawa in the remote and inaccessible cedar forest, in their arrogance they have treated a great goddess with disdain, and in killing the bull of heaven they have proved they could get the better of her. There seems to be nothing they cannot do.

Now, however, things begin to catch up with them. Huwawa was appointed guardian of the cedar forest by Enlil, and in killing him Gilgamesh and Enkidu have incurred Enlil's anger. In a dream that night Enkidu sees the gods assembled to pass judgment on him and Gilgamesh for killing Huwawa. Enlil demands the death penalty but the sun god — god of fairness and moderation — intercedes and is able to save Gilgamesh. Enkidu, however, perhaps as the more palpably guilty one, has to die. And so Enkidu falls ill. Horror-stricken at what he knows is happening to him, he wishes he had never come to Uruk and curses the trapper and the harlot who brought him. The sun god, again speaking up for fairness, points out to Enkidu how much he has gained in his new life of luxury with Gilgamesh for a friend, and Enkidu then balances the harlot's curse with a long blessing. But, reconciled or not, Enkidu is doomed and dies.

Up to this point, it will have been noted, Gilgamesh has lived by the heroic values of his times. Death was a part of the scheme of things, so, since you had to die anyway, let it be a glorious death in battle with a worthy foe so that your name and fame would live. Thus, when he proposed their venturing against Huwawa to Enkidu, and Enkidu proved reluctant, he sternly upbraided his friend in just such terms:

Who, my friend, was ever so high
    (that he could)
rise up to heaven
    and lastingly dwell with Shamash?
Mere man, his days are numbered,

whatever he may do, he is but wind.
You are — already now — afraid of death.
What about the fine strength of your courage?
Let me lead,
and you (hanging back) can call out to me:
   "Close in, fear not!"
And if I fall I shall have founded fame
"Gilgamesh fell (they will say)
   in combat with terrible Huwawa"

He goes on imagining how in later years his children will climb on
Enkidu's knee, and how Enkidu will then tell them how bravely their
father fought and what a glorious death he died.

But all of this was when death was known to Gilgamesh only in the
abstract. Now, with the death of Enkidu, it touches him in all its stark
reality, and Gilgamesh refuses to believe it:

My friend, the swift mule,
   the wild ass of the mountain,
   the panther of the plain,
Enkidu, my friend, the swift mule,
   the wild ass of the mountain,
   the panther of the plain,
who with me could do all,
   who climbed the crags,
seized, killed the bull of heaven,
undid Huwawa dwelling in the cedar forest,
now — what sleep is this that seized you?
You have grown dark and cannot hear me!
But he was not raising his eyes,
(Gilgamesh) touched his heart,
   it was not beating.
Then he covered the face of his friend,
   as if he were a bride . . .
Like an eagle he was circling around him;
as does a lioness when (returning and) meeting its whelps,
he kept circling in front and back of his friend;
tearing the while his hair and scattering the tufts,
stripping and flinging down the finery off his body.

The loss he has suffered is unbearable. He refuses with all his soul to
accept it as real:

He who ever went through all hazards with me,
Enkidu whom I love dearly,
who ever went through all hazard with me,
the fate of man has overtaken him.
All day and night have I wept over him,

and would not have him buried —
as if my friend might yet rise up
   at my (loud) cries —
for seven days and nights,
until a maggot dropped from his nose.
Since he is gone I can no comfort find,
keep roaming like a hunter in the plains.

Death, fear of death, has become an obsession with Gilgamesh. He can
think of nothing else; the thought that he himself must die haunts him day
and night and leaves him no peace. He has heard about an ancestor of his,
Utanapishtim, who gained eternal life and now lives far away at the ends
of the world. He decides to go to him to learn the secret of immortality.

So Gilgamesh sets out on his quest. It takes him through the known
world to the mountains where the sun sets in the West. The gate the sun
enters is guarded by a huge scorpion man and his wife, but when Gilgamesh tells them of Enkidu's death and his quest for life, they take pity
on him and let him enter the tunnel into the mountains through which the
sun travels by night. For twelve double miles, then, Gilgamesh makes his
way through the dark tunnel; only as he nears the gate of sunrise at the
other end does he feel the wind on his face then at last sees the daylight
ahead. At the gate of sunrise is a wondrous garden in which the trees bear
jewels and precious stones as fruits, but its riches hold no temptation for
Gilgamesh whose heart is set on one thing only, not to die. Beyond the
gate lie vast deserts over which Gilgamesh roams, supporting himself by
killing wild bulls, eating their flesh, and dressing in their skin. To get
water he digs wells where wells never were before. Without any goal he
follows the prevailing winds. Shamash, the sun god — always the soul of
moderation — becomes vexed at seeing him thus, and he reasons with
Gilgamesh from the sky. But Gilgamesh will not listen to reason, he just
wants to live:

Is it (so) much — after wandering and roaming
   around in the desert —
to lie down to rest in the bowels of the
   earth?
I have lain down to sleep full many a time
   all the(se) years!
(No!) Let my eyes see the sun
   and let me sate myself with daylight!
Is darkness far off?
   How much daylight is there?
When may a dead man ever see the sun's splendor?

Roaming thus, Gilgamesh eventually comes to the shore of the sea that
encircles the earth and here he finds an inn kept by an alewife. His

unkempt looks and hide clothing frighten the alewife and she hastens to lock her door, thinking him a bandit. As Gilgamesh comes close, however, he tells her who he is and speaks of Enkidu who died and of his own quest for eternal life, the secret of which he hopes to learn from Utanapishtim. The alewife — as had Shamash — sees the hopelessness of his quest and tries to dissuade him:

> Gilgamesh, whither are you roaming?
> Life, which you look for, you shall
>   never find.
> (For) when the gods created man, they set
> death as share for man, and life
> snatched away in their own hands.
> You, Gilgamesh, fill your belly,
> day and night make merry,
> daily hold a festival,
> dance and make music day and night.
> And wear fresh clothes,
> and wash your head and bathe.
> Look at the child that is holding your hand,
> and let your wife delight in your embrace.
> These things alone are the concern of man.

But Gilgamesh cannot be reached:

> Why, my (good) alewife, do you talk thus?
> My heart is sick for my friend.
> Why, my (good) alewife, do you talk thus?
> My heart is sick for Enkidu!

and he asks her to tell him the way to Utanapishtim. She does so. The boatman of Utanapishtim, Urshanabi, happens to be on the mainland to cut timber, perhaps he will let Gilgamesh cross over with him. Gilgamesh finds him, but there are difficulties at first. Gilgamesh, it seems, has broken in anger the stone punting poles that Urshanabi uses to propel his boat across the waters of death, probably because Urshanabi did not immediately grant his request for passage. So now he has to cut a considerable number of wooden (and so perishable) punting poles needed to make up for the durable stone ones. But in the end he is taken across to the island on which Utanapishtim lives.

And so at long last, after incredible hardships, Gilgamesh has reached his goal. There on the shore of the island is his forbear Utanapishtim, and he can ask him how one obtains eternal life.

Yet, the moment Gilgamesh lays eyes on him, he senses that things are not quite what he had thought, something is subtly wrong:

> I look at you Utanapishtim,
> your proportions are not different,
>   you are just like me!
> Nor are you different,
>   you are just like me!
> My heart was all set
>   on doing battle with you,
> but you in idleness lie on your back.
> Tell me, how came you to stand
>   in the assembly of gods and seek life?

Utanapishtim then tells him the story of the flood, how he alone was warned by his lord Ea, built an ark and saved his family and pairs of all animals in it and eventually, after the flood, was granted eternal life by the gods as a reward for having saved human and animal life. It is the story of a unique event which will never recur, not a secret recipe or set of instructions for others to follow. It has no relevance for Gilgamesh and his situation, and so destroys utterly all basis for the hope that drove him on his quest:

> But for you, now, who will assemble
>   the gods for you,
> that you might find life, which you seek?

Utanapishtim leaves Gilgamesh no time to answer. Perhaps this is because he wishes to bring his point home through an object lesson, the contest with sleep that is to follow, perhaps it is merely an indication that the flood story was a not too skillful insertion in a shorter tale that originally had only the object lesson. At any rate, Utanapishtim immediately suggests to Gilgamesh that he try not to sleep for six days and seven nights. Gilgamesh accepts the challenge — a contest, it would seem, with Death's younger brother Sleep — but as he sits down Sleep sends a blast down over him and Utanapishtim sardonically says to his wife:

> Look at the strong man who craved life!
> Sleep is sending a blast down over him
>   like a rainstorm.

Utanapishtim's wife, however, takes pity on Gilgamesh, knowing that from this sleep he will never waken by himself, that fighting it is in fact fighting death; and she begs her husband to wake him, that he may go back in peace. Utanapishtim is not too keen. He knows only too well that man is by nature deceitful, and he expects that Gilgamesh will prove no exception. He therefore tells his wife to prepare food for Gilgamesh each day and to mark the days on the wall behind him. She does so, and on the seventh day Utanapishtim touches him and he wakes. His first words — as Utanapishtim had foreseen — are:

> As soon as sleep poured down over me
>   you quickly touched me
>   so that you awakened me.

but the marks on the wall and the food portions in various states of
staleness bear witness to a different truth. There is no hope, then, and
terror holds Gilgamesh in its grip more desperately than ever.

> Gilgamesh said to him, to the faraway Utanapishtim:
> "What can I do, Utanapishtim, where will I go?
> The one who followed behind me,
>   the rapacious one,
> sits in my bedroom, Death!
> And wherever I may turn my face,
>   there he is, Death!"

Utanapishtim has no solace to offer, only tells the boatman Urshanabi
to take Gilgamesh to a place where he can wash, and to give him clean
clothes for the return journey. These clothes will stay fresh until he gets
home. Then Gilgamesh and Urshanabi launch the boat once more, but as
they move off, the wife of Utanapishtim again intercedes for Gilgamesh,
asking her husband what he will give Gilgamesh now that, after so many
hardships, he is on his way home. Gilgamesh brings the boat back to shore
and Utanapishtim tells him of a thorny plant growing in the Apsû, the
sweet waters deep under the earth, which has power to rejuvenate. Its
name is "As Oldster Man Becomes Child." Gilgamesh, overjoyed, makes
haste to open the valve down to the Apsû, ties stones to his feet, as do the
pearl divers in Bahrein, to drag him down, finds the plant and plucks it,
through it stings his hand, cuts loose the stones, and lets the flood carry
him up and cast him ashore. Delighted, he shows the plant to Urshanabi
— both, apparently, are now on the shore of the Persian Gulf rather than
at Utanapishtim's island — and tells him of its qualities and how he is
taking it back to Uruk where he will eat it when he grows old and thus
return to childhood.

But the weather is warm and as he travels back Gilgamesh sees an
inviting, cool pond, doffs his clothes, and goes in to bathe. A serpent
smells the odor of the plant which he has left with his clothes, comes out of
its hole, snatches, and eats it. As it disappears again into its hole it sloughs
off its old skin and emerges new and shiny and young.

This spells the end of Gilgamesh's quest. It has come to nothing. The
serpent, not he, has obtained the power of rejuvenation. And so at last he
has to admit defeat, final and utter defeat:

> On that day Gilgamesh sat down and wept,
> tears streaming down his cheeks:
> "For whose sake, Urshanabi, did my arms tire?

> For whose sake has my heart's blood been spent?
> I brought no blessing on myself,
> I did the serpent underground good service!"

The mood in which he meets this final defeat, however, is new and other than what he has been capable of before; it is one of composure, one of resignation, even humorous, self-ironical resignation, not of terror and despair. It is a mood not unlike Dryden's:

> Since ev'ry man who lives is born to die,
> And none can boast sincere felicity,
> With equal mind, what happens, let us bear,
> Nor joy nor grieve too much
>   for things beyond our care.
> Like pilgrims to th' appointed place we tend;
> The world's an inn, and death the journey's end.[346]

This late and dearly won resignation, this acceptance of reality, finds symbolic expression in the epic in a return to where we began, to the walls of Uruk which stand for all time as Gilgamesh's lasting achievement. Man may have to die, but what he does lives after him. There is a measure of immortality in achievement, the only immortality man can seek.

And so, when Gilgamesh finally arrives home, his first act is to show the walls to Urshanabi.

> Gilgamesh said to the boatman, Urshanabi:
> "Go up, Urshanabi, on the wall of Uruk,
>   walk around!
> Examine the terrace, look closely at the
>   brickwork!
> Is not the base of its brickwork of baked
>   brick?
> Have not seven masters laid its foundations?
> An acre town and an acre orchards,
> an acre riverbed,
>   also precinct of the Ishtar temple.
> Three acres and the precinct comprises Uruk."

This ends the story.

Sources

To clarify to ourselves what this ancient story is about and what its author was driving at, we may profitably ask two fundamental questions, one about sources and another about the theme. The question about sources asks what the author had to work with or — if the Old Babylonian fragments do not yet represent an epic, merely a cycle of tales — within what frame of reference, within what world of traditional Gilgamesh lore, the telling of these tales moved. The question about theme probes further. It asks what the author (or authors) did with those materials: how they were aimed, what meanings were seen in them or given to them. What made them the stuff of poetry?

The sources — what is known about them or can be surmised — we have tried to present succinctly in a diagram headed "Gilgamesh Tradition." It begins with the "historical Gilgamesh," a ruler of Uruk at circa 2600 B.C., in the period known as Early Dynastic II. The reason we assume that the Gilgamesh traditions cluster around an actual historical figure is that the tradition seems to be remarkably informed about the period with which it deals. Personages encountered in the episodes, such as Enmebaragesi, the father of Agga of Kish, mentioned in the tale "Gilgamesh and Agga," have been proved to be historical by contemporary inscriptions.[347] The name Gilgamesh itself is composed of elements that were current in proper names at that time, but fell out of use later; the custom of burying a ruler's court with him when he died, implied in the tale of "The Death of Gilgamesh," is actually known to us from the only slightly younger Royal Tombs at Ur, after which time it was abandoned.

As ruler of Uruk in the Early Dynastic period the historical Gilgamesh would have had the title of e n and would have united in his person the two distinct aspects of that office, magical and martial, which we have called on the chart respectively, the Heros and the Hero aspects.

The magical, or Heros, aspect of the office of e n we have touched upon earlier, in our discussion of the yearly rite of the sacred marriage, in which a human e n priest or priestess married a deity. In Uruk, the e n was male and was the ruler of the city. In the rite he took on the identity of Dumuzi-Amaushumgalanna and married the goddess Inanna, or Ishtar. Their union magically ensured fertility and plenty for all. As shown by the famous Uruk Vase on which the rite is pictured, it was celebrated in that city as early as Protoliterate times.

The magic powers of the e n were not limited to his ritual role in the sacred marriage. They belonged to him in his own right and continued to be effective after his death when he dwelt in the underworld, in the earth from which emanated the powers that made trees and plants, orchards, fields, and pasturage all grow and thrive. Notably successful e n priests, in whose time there had been years of plenty, continued, therefore, to be worshiped with funerary offerings after their death to insure that they would continue their blessings. The historical Gilgamesh, we may assume, was such a figure, credited with the power to produce plentiful years and continuing to be worshiped after his death. Our first tangible indication that this was so comes from account texts from Girsu of around 2400 B.C. They show that funerary offerings for successful dead e n priests and

Gilgamesh Tradition

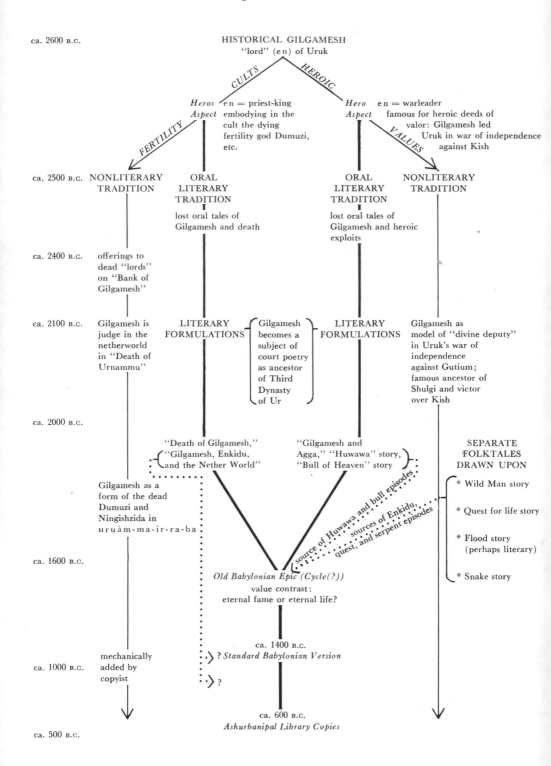

ca. 2600 B.C.
HISTORICAL GILGAMESH
"lord" (e n) of Uruk

CULTS　　　*HEROIC*

Heros Aspect e n = priest-king embodying in the cult the dying fertility god Dumuzi, etc.

Hero Aspect e n = warleader famous for heroic deeds of valor: Gilgamesh led Uruk in war of independence against Kish

FERTILITY　　　*VALUES*

ca. 2500 B.C. NONLITERARY TRADITION　ORAL LITERARY TRADITION　ORAL LITERARY TRADITION　NONLITERARY TRADITION

lost oral tales of Gilgamesh and death

lost oral tales of Gilgamesh and heroic exploits

ca. 2400 B.C. offerings to dead "lords" on "Bank of Gilgamesh"

ca. 2100 B.C. Gilgamesh is judge in the netherworld in "Death of Urnammu"　LITERARY FORMULATIONS　{ Gilgamesh becomes a subject of court poetry as ancestor of Third Dynasty of Ur }　LITERARY FORMULATIONS　Gilgamesh as model of "divine deputy" in Uruk's war of independence against Gutium; famous ancestor of Shulgi and victor over Kish

ca. 2000 B.C.

"Death of Gilgamesh," "Gilgamesh, Enkidu, and the Nether World"　"Gilgamesh and Agga," "Huwawa" story, "Bull of Heaven" story　SEPARATE FOLKTALES DRAWN UPON

Gilgamesh as a form of the dead Dumuzi and Ningishzida in u r u à m - m a - i r - r a - b a

* Wild Man story

* Quest for life story

source of Huwawa and bull episodes

sources of Enkidu, quest, and serpent episodes

* Flood story (perhaps literary)

ca. 1600 B.C.

* Snake story

Old Babylonian Epic (Cycle(?))
value contrast: eternal fame or eternal life?

ca. 1400 B.C.
? *Standard Babylonian Version*

ca. 1000 B.C. mechanically added by copyist　?

ca. 600 B.C.
Ashurbanipal Library Copies

ca. 500 B.C.

other figures credited with fertility powers were made at a sacred locality called "The (River-)Bank of Gilgamesh." [348] Further evidence of Gilgamesh's prominence as a power in the netherworld comes in a composition of about 2100 B.C. dealing with the death of the first king of the Third Dynasty of Ur, Urnammu.[349] Here Gilgamesh appears as a judge in the realm of the dead. He occurs again in that role much later, in magical texts of the first millennium, where he is appealed to for judgment against wayward ghosts and other evils.[350] Lastly, copies of laments, which may have been composed in the first half of the second millennium, mention Gilgamesh as a form of the dying god Dumuzi side by side with the god Ningishzida.[351]

It is clear, thus, that there was a vigorous and continuous nonliterary religious tradition arising from the magical aspect of the historical Gilgamesh's office as e n.

The martial aspect of the office of e n implies that the historical Gilgamesh must have headed the army of Uruk, and here again the fact that traditions cluster around his name suggests that he was a military leader of extraordinary stature. Whether the later literary tradition celebrating him as leader in a war of liberation against Kish actually contains a historical kernel is not easy to say, though it is not implausible. At any rate, the role of liberator ascribed to him would seem to be the reason why the god Dumuzi-Amaushumgalanna chose to model himself on Gilgamesh when he served as divine deputy with the army of Uruk in a later war of independence, the one against the hated Gutian mountaineers in about 2100 B.C. Utuhegal, who led that army to victory, tells us in his inscription how he reported this decision of Dumuzi-Amaushumgalanna to his troops in a speech to them when they set out.[352]

The tradition about Gilgamesh's war with Kish is referred to also in a royal hymn written for Shulgi of Ur[353] only a generation or so after Utuhegal, and another military achievement, the building of the city walls of Uruk, is ascribed to him in a tradition attested to around 1800 B.C. in an inscription of the ruler Anam who made repairs on them.[354]

Against the background of these two nonliterary lines of tradition, one about a power for fertility in the netherworld (the Heros line), one about a famed warrior and wall builder of old (the Hero line), we may then set what we might call the literary development. Of its beginnings we know nothing at all, but we may surmise a body of oral tales and songs handed down and lost to us, except as they furnished material for later written compositions.

It seems such written compositions appear[355] first with the accession of the Third Dynasty of Ur around 2100 B.C. The kings of that dynasty not only took great interest in literature and the preservation of old works generally, but considered themselves descendants of Gilgamesh, so that

traditions and works about him would have special claim to their attention. What we have preserved (almost all in later copies) are separate short
epic compositions in Sumerian, and they divide quite neatly into the
Heros and Hero lines of tradition, with works where Gilgamesh confronts
the problem of death and works celebrating his martial prowess. Among
the former is the tale called "The Death of Gilgamesh,"[356] which tells how
death came to him in due time, how he violently protested, and how Enlil
himself personally argued with him that there was no way for man to
avoid it. The story is known to us only in fragments and its full meaning
may only become clear through future lucky finds. Another Gilgamesh
story concerned with death is called "Gilgamesh, Enkidu, and the
Netherworld."[357] It tells how in the beginning of time the goddess
Inanna, wandering along the banks of the Euphrates, found a tree floating
on it, pulled it ashore, and planted it with the hope that when it grew to
maturity she could have a table and a bed made from its wood. The tree
grew apace, and when it had reached the proper size Inanna wished to fell
it but found that the thunderbird Imdugud had built its nest in the crown,
the demoness Kiskillilla had made her abode in its trunk, and a huge
serpent nestled at its root. Poor Inanna, therefore, could not get to her
tree and appealed to her brother Utu, the sun god, for help, but he
refused. She then turned to Gilgamesh, who gallantly took up arms and
drove the intruders away, felled the tree, gave her its wood for a table and
a bed, and made for himself a puck and stick — for a game which seems to
have resembled modern hockey — out of its roots. Uruk played and
feasted, celebrating the victory, and all were happy except a poor waif, a
little girl who had neither father, mother, or brother, and felt left out and
lost. In her anguish she cried out to the sun god, the god of justice and
fairness, with the dread "i - U t u," and he heard her. The earth opened
and the playthings Gilgamesh had made for himself fell down into the
netherworld as a reproof to the thoughtless revelers. Gilgamesh was
disconsolate and Enkidu rashly offered to bring them back up. Accordingly, Gilgamesh gave him elaborate instructions about how to conduct
himself in the netherworld, to be very quiet, not to call attention to himself
by wearing fine clothes and anointing himself, not to show emotion by
kissing the dead child and wife he had loved or striking the dead child or
wife he had hated. As it turned out, Enkidu did all these things and the
netherworld held him fast. Gilgamesh appealed to the gods but all they
could do for him was to open a vent to allow Enkidu's ghost to come up to
speak with him. The friends embraced, and at Gilgamesh's questioning
Enkidu told in detail what the netherworld was like. Conditions were
dismal, although there were gradations of misery. Those with large
families, those who fell in battle, those who had lived a good life, were
better treated than the rest. But no clear general principles of a moral or
ethical nature seem to have governed the infernal regions.

Among the compositions belonging to the Hero line of the tradition are, first of all, "Gilgamesh and Agga of Kish,"[358] a short Sumerian composition which tells how Gilgamesh led Uruk in a war of freedom against Kish. After Uruk had refused to do the usual corvée work, Agga's shipborne troops appeared before its walls and began a siege. A first sortie by the warrior Birhurturra proved unsuccessful. A second by Enkidu and Gilgamesh cut its way to Agga's boat and took him captive. The story raises intricate problems of heroic honor and loyalty. Gilgamesh had at one time, it appears, been a fugitive whom Agga received kindly. In fact, it would seem likely that it was Agga who made Gilgamesh his vassal ruler in Uruk, the position from which Gilgamesh now foments a rebellion against him. As a true hero, Gilgamesh cannot bear to owe anything to the largess of another, but must win what he has through his own prowess in battle, must prove himself by defeating Agga. Only after he has taken Agga captive can he acknowledge his debt to him: he sets him free and of his own free will promises to recognize him as overlord. The largess is now his: he is repaying the good turn Agga originally did him and is no more in his debt.

Gilgamesh's Hero aspect also dominates the Sumerian tale about his expedition against Huwawa which we have in two different versions, one elaborate, the other brief.[359] The adventure is undertaken so that Gilgamesh may establish a name for himself, but the tale differs from the one about Agga in its more romantic, almost fairy tale setting. Unlike Agga, who is an entirely human opponent, Huwawa seems more ogre than warrior. Altogether mythical in character, finally, is the Sumerian tale about "Gilgamesh, Inanna, and the Bull of Heaven."[360] Here, as in the corresponding episode in the epic,[361] Gilgamesh's valor is pitted against a deity and a mythical monster.

As will be seen, then, the two lines of the Gilgamesh tradition find literary expression in compositions showing diametrically opposed attitudes toward death. In the Hero tales death is almost recklessly courted by the hero: to repay Agga and no longer feel in his debt, to establish a name by killing Huwawa, to stand up to Inanna. In the Heros tales death is the great unavoidable evil: "the darkness that cannot be resisted has arrived for you,"[362] Gilgamesh is told in the "Death of Gilgamesh." "If I instructed you about the netherworld, you sitting down weeping, I would want to sit down and weep,"[363] Enkidu tells him in "Gilgamesh, Enkidu, and the Netherworld." These contradictory attitudes united in the person of Gilgamesh prefigure, as it were, what was to become the theme of the later epic: the change from an earlier disdain for death to the obsessive fear of it which drives Gilgamesh on his quest after Enkidu's death.

If we ask more specifically which parts of the Sumerian literary Gilgamesh tradition were used in the epic we would point to the Huwawa story and the "Gilgamesh, Inanna, and the Bull of Heaven" story as obvious prototypes of the corresponding episodes in the epic. Both of these episodes are represented in the Old Babylonian materials. No Sumerian prototypes, on the other hand, have been found for the "Coming of Enkidu" and the "Quest for Life" episodes, which also are part of the Old Babylonian materials; and it may in fact be doubted whether these tales ever did form part of the Sumerian Gilgamesh tradition. The likelihood is that they came from elsewhere.

In the case of the "Coming of Enkidu" tale, the motif of the hairy wild man who lives with the animals and is lured into human society by a woman is found in many forms in the folklore of Asia, and has been studied in detail by Charles Allyn Williams in his dissertation, *Oriental Affinities of the Legend of the Hairy Anchorite* (Urbana, 1925–26). His data show that the basis of the story is wonder at the orangutan, which was seen as a "wild man" deliberately shunning the company of other men. Its origin must therefore be looked for in the Far East.

The motif of the "Quest for Life" is also well known outside Mesopotamia. We find it in the story of "The Water of Life" in Grimm's *Hausmärchen*, which tells about a dying king whose three sons set out to find the water of life to revive him. Only the youngest son, helped by animals to whom he has been kind, succeeds in reaching the island where the water of life is and bringing it back. He also, of course, wins a princess and, after further trials, lives happily ever after.

Lastly, there is the motif of the serpent stealing the plant of rejuvenation. This motif has been convincingly traced to Melanesian and Annam folklore by Julian Morgenstern in a study called "On Gilgamesh — Epic XI" in *Zeitschrift fur Assyriologie* 29, pp. 284–300.

At what time these Far Eastern folktale motifs spread to Mesopotamia is not easy to determine. The first two must have been there in Old Babylonian times, as shown by the Gilgamesh materials, and there is no reason to assume that they had come in earlier. Why they were drawn into the Gilgamesh tradition is a further puzzle. The simplest answer — which can of course be no more than a surmise — is clearly to assume that the Old Babylonian materials do indeed belong to an epic, the author of which obtained his theme from the contrastive attitudes to death in the Gilgamesh tradition but supplemented his materials with other tales he knew that would serve to develop it. If one would see, rather, the Old Babylonian materials as representing merely a loose cycle of independent tales, it becomes more difficult to imagine what, if anything, about these tales could have made anybody think they referred to Gilgamesh.

If we are right in surmising the existence of an Old Babylonian Epic of Gilgamesh, that epic would almost certainly have been shorter than the version credited to Sîn-liqi-unninī from perhaps the end of the second millennium, and that shorter again than the version in twelve tablets we have from the library of Ashurbanipal. To begin with the latter, the twelfth tablet is a mechanical addition of an Akkadian translation of the last half of "Gilgamesh, Enkidu, and the Netherworld," a tale which has no organic connection with the rest of the epic. The adding on has indeed been done so mechanically that the first lines make no sense and can only be understood in the light of those parts of the original story which were dropped when it was attached to the Gilgamesh Epic. Without this addition — which seems more the work of a copyist than an editor — the epic shows a frame: it begins and ends with the same hymn in praise of the walls of Uruk. Probably this was the form Sîn-liqi-unninī gave it, and to his version belongs probably also the long account of the flood which is put in the mouth of Utanapishtim and which takes up almost half of the eleventh tablet. That it belongs with the frame is suggested by the stress which the introduction to the epic places upon it, for in a passage omitted in our retelling of the story the introduction lists as one of Gilgamesh's achievements that he brought back information from before the flood. On the other hand the unwieldy length of the flood story, which badly upsets the flow and balance of the quest narrative, and the fact that it duplicates — in fact renders meaningless — the following contest of Gilgamesh with Sleep, strongly suggests that it is an addition and not part of the original story. Its source is obviously the tradition about the flood represented both by the Sumerian flood story and the elaborate account in the Atrahasīs Myth. In neither of these settings, of course, does the flood have any relation to the traditional Gilgamesh materials. Probably, therefore, we should imagine the Old Babylonian epic (or story of the quest) as not yet having it — at least not at such length — and assume that it was included because of its intrinsic interest by Sîn-liqi-unninī in his version.

Structural Analysis: Themes

The question about the sources of the Gilgamesh Epic, which led us back to a historical Gilgamesh, e n of Uruk and point of origin for two lines of tradition with contrasting attitudes toward death, suggests that precisely in this contrast lay, *in nuce*, the central theme of the later epic. The further question about how that theme was developed, what the author did with his materials and how he focused them, is perhaps best asked in terms of Sîn-liqi-unninī's version. It may be phrased either in positive terms as a quest for achieving immortality or in negative terms, as a flight, an attempt to avoid death. In the accompanying diagram we have indicated progress toward the story goals by upward movement of the story curve, and shown hindrance by a downward turn.

As the story begins Gilgamesh shares the heroic values of his times, and

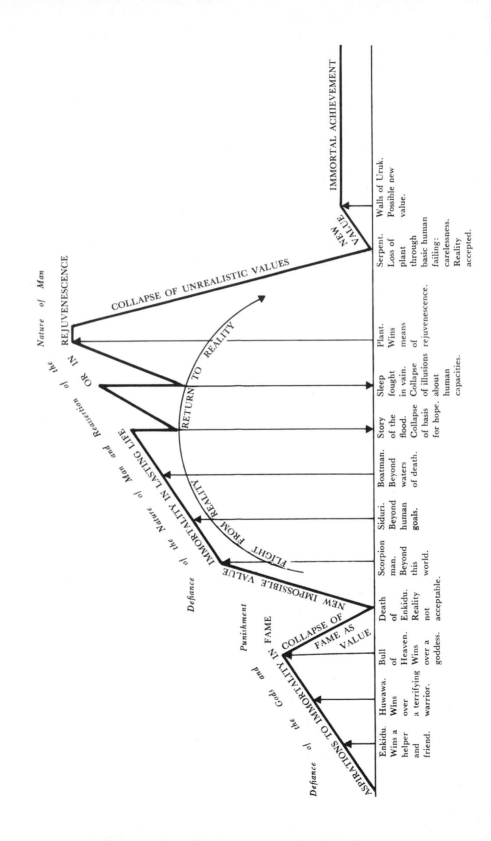

his aspirations to immortality take the form of a quest for immortal fame. Death is not yet truly the enemy; it is unavoidable of course but somehow part of the game: a glorious death against a worthy opponent will cause one's name to live forever. In his pursuit of this goal Gilgamesh is extraordinarily successful and scores one gain after another. He fights Enkidu and gains a friend and helper. Together they are strong enough to overcome the famed Huwawa and to treat with disdain the city goddess of Uruk, Ishtar. At that point they have undoubtedly reached the pinnacle of human fame. And at that point their luck changes. In ruthlessly asserting themselves and seeking ever new ways to prove their prowess they have grievously offended the gods, paying no heed to them whatever. Huwawa was the servant of Enlil, appointed by him to guard the cedar forest; their treatment of Ishtar was the height of arrogance. Now the gods' displeasure catches up with them, and Enkidu dies.

When he loses his friend, Gilgamesh for the first time comprehends death in all its stark reality. And with that new comprehension comes the realization that eventually he himself will die. With that all his previous values collapse: an enduring name and immortal fame suddenly mean nothing to him any more. Dread, inconquerable fear of death holds him in its grip; he is obsessed with its terror and the desirability, nay, the necessity of living forever. Real immortality — an impossible goal — is the only thing Gilgamesh can now see.

Here, then, begins a new quest: not for immortality in fame, but for immortality, literally, in the flesh. As with his former quest for fame Gilgamesh's heroic stature and indomitable purpose take him from one success to another. Setting out to find his ancestor, Utanapishtim, in order to learn how to achieve, like him, eternal life, he gains the help of the scorpion man and his wife, Sidûri, the alewife, and Urshanabi. When after great travail he stands before Utanapishtim it is only to have the whole basis for his hopes collapse. The story of the flood shows that the case of Utanapishtim was unique and can never happen again and — to make his point — Utanapishtim's challenging him to resist sleep, proves how utterly impossible is his hope for vigor strong enough to overcome death.

However, at the point of the seemingly total and irreversible failure of his quest, new hope is unexpectedly held out to Gilgamesh. Moved by pity, Utanapishtim's wife asks her husband to give Gilgamesh a parting gift for his journey home, and Utanapishtim reveals a secret. Down in the fresh watery deep grows a plant that will make an oldster into a child again. Gilgamesh dives down and plucks the plant. He has his wish. He holds life in his hand. Any time he grows old he can again return to childhood and begin life anew. Then on the way back there is the inviting pool and the serpent who snatches the plant when he carelessly leaves it on the bank.

Gilgamesh's first quest for immortality in fame defied the gods and brought their retribution on him; this quest for actual immortality is even more deeply defiant; it defies human nature itself, the very condition of being human, finite, mortal. And in the end it is Gilgamesh's own human nature that reasserts itself; it is a basic human weakness, a moment of carelessness, that defeats him. He has nobody to blame but himself; he has ingloriously blundered. And it is perhaps this very lack of heroic stature in his failure that brings him to his senses. The panic leaves him, he sees himself as pitiful and weeps; then as the irony of the situation strikes him, he can smile at himself. His superhuman efforts have produced an almost comical result. This smile, this saving sense of humor, is the sign that he has, at last, come through. He is finally able to accept reality and with it a new possible scale of value: the immortality he now seeks, in which he now takes pride, is the relative immortality of lasting achievement, as symbolized by the walls of Uruk.

The movement from heroic idealism to the everyday courage of realism illustrated by the Gilgamesh story gains further in depth if one analyzes it not only positively as a quest, but also negatively as a flight, an avoidance. A flight from death rather than a quest for life — but a flight in what terms?

Throughout the epic Gilgamesh appears as young, a mere boy, and he holds on to that status, refusing to exchange it for adulthood as represented by marriage and parenthood. Like Barrie's Peter Pan he will not grow up.* His first meeting with Enkidu is a rejection of marriage for a boyhood friendship, and in the episode of the bull of heaven he refuses—

---

* Note Harry Stack Sullivan, *The Interpersonal Theory of Psychiatry* (New York, 1953), p. 245: "The beginning of preadolescence is equally spectacularly marked, in my scheme of development, by the appearance of a new type of interest in another person. . . . This new interest in the preadolescent era is . . . a specific new type of interest in a *particular* member of the same sex who becomes a chum or a close friend. This change represents the beginning of something very like full-blown, psychiatrically defined *love*. In other words, the other fellow takes on a perfectly novel relationship with the person concerned: he becomes of practically equal importance in all fields of value." And ibid., p. 264: ". . . the change from preadolescence to adolescence appears as a growing interest in the possibilities of achieving some measure of intimacy with a member of the other sex, rather after the pattern of the intimacy that one has in preadolescence enjoyed with a member of one's own sex."

The appearance of Enkidu provides Gilgamesh with a "chum" and allows him to remain in preadolescence rather than moving on to a heterosexual relationship such as is characteristic of adolescence and adulthood. Note that in explaining Gilgamesh's dream about Enkidu's arrival his mother says (Gilgamesh Epic Tablet I vi 17–20; cf. Pennsylvania Tablet i. 39–ii. 1): "The axe you saw is a man, you will love him as (you would) a wife, so that I will make him your compeer" and that at his arrival Enkidu prevents Gilgamesh's marriage to Ishhara (Pennsylvania Tablet v; cf. Landsberger, "Jungfräulichkeit," pp. 83–84). Also when he rejects the adult goal of marriage and children urged by the alewife he does so in terms of his attachment to Enkidu: "Why, my (good) alewife do you talk thus? / My heart is sick for my friend! / Why, my (good) alewife do you talk thus? / My heart is sick for Enkidu!" Throughout the epic the relationship with Enkidu competes with, and replaces, marriage.

almost unnecessarily violently — Ishtar's proposal of marriage. She spells disaster and death to him. So when Enkidu dies, he does not move forward seeking a new companionship in marriage, but backward in an imaginary flight toward the security of childhood. At the gate of the scorpion man he leaves reality; he passes literally "out of this world." In the encounter with the alewife he again firmly rejects marriage and children as an acceptable goal, and eventually, safely navigating the waters of death, he reaches the ancestors, the father and mother figures of Utanapishtim and his wife, on their island where, as in childhood, age and death do not exist. True to his images, Utanapishtim sternly attempts to make Gilgamesh grow up to responsibility; he proposes an object lesson, the contest with sleep, and is ready to let Gilgamesh face the consequences. The wife of Utanapishtim, as mother, is more indulgent, willing for Gilgamesh to remain a child, and she eventually makes it possible for him to reach his goal with the plant "As Oldster Man Becomes Child." Gilgamesh is fleeing death by fleeing old age, even maturity; he is reaching back to security in childhood. The loss of the plant stands thus for the loss of the illusion that one can go back to being a child. It brings home the necessity for growing up, for facing and accepting reality. And in the loss Gilgamesh for the first time can take himself less seriously, even smile ruefully at himself; he has at last become mature.

> For whose sake, Urshanabi, did my arms tire?
> For whose sake has my heart's blood been spent?
> I brought no blessing on myself,
> I did the serpent underground good service!

The Gilgamesh Epic is a story about growing up.

Epilogue

A wall relief of Assyrian soldiers returning from a raid with captives—men, women, and children. The relief is from Sennacherib's palace, Ninevah.

In terms of insight and depth, the second millennium B.C. can rightly be said to mark the high point of ancient Mesopotamian religious achievement. The millennium that followed contributed no major new insights, rather, it brought in many ways decline and brutalization. With the second millennium, therefore, we may appropriately end our presentation and leave it to an epilogue to summarize what those religious achievements were and to outline how they fared in the course of the first millennium with which ancient Mesopotamian civilization itself came to an end.

Assessment of Second Millennium Religious Achievement

The Great Critiques

To sum up what the second millennium achieved, one must point, of course, to the myths and epics, to which it gave rise but even more so to its lighting upon a new, profound religious metaphor, the parent metaphor that was truly and vividly suggestive of essential elements in the human response to numinous experience.

The great existential myths and epics, the critiques in which man took stock of himself and the universe around him, are "The Story of Atrahasīs," the Gilgamesh Epic, and Enûma elish. Each in its own way considers traditional attitudes — evaluating, modifying, rejecting, or wholeheartedly embracing them.

"The Story of Atrahasīs" comes to grips with some of the oldest attitudes in the religious heritage. It examines man's relations to nature in a mood keenly aware that the powers on which he depends for his life may not only die and disappear, leaving him orphaned or widowed, but can show themselves unfriendly and willful. In epidemics and famines one may even discern a will to hold man's numbers down, a will that could lead to his extinction in a cataclysm like a general flood.

This will, the god Enlil and his power to bring about something as staggeringly immense as the flood, paradoxically does not alienate man. It holds an odd and perverse fascination for him, for "In the human soul . . . Power awakens a profound feeling of awe which manifests itself both as fear and as being attracted."[364] Thus "The Story of Atrahasīs," on the deepest level, is well aware that it is told in praise of the adversary, Enlil, awed at the power he can unleash, however much on the surface it may seem to shortchange him. It becomes a critique and an adjustment of that simple attitude of human solidarity with the powers of nature that generally characterizes the fertility cults, it brings into play the growing insight into power — and so into the ambivalence of tremendum — that had come with the third millennium ruler metaphor.

Compared to this, the surface play of the story, the clever maneuvering of the weak (Enki and man) to avoid destruction, is almost trivial. Man has but one immediate recourse: increased devotion, the massing of offerings and services in the hope that so much loyalty and attachment will shame the power directly involved and make him desist. There is likewise only one long-range solution: man is a servant and as a servant has to "know his place." He must see to it that he does not come unpleasantly to the notice of his masters — if only by multiplying and being too much in evidence; he must exercise a prudent self-restraint, avoiding all excesses. The motto of the story could have been that of Delphi: μηδὲν ἄγαν ("Nothing in excess").

The Early Dynastic period at the beginning of the third millennium was, as we suggested, a "heroic period" in which war — the war of all against all — became the order of the day. In those parlous circumstances man tended to look to human martial prowess for salvation, and the idea of the human hero — subject of the epic and the heroic tale — tempted him to rely on man and human feats rather than on the gods for salvation. This trend is recognizable in much of the early Gilgamesh materials and finds its exemplar in Naramsîn of Agade, of whom warning tales were told at a later date.

The Akkadian Gilgamesh Epic of the second millennium — like the Sumerian and Akkadian tales about Naramsîn — takes this heroic attitude of human self-reliance to task. As we have indicated, the sources for the Akkadian Gilgamesh Epic go back in part to traditions that come down from well into the Early Dynastic period and are imbued with the heroic outlook of those times: the Huwawa tradition, for instance, and the story of the "Bull of Heaven." The second millennium critique — clearly born of experience — not only mercilessly collapses the self-reliant, death-defiant, heroic mood (the death of Enkidu makes death real), it also vigorously contests the opposite attitude of excessive fear of death, an attitude which — with paranoiac overtones — assumes a quixotically heroic stance in a quest for an impossible goal: life everlasting.

Thus, in its own way the Gilgamesh Epic comes to conclusions much like those of the Atrahasîs story: "nothing in excess" or, with Dryden, "nor joy nor grieve too much for things beyond our care." [365] It is, curiously enough, not inappropriate to quote Dryden for the Gilgamesh Epic in its final version. Despite its sources, it is as rationalistic and antiheroic as *Palamon and Arcite.*[366] As one commentator put it in speaking of the serpent episode: "here the author betrays his hero." He does so, though, because he is committed to sanity and normalcy. He speaks to us throughout his work in the voice of the sun god urging in all things balance, fairness, the seeing of both sides, and nothing extreme.

Though he speaks so freely with the tongue of a god, the author of the late Gilgamesh Epic does not quite manage to make his work a religious document. He warns in its first part against that hubris that invites divine retribution and in its latter part against challenging the nature of things. This latter challenge, as one listens, seems more real, less literary: the late Gilgamesh Epic is a refutation of human hubris, not in religious terms, but rationalistically by an ancient humanist.

The tendency to trust in human prowess, which still echoes in the Gilgamesh Epic, was countered early in the third millennium by a transfer of the heroic image to the world of the gods, thus creating the characteristic religious metaphor of that millennium: the Numinous as ruler. Enûma elish, the third great existential critique, deals with that metaphor. Enûma elish is a committed critique. In it the concept of rulership (specifically, monarchy) is embraced unquestioningly and is seen as the unifying and ordering principle to which all existence conforms and by way of which existence may be understood.

In tracing the implication of the ruler metaphor, explaining how the cosmic monarchy came into being and in describing his hero, Marduk, the author of Enûma elish is at pains to stress both the fascinosum and the tremendum aspects of the metaphor — the benefits monarchy conveys no less than the respect and awe the monarch commands. If anything, the benefits are perhaps a bit too much in evidence: terrors and dangers are all overcome, no more a threat to anybody. There is little of that fascinated horror before powers of nature that one feels in Atrahasīs in the accounts of famines and the flood, or at the divine destruction by force of arms in the great "Lament for Ur" of the previous millennium. In part this may be because of the determinedly theocentric viewpoint of the story. Man plays no role except as one of several benefactions for the gods, a drudge to free them from work with no standing in and for himself. Form and function of the universe, not the finite human situation, is the author's theme.

The New Metaphor

Atrahasīs, the Gilgamesh Epic, and Enûma elish all deal with ways of religious understanding developed earlier — in particular with the provider and ruler metaphors of the preceding millennia. They test these metaphors and their implications in dramatic narratives that let the listener — vicariously — have vivid, trenchant experience of them. Frequently they invite special attitudes toward them and judgments of them, modify, or accept; and in all of this they intellectually and emotionally refine and explore to the limit the capacities inherent in them. But on the most basic level they do not add anything new.

The truly new, the fundamentally new achievement of the second millennium was its genius in lighting upon a new metaphor truly suggestive of essential elements in the human response to numinous experience. This parent metaphor, which saw the Numinous as a father or a mother, significantly enhanced and deepened the sense of fascinosum that was present already in the worship of the fertility gods, was paradoxically sensed behind the tremendum in Atrahasīs, and more rationalistically in the benefits of divine monarchy in Enûma elish. It enhanced and deepened it by recognizing and expressing a personal relationship to the divine, a sense of attraction being reciprocal. Man, who under the ruler metaphor was subject and slave, gained sonship.

The parent metaphor adds a new dimension also to the sense of tremendum by seeing it in tension with underlying love as in a stern but loving father; and eventually this new metaphor precipitated man into the religious dilemma of mysterium through the problem of the just sufferer, which it posed in such an acute form: inescapable confrontation with the wholly other in the Numinous, incommensurable with anything else, incommensurable in the last analysis even with human moral and ethical rules. It compelled what Sapir saw as the essence of religion, the "haunting realization of ultimate powerlessness in an inscrutable world, and the unquestioning and thoroughly irrational conviction of the possibility of gaining mystic security by somehow identifying oneself with what can never be known." [367]

First Millennium

Powers of Death

The first millennium that followed began badly:

> The mounting tide of Aramean invasion, the desperate efforts made by the Assyrians to dam it up, the irremediable decadence of Babylon, Sumer and Akkad wide open to the Sutu, and the Arameans, foreign wars, civil wars, floods, famine, such is the pitiful picture offered by Iraq during the tenth and ninth centuries B.C.[368]

A world, barely livable before, had now collapsed and become rank jungle.

In thoroughly disturbed times like these — as we have noted before — men in their despair are apt to turn to force for salvation, to the warlike hero, and the turn of the millennium produced a heroic epic celebrating the prowess of Tukulti-Ninurta I, much as in Early Dynastic times similar conditions had given rise to the heroic traditions about Gilgamesh.

The trend to trust in human prowess alone had been countered in Early Dynastic times, we suggested, by a complete transfer of the image of the human king and hero to the gods, a transfer that gave rise to the religious metaphor characterizing the third millennium, the ruler metaphor. In the first millennium something similar and yet oddly different took place. Here too, the image of the warrior king and hero was applied to the gods; but where the third millennium had idealized the heroic image as protector and ruler, the first millennium does almost the opposite: it sees the warrior not as a protector but as a threat, a wild man, a killer, dangerous to friend and foe alike, part and parcel of the turmoil, even a prime cause of it — to be appeased, if at all, by abject flattery of his frightfulness. Accordingly, as this image is applied to the gods, it is the divine that conforms down to the image rather than the image that rises up to approach the divine. The god of riot and indiscriminate slaughter, Erra, moves into a position of central importance; he fits the picture of a will to make the world what it now has become and he is given supreme command.

The work telling how he was ceded these powers, the Erra Epic,[369] was revealed to its author, one Kabti-ilī-Marduk, in a dream not long after 1000 B.C. and may not have been orthodox doctrine everywhere. Numerous copies of the epic, or parts of it, however, are eloquent testimony to its popularity and the spread of its teachings, so that in many ways it must have been generally representative of popular contemporary attitudes.

The god, Erra — originally seemingly an Akkadian god of "scorched earth," raids and riots[370] — was in the first millennium identified with Nergal, god of war and sudden death and the ruler of the realm of the dead.

The epic tells how he was roused from dalliance with his wife by his weapon, the "heptad" or "seven gods," who wanted to go on a campaign, how he managed to fast-talk Marduk — depicted as an old fuddy-duddy — into leaving him in charge of the universe while Marduk went off to have his crown jewels cleaned, and how Erra then settled down to stir things up. Taking human shape as an agitator, he began fomenting rebellion in Babylon, getting its citizens, unskilled in the use of weapons, to take to arms as best they could:

> The citizens of Babylon, who, like the reeds of the canebrake,
>> had none to take care of them,
>> gathered around you:
> He who knew not (wielding a combat) weapon
>> had his dagger drawn,
> he who knew not (how to handle) a longbow
>> had ready his (ordinary) bow
>> fitted (with arrow),
> he who knew not (how to wage) a war
>> engaged in hand-to-hand fighting,
> he who knew not (how to cross) a river
>> flew like a bird.

> The weak kept pace with the swift,
>> the cripple gave cover to the strong,
> about the commandant, the support of their city,
>> they had been told gross calumny.[371]

Next he drove the commandant to order his troops in to take savage repressive action:

> Respect no god! Fear no man!
> Put to death young and old alike,
> the suckling and the babe — leave not anyone! [372]

Soon he had made disorders and wars spread all over the known world. He might have devastated the world completely in his frenzy, but his van-courier Ishum was able to calm him down enough to leave a remnant. Even so Erra had few regrets and might clearly at any time relapse into another homicidal fit. His address to the assembled gods after he had been calmed begins — not exactly contritely:

> Listen, all of you, mark my word!
> (So) maybe I did plot evil
>> because of the sins of yore —
> my heart waxed hot in me,
>> and I ploughed the people under,
> like a hireling I let go
>> the bellwether from the fold,
> like a nonorchardman
>> I was careless in felling,
> like a despoiler of a country
>> I distinguished not good from bad, laid (all) low,
> from the maw of a roaring lion,
>> no one gets a carcass away,
> nor, when one is raging,
>> can another (ever) reason with him.[373]

The ubiquity of the powers of sudden death led understandably to an increased interest in what these powers and their domain, the netherworld, were like; stories and descriptions of them became popular. The netherworld was of old imagined as a city ringed securely around by seven walls and so entered through seven successive gates. The rulers of it were Nergal (also called Meslamtaea, Ugur, or Erra) and his consort Ereshkigal. Earlier traditions mention instead of Nergal, "The great bull of heaven," Gugalanna, or the god Ninazu, as Ereshkigal's consort. The netherworld had a judicial assembly, the Anunnaki which was sometimes presided over by visiting judges from the world above, such as the sun god (at night) or the moon god (on the day the moon is invisible), and sometimes by Ereshkigal or Gilgamesh. There was a high constable or sheriff, Ningishzida, and many deputies. The vizier and messenger of Ereshkigal was Namtar, "fate." A gatekeeper, Nedu, kept the gates locked, partly against unwelcome visitors, but mainly so that none of the inhabitants would escape to prey upon the living.

The heightened interest in the netherworld around the turn of the first millennium is attested to by the mechanical addition to the Gilgamesh Epic of an Akkadian translation of the latter half of the Sumerian story of "Gilgamesh, Enkidu, and the Netherworld," as its twelfth tablet. The addition, as we have mentioned earlier (see above, p. 215), has no connection whatever with the tale told by the epic and is so ineptly done that the first lines make no sense. Only intense interest in its subject matter, a detailed description of how people were treated after death, can account for its being appended in that way.

The meeting, hate/love courtship, and eventual marriage of the ruling couple of the netherworld is the subject of the myth "Nergal and Ereshkigal" which we have in a brief version in an Amarna tablet[374] of about 1350 B.C. and in a much more elaborate version from the early half of the first millennium.[375]

This story tells how once the gods were feasting and sent a messenger down to Ereshkigal inviting her to send up Namtar so that he might take some of the delicacies to her. Namtar arrived and the gods all rose as a polite gesture to his mistress. Only one god, Nergal, rudely refused to do so. When Namtar returned and reported the slight, Ereshkigal furiously sent him back to bring the offender down to her that she might kill him. Namtar went, but Ea had changed Nergal's appearance and made him appear bald. Namtar, therefore, did not recognize him and returned empty-handed. Ea, however, in his uncanny knowledge of the human — and divine — heart, fashioned a chair and told Nergal to take it down to Ereshkigal to get her in a better mood. Nergal, understandably, demurred on the grounds that she would surely kill him; but Ea heartened him and assigned seven demons to help him. When he arrived in the netherworld he stationed these demons in its seven gates and told them to keep the gates open in case he had to beat a quick retreat. That proved unnecessary however. When he went into the house where Ereshkigal sat he met with no resistance. He seized her by the hair, pulled her from her throne, and threw her on the ground the better to cut off her head. She, however, pleaded with him for her life and offered him both marriage and rule over the netherworld. He listened to her, picked her up, kissed her, and wiped away her tears, saying — in sudden enlightenment: "It was but love you wanted of me from months long ago to now!"[376]

As a tale of sexual attraction, of the adolescent gambit of attracting attention and challenging by rudeness, and of the thin line between the wish to kill and passionate surrender, the story is not difficult to interpret.

As a myth, the savage courtship it tells of seems somehow right for the forbidding powers of death; but beyond that, as one looks for a more ultimate meaning, it appears almost impenetrable, and we do not pretend to offer even a reasonable suggestion.

The later version of the story has been greatly elaborated. After the episode of not rising, Nergal visits the netherworld and, disregarding Ea's advice, goes to bed with Ereshkigal. After seven days he makes his getaway. She, disconsolate, demands of the great gods that they restore him to her and make him marry her since impure as she now is by reason of her affair, she is incapable of fulfilling her duties of judging the cases of the great gods below. Her plea, touching and threatening at the same time, runs:

> When I, your daughter, was little, and since
> I never knew girls' play,
> I never knew the frolicking of little ones.
> That god you sent me, who lay with me,
>   let him bed down with me,
> send me that god: he shall be my bridegroom
>   taking me in marriage!
> I am defiled, unclean, can not judge the
>   cases of the great gods,
> the great gods of the netherworld.
> If you send me not that god
> I shall let the dead up to eat the living,
> shall make the dead more than the living![377]

It seems that she gets her wish, and Nergal returns to her in a passionate embrace.

A last work concerned with the netherworld is a curious tale about an Assyrian prince who,[378] because of his burning desire, is allowed to visit the netherworld where Nergal — who at first threatens to kill him — is persuaded to let him go after a fierce admonition which seemingly carries a distinct political message. The story does, however, take evident pains to give a most detailed and frightening description of each of the various demonic figures who form Nergal's court.

Growing Brutalization

That the parlous character of life in the early first millennium should have focused interest on death and its powers is very understandable. So is also, regrettably, that its climate of constant wars, riots, and disorders could not but slowly and insidiously inure men to the sufferings of others, brutalize them, and bring out any latent strain of cruelty in them. The religious outlook and the expression of the age show this only too plainly.

The image of the gods on occasion became remarkably crude. We have mentioned the description of Erra as a ruthless killer; but far more crudely drawn are the gods of the older generations whose doings are chronicled in a myth we have called the "Dynasty of Dunnum."[379] Actually this myth seems to go back to a rather simple and rustic herdsman's cosmogony of the early second millennium after which it became popular and spread beyond the borders of Mesopotamia in the middle of that millennium; and it continued to be copied throughout the first millennium. It tells a strange tale of succeeding generations of gods, each taking power through parricide and living in incest with mother, sister, or both. The end of the story is not preserved, but it is possible that it recorded a gradual improvement in divine mores as it approached the later, contemporary, generations of gods. Such an intent is not incompatible with what we know if its offshoots in Phoenician, Greek, and Hurrian mythology; but even so the picture it presents still remains remarkably crude.

Not only were such myths as the Erra Epic and the "Dynasty of Dunnum" crude, but ritual in the first millennium had become remarkably lacking in sensitivity. Not only are such divine opponents as Ti'āmat, Kingu, Azag, and Anzu more or less cruelly killed by Marduk and Ninurta and their deaths ritually celebrated, but high gods such as An and Enlil are most brutally dealt with. An, for instance, is flayed and his head is cut off, Enlil has his eyes plucked out,[380] and we are informed in a royal ritual that: ". . . the king who has the bishop bounce a loaf baked in ashes with him: they are Marduk and Nabû. Marduk bound Anu and broke him — the loaf baked in ashes that they bounce is the heart of Anu as he (i.e., Marduk) pulled it out with his hands." Presumably this cruelty goes hand in hand with the growing politization of the gods who come to embody more and more the political interests of their cities and countries. Enlil of Nippur was, like his city, on the side of the Sealand, the land of Ti'āmat- and so an enemy of Marduk of Babylon. The same was true of Anu of Uruk, so much so that when Enûma elish was read at New Year in Babylon the faces of these two deities were kept covered, while at Borsippa an incantation priest passed a cedar cutting victoriously over the crown of Anu's statue in a symbolic gesture of killing him while the statue of Nabû was set in Anu's garden as a sign of his having taken the kingship from Anu. The gods of political enemies had become enemies themselves and were treated as such, with all the brutality of the times. It is no wonder then, that the gods were credited with comparable callousness and ferociousness where it was a matter of human adversaries. Esarhaddon for instance, is encouraged by the goddess Ishtar in an oracle where she says "I am Ishtar of Arbela. I will flay your enemies and present them to you,"[381] and Ashurbanipal describes how he soothed the hearts of the great gods, angered at the disrespect shown them by Babylon and other major cities in Babylonia:

> (as for) the rest of the people: guided by the guardian spirits, (guided by whom) my grandfather Sennacherib ploughed under, I now — as a funerary offering to him — ploughed those people under alive. Their flesh I fed to the dogs, pigs, vultures, eagles — the birds of heaven and the fishes of the deep. After I had done these deeds (and so) calmed the hearts of the great gods, my lords, I took the corpses of the people whom Erra had laid low or who had laid down their lives through hunger and famine and the remains of the dog and pig feed, which blocked the streets and filled the broad avenues; those bones (I took) out of Babylon, Kutha, and Sippar and threw them on heaps. By means of purification rites I purified their (holy) daises and cleansed their defiled streets. Their angry gods and incensed goddesses I calmed with hymns and penitential psalms.[382]

Since the gods were in large measure identified with their main places of worship as local and national gods, they became, of course, unavoidably drawn into political conflicts as partisans; and they, their statues and their temples were felt to be at the mercy of the conqueror. Sennacherib, for instance, tells how he sends his army into rebellious Southern Babylonia:

> They marched as far as Uruk. Shamash of Larsa . . . Bêltu of Uruk, Nanâ, Ussur-amassa, Bêlit-balāti, Kurunnam, Kashshītu, and Nergal, the gods dwelling in Uruk, as well as their countless effects and belongings, they carried off as spoil.[383]

Similarly, when he conquered Babylon after the city had long and bitterly opposed him, he was merciless:

> . . . I left not (a single one) young or old, with their corpses I filled the city's broad streets. . . . The belongings of that city: silver, gold, precious stones, effects, belongings, I counted as my people's share and they took them for their own. The gods living in its midst the hands of my people seized and smashed, taking their effects and belongings.[384]

Most bitter of all was the abuse in the political-religious pamphlets. In one such (apparently meant to discredit the New Year Festival of Babylon in the eyes of the Assyrian garrison) we have ritual directions for a trial of the god Marduk for his sins against Ashur;[385] and another pamphlet descends to the lowest depths of blasphemy in heaping obscene abuse upon the goddess Ishtar of Babylon.[386]

The Heritage

As one comes from the religious materials of the older periods to those of the first millennium, the focus on death and signs of a blunting of sensibilities are the new traits that first come to notice. Actually, of course, there are a great many other complex and, in part, very subtle, developments — for instance, a strong trend to identify the gods with stars — and a massive, albeit somewhat vaguely contoured, body of survivals that make up the complete picture.

Here we shall merely look briefly at some of the modifications which may be observed in the major religious metaphors of the previous ages as they continued as vehicles of religious expression into the first millennium B.C.

The earliest such, the provider metaphor, seems on the whole to have lost ground considerably to the ruler metaphor and its social and political concerns. A great deal of this development probably lies in the third and second millennia. The provider metaphor as it survives into the first millennium tends to cast the power — the god — in the form of an official in charge of a beneficent phenomenon of nature. Two prayers of Sargon II of Assyria, one to Ea, whom he calls by his Sumerian epithet N i n - i g i - k u g, and another to Adad, may serve as examples. The first reads:

> O N i n - i g i - k u g, expert, fashioner of all and everything,
> for Sargon, king of the world, king of Assyria,
>   commandant of Babylon,
> king of Shumer and Akkad, builder of your
>   sanctum, cause your spring (of the deep)
>   to open up,
> let its fountainheads bring waters of fecundity
>   and abundance, have his commons watered!

The second says

> O Adad, canal inspector of heaven and earth,
>   who(se flash of lightning) lights up the
>   thronc-daiscs,
> for Sargon, king of the world, king of Assyria,
>   commandant of Babylon,
> king of Shumer and Akkad, builder of your sanctum,
> bring him in season rain from heaven, floods
>   from the spring (of the deep),
> heap up emmer-wheat and leeks in his common,
> let his subjects lie down securely amid plenty
>   and abundance.[387]

It is more difficult to gauge what happened to the ruler metaphor, or how to account for what appears to have been essentially a change in emphasis. Such a change is not easily pinned down for it may have differed from person to person and from occasion to occasion. Any comments one might make are therefore bound to be highly subjective and tentative.

Subject to this caveat, we would hesitantly suggest, however, that the trend toward absolutism in kingship on earth which became dominant already in the third millennium, is likely in time to have colored the concept of king and ruler and so to have lent its peculiar emphasis to its use in the metaphor. A result of this is an urge to sense, when the metaphor was applied to a deity, a concentration of power similar to that of the absolute monarch on earth. Such an urge accords well with the unlimited power of the tremendum, but runs counter to the tenets of a polytheistic system in which power is widely and variously distributed among many deities. Therefore, to assert itself it must seek ways of unifying and consolidating. Actually various such unifying and consolidating tendencies seem attested to in our materials.

One fairly obvious way of consolidating power, fully compatible with the view of the gods as officials in a cosmic state, was to assume delegation of power to a single deity. Such delegation is described as early as Enûma elish where all the major gods delegate their various authorities to Marduk, and in the bilingual "Elevation of Inanna"[388] where successively An, Enlil, and Ea delegate their powers to Inanna. Both of these compositions reach back into the second millennium B.C. An example from the first millennium is the hymn of Ashurbanipal to Marduk, which states:

> You hold the Anuship, the Enlilship, and Eaship,
>   the lordship and the kingship
> you hold gathered all (good) counsel
>   O you, perfect in strength![389]

A similar example, seeking to find a formula, for reconciling the conflicting claims to universal rule of Marduk and Ashur, is a passage in an inscription of Sargon II of Assyria in which he has Marduk delegate authority and claim to tribute from all other gods to Ashur.

> Ashur, father of the gods, lord of (all) lands,
> king of the whole heaven and earth, the begetter,
> lord of lords, to whom from days of old the Enlil
> of the gods, Marduk, submitted the gods of the
> level land and the mountains of the four quarters
> (of the world) to pay homage to him and — no one
> escaping — have them enter Ehursaggal with their
> heaped up treasure.[390]

A more radical way of consolidating powers was to unify them by identifying their several divine bearers as but aspects of one and the same deity. This was not new; in all periods the line between the epithets and names of a deity had been fluid, and the decision in a given case as to whether one or more gods were involved must already have been a difficult one for the ancients. What is new in the first millennium, though, is a remarkable readiness to bring such uncertainty about separateness or identicalness, to bear upon major, well defined, clearly distinct deities. As an example, a text that baldly states:

> Ninurta is Marduk of the hoe,
> Nergal is Marduk of the attack,
> Zababa is Marduk of the hand-to-hand fight,
> Enlil is Marduk of lordship and counsel,
> Nabium is Marduk of accounting,
> Sîn is Marduk, the illuminator of the night,
> Shamash is Marduk of justice,
> Adad is Marduk of rains. . . .[391]

As will be seen even from this excerpt a remarkable number of major gods. are here simply identified with aspects of Marduk, that is to say, with functions of his that correspond to their own characteristic natures, functions, and powers.

A similar set of identifications, in some ways perhaps odder still is presented in a hymn[392] to the god Ninurta in which a long list of major gods are blithely identified with parts of Ninurta's body.

> O lord, your face is the sun god, your hair, Aya,
> your eyes, O lord, are Enlil and Ninlil.
> The pupils of your eyes are Gula and Bêlit-ilī,
> the irises of your eyes are the twins, Sîn
>   and Shamash,
> the lashes of your eyes are the rays of the sun
>   god that. . . .
> The appearance of your mouth, O lord, is Ishtar
>   of the stars
> Anu and Antum are your lips, your command . . .
> your tongue (?) is Pabilsağ of the above. . . .
> The roof of your mouth, O lord, is the vault
>   of heaven and earth, your divine abode,
> your teeth are the seven gods who lay low
>   the evil ones.

The hymn travels down Ninurta's body leisurely and in great detail. As with the preceding text, there is a correspondence of function between the part of Ninurta's body and the deity identified with it: his lashes are rays, his lips, with which he gives commands, are identified with the embodiments of authority, Anu and Antum, the roof of his mouth is the vault of heaven, which, since it rests on earth, is also "of" earth, and so forth.

Exactly what one is to make of the kind of unity toward which these texts and others like them seem to strive is not, perhaps, as simple as it may at first appear. If we were to take them at face value we should probably have to assume that they reflect the idiosyncracies of a very few individuals, for nowhere else is there any indication that the gods here identified with aspects of Marduk or parts of Ninurta's body ceased to be depicted, described, addressed, or worshiped as anything other than themselves. More likely, therefore, the unity which these texts seek is of a different kind: a unity of essence, as it were, a recognition of sameness of will and power in the bewildering variety of divine personalities — also, no doubt, a delight in voicing the versatility and many-faceted endowments of a favorite deity. In favor of such interpretation of the "identification" is perhaps the proclivity of Akkadian for using proper names metaphorically — as common names — across the division line, personal-neuter, that we do not share. While we may easily describe a financier as a "Napoleon of Wall Street," we can not idiomatically indicate the masterful character of his orders to buy or sell by calling them "Napoleons." Akkadian, unlike English, can cross that line and can indicate the decisive character of Marduk's commands by stating that "your command is Anu."[393] What is implied, presumably is that the immediate and instinctive reaction to Marduk's word is the same — a will to full, unconditional obedience — as the one produced in gods and men by Anu. To say, for example, that Marduk in his role of helper in battle to the kings of Babylon is Ninurta, is as much as saying that the enemy reaction to him and his martial prowess is the same as the one Ninurta would have produced, while to maintain that Ninurta's lips are Anu and Antum amounts to much the same thing as when Enûma elish says that Marduk's command is Anu.

Tentatively, we would therefore suggest caution in assessing the implications of the identifications made in these texts. It does seem likely that the development of absolute monarchy in the third and second millennia invested the terms for "king" and "ruler" with a sense of supreme and general power and that this sense was distinctly felt also when these terms were used as religious metaphors. With favorite gods, therefore, a trend away from specialization of power developed and endowed such gods with more extensive, or even all-embracing, control: either by assumed delegation from other divine potentates or by seeing the favorite god as sharing in — and equaling — the special competences of major gods. In neither case, however, do the delegating or sharing gods appear to have suffered any observable diminution of either the powers or the identities they held before.

As a last question we may inquire into the fortunes of the parent metaphor in the first millennium. Within its own original sphere, the penitential psalms, it continued to flourish throughout the first millennium in rites of contrition by kings and commoners alike, still caught up in its dilemma of the just sufferer, not yet able to say: "Nevertheless, not as I will, but as Thou wilt." Outside of this ritual influence this attitude is discernible in the stance of the king to the deities who advise and encourage him in dreams and prophesies. Esarhaddon, for instance, was told by Ishtar of Arbela in an oracle,[394] how she had stipulated for him many days, long-lasting years. In presenting herself to him she comes very close to a mother image: "I was the senior midwife (at) your (birth)" and "I am your kindly wetnurse." Similarly, when Ashurbanipal turned to her in tears because Teumman of Elam threatened to attack him, Ishtar acted very much the overprotective mother. She "had compassion on his eyes that filled with tears"[395] and — as witnessed by a seer that night in a dream — talked with him as if she were the mother who bore him,[396] telling him that she would take care of everything:

> You (better) stay here where you are, eat food, drink dark beer, make merry and praise my godhead while I go and do that job and achieve your heart's desire — your face shall not blanch, your legs not tremble, you shall not (have to) wipe off your sweat in the midst of battle.[397]

She treats him like a child:

> She coddled you in the cozy crook of her arm
> so that she protected your entire body.[398]

Ashurbanipal's attitude of childlike helplessness as he weeps before Ishtar was apparently — by virtue of the complete trust it expressed and its utter lack of self-assertiveness and reliance on own powers — most highly regarded as truly meritorious and pious. It stands for an attitude which may be termed quietistic, in that it holds that only by refraining from all action of one's own and thereby showing complete unflinching trust in divine help does one prove deserving of it.

This attitude (familiar from the Old Testament where it underlies the axiom of "Holy War") generally demands that few or no preparations to meet the enemy be made, that trust be placed entirely in divine help. Besides the instance of Ashurbanipal and Teumman just quoted, there is a similar episode concerning Urtaku, which Ashurbanipal records as follows.[399]

> They (i.e., the gods) judged my lawsuit against Urtaku, king of Elam, whom I had not attacked (yet) he attacked me. . . . In my stead they brought about his defeat, smote his vanguard and expelled him (back) to the border of his own land. In the same year they destroyed his life through a wicked death, and gave him in charge to the "Land of no Return," from which there is no coming back. The heart of the great gods, my lords, came not to rest, their raging lordly temper quieted not down. They overthrew his rule (kingship), removed his dynasty and let another assume the rulership of Elam.

Most striking of all, perhaps, is the account which Esarhaddon gives of his defeat of his hostile brothers after they had murdered Sennacherib and seized power:[400]

> I raised my hands (in prayer) to Ashtur, Sīn, Shamash, Bêl, Nabû and Nergal, Ishtar of Nineveh and Ishtar of Arbela, and they agreed with what I said. In (token of) their firm "Yes!" they repeatedly sent me a reliable omen (signifying): Go! Hold not back! We shall go at your side and slay your foes! I did not tarry one, (much less) two days, waited not for my troops, did not look to the rear guard, did not see to the assigning of teams of horses or battle implements, did not stock campaign provisions; the snow and the cold of the month of Shabat, the hardships of winter, I feared not, like a flying eagle I spread my wings bent on the overthrow of my enemies, arduously I pressed on along the road to Nineveh — when, in front of me, in the region of Hanigalbat, all of their tall warriors, blocking my path, were whetting their weapons.
>
> Fear of the great gods, my lords, overwhelmed them, they saw my powerful storm troops and became crazed (with fright). Ishtar, queen of attack and hand-to-hand fighting, who loves my priesthood, stepped to my side, broke their bows, and dissolved their battle formation so that they all said: "This is our king!" At her exalted command they came over, one after the other, to my side and took up positions behind me, gamboled like lambs, and invoked me as lord.

The application of quietistic piety to war — often to ruthless and cruel war — is of course an extreme. In the peaceful aspects of life it showed to greater advantage, enhancing such truly religious attitudes as sincere humility before the divine and trust, not only in miraculous assistance and intervention, but in greater divine wisdom. In that respect it may perhaps be considered the only real religious insight that can be credited to the first millennium in Mesopotamia. As we find it around the middle of the millennium in inscriptions of Neo-Babylonian rulers it seems, however, less a part of Mesopotamian religious tradition than a new impulse from the simple piety of the Aramean tribesmen to whom the Neo-Babylonian rulers traced their lineage. Similarly, the noble faith of the Achaemenids who followed them was a new impulse with its roots in the belief of Iranian herdsmen. To illustrate this new, foreign, Neo-Babylonian piety in its most attractive form, we may quote a prayer to Marduk by Nebuchadnezer of the early sixth century B.C.,[401] thus bringing our consideration of ancient Mesopotamian religion to a positive conclusion. The prayer reads

> Without Thee, Lord, what hath existence?
> For the king Thou lovest, whose name Thou
>   didst call,
> who pleaseth Thee, Thou advancest his fame,
> Thou assignest him a straightforward path.
>
> I am a prince Thou favorest, a creature of
>   thine hands,

Thou madest me, entrusted to me the kingship
  over all people.
Of Thy grace, O Lord, who providest for all
  of them,
cause me to love Thy exalted rule,
Let fear of Thy godhead be in my heart,
grant me what seemeth good to Thee;
  Thou wilt do, verily, what profiteth me.

Abbreviations

CyS	H. Frankfort, *Cylinder Seals. A Documentary Essay on the Art and Religion of the Ancient Near East*, London, 1939.
DT	Tablets in the Daily Telegraph collection in the British Museum.
EI	W. W. Hallo and J. J. A. van Dijk, *The Exaltation of Inanna*, New Haven, 1968.
FTS	S. N. Kramer, *From the Tablets of Sumer*, Indian Hills, Colorado, 1956.
Gudea, *Cylinder*	F. Thureau-Dangin, *Les Cylindres de Goudéa découverts par Ernest de Sarzec à Tello*, *TLC* VIII, Paris, 1925.
Gudea, *St.*	*Statues of Gudea*, F. Thureau-Dangin, *VAB* I, pp. 66–88 for *St.* A-L. For *St.* L-P (& Q) see the bibliography by A. Falkenstein, *AnOr* 28, p. 5.
HRET	Nies and Keiser, *Historical, Religious and Economic Texts and Antiquities*, New Haven, 1920.
IM	Tablets in the collection of the Iraq Museum, Baghdad.
*IV R*₂	H. C. Rawlinson, *The Cuneiform Inscriptions of Western Asia*, 4, 2d ed., ed. T. G. Pinches, London, 1891.
JCS	*Journal of Cuneiform Studies.*
JNES	*Journal of Near Eastern Studies.*
JRAS	*Journal of the Royal Asiatic Society.*
K	Tablets in the Kouyunjik collection of the British Museum.
KAR	E. Ebeling, *Keilinschriften aus Assur religiösen Inhalts*, *WVDOG* 28 and 34 (Leipzig, 1915–23).
KAV	O. Schroeder, *Keilschrifttexte aus Assur verschiedenen Inhalts*, *WVDOG* XXXV (Leipzig, 1920).
KK	B. Landsberger, *Der kultische Kalender der Babylonier u. Assyrer. Erste Hälfte*, Leipzig, 1915.
LE	Claus Wilcke, *Das Lugalbandaepos*, Wiesbaden, 1969.
LKU	A. Falkenstein, *Literarische Keilschrifttexte aus Uruk*, Berlin, 1931.
Lugal-e	Lugal-e ud me-lám-bi nir-ğál. An edition by E. Bergmann (†) and J. van Dijk is in preparation.
MBI	G. A. Barton, *Miscellaneous Babylonian Inscriptions*, New Haven, 1918.
MNS	Åke Sjöberg, *Der Mondgott Nanna-Suen in der sumerischen Überlieferung. I. Teil: Texte*, Stockholm, 1960.
Ni	Tablets from Nippur in the collection of the Museum of the Ancient Orient at Istanbul.
OECT	*Oxford Editions of Cuneiform Texts.*
OIP	*Oriental Institute Publications*, Chicago.
PAPS	*Proceedings of the American Philosophical Society Held at Philadelphia for Promoting Useful Knowledge*, Philadelphia, 1838–.*
PBS	*Publications of the Babylonian Section, University Museum, University of Pennsylvania.*

PRAK   H. de Genouillac, *Premières recherches archéologiques à Kich* I-II, Paris, 1924–25.

PSBA   *Proceedings of the Society of Biblical Archaeology.*

R   H. C. Rawlinson, *The Cuneiform Inscriptions of Western Asia*, vols. I-V, London, 1861–1909.

RA   *Revue d'assyriologie et d'archéologie orientale.*

SAHG   A. Falkenstein and W. von Soden, *Sumerische und akkadische Hymnen und Gebete*, Zürich/Stuttgart, 1953.

SBH   G. A. Reisner, *Sumerisch-babylonische Hymnen nach Thontafeln griechischer Zeit*, Berlin, 1896.

Sculptures   W. A. Wallis Budge, *Assyrian Sculptures in the British Museum, Reign of Ashur-naṣir-pal*, 885–860 B.C., London, 1914.

SEM   E. Chiera, *Sumerian Epics and Myths*, OIP XV (Chicago, 1934).

SETP   Muazzez Çiğ and Hatice Kizilyay, *Sumer Edebî Tablet ve Parçalari* 1, Ankara, 1969.

SGL   *Sumerische Götterlieder*, vols. I-II. Abhandlungen der Heidelberger Akademie der Wissenschaften phil.-hist. Klasse 1959–60.

SK   H. Zimmern, *Sumerische Kultlieder aus altbabylonischer Zeit* I-II, *VS* II, X (Leipzig, 1912–13).

SLTN   S. N. Kramer, *Sumerian Literary Texts from Nippur*. Annual of the American Schools of Oriental Research 23, New Haven, 1944.

SM   S. N. Kramer, *Sumerian Mythology*. Memoirs of the American Philosophical Society, vol. XXI, Philadelphia, 1944.

SRT   E. Chiera, *Sumerian Religious Texts*, Upland, Pa., 1924.

Stones   C. J. Gadd, *The Stones of Assyria, the Surviving Remains of Assyrian Sculpture, Their Recovery and Their Original Positions*, London, 1936.

STVC   E. Chiera, *Sumerian Texts of Varied Contents*, OIP XVI (Chicago, 1934).

Surpu   E. Reiner, *Šurpu. A Collection of Sumerian and Akkadian Incantations*, *AOF*, Supplement Z (Graz, 1958).

TCL   *Textes cunéiformes. Musée du Louvre.*

TH   Å. Sjöberg and E. Bergmann (†), *The Collection of the Sumerian Temple Hymns*, New York, 1969.

TIT   Thorkild Jacobsen, *Toward the Image of Tammuz*, edited by W. L. Moran, Cambridge, Mass., 1970.

Tr. D   H. de Genouillac, *La trouvaille de Drehem*, Paris, 1911.

TRS   H. de Genouillac, *Textes religieux sumériens du Louvre*, *TCL* XV-XVI (Paris, 1930).

TuMnF   *Texte und Materialien der Frau-Professor-Hilprecht-Sammlung Vorderasiatischer Altertümer im Eigentum der Friedrich-Schiller-Universität Jena. Neue Folge*, Leipzig/Berlin, 1937–.

UE(T)   *Ur Excavations (Texts)* I-VIII, London, 1928–.

VAB	*Vorderasiatische Bibliothek*, Leipzig, 1907–16.
VAT	Text in the Near Eastern section of the Kaiser Friedrich Wilhelm Museum in Berlin.
VS	*Vorderasiatische Schriftdenkmäler der Königlichen Museen zu Berlin.*
"Weltordnung"	Bernhard and Kramer, "Enki und die Weltordnung," *Wissenschaftliche Zeitschrift der Friedrich-Schiller-Universität Jena*, gesellschafts- und sprachwissenschaftliche Reihe IX (1959/60), pp. 231 ff.
WVDOG	*Wissenschaffentliche Veröffentlichungen der Deutschen Orient Gesellschaft.*
WZKM	*Wiener Zeitschrift für die Kunde des Morgenlandes.*
YOS	*Yale Oriental Series, Babylonian Texts.*
ZA	*Zeitschrift für Assyriologie.*
3N-T	Field catalogue of tablets found at Nippur by the joint expedition of the Oriental Institute, University of Chicago, and the University Museum, University of Pennsylvania, third season.

Notes

Notes have been held to a minimum. They are intended primarily to furnish scholars with a clue to the compositions and text passages referred to in the text. Editions or references where further literature may be found have been quoted whenever possible, but no attempt at full bibliographical reference has been even approximated. It is hoped that the many editions cited as "in preparation" may, when published, be identified from the references here given.

The general reader will find English translations of many of the texts cited in *ANET*, *ANET* Suppl., *BWL*, and in S. N. Kramer's various publications. A particularly valuable Collection of Translations in German is *SAHG*. Translations of major compositions such as Atrahasīs, Enûma elish, and the Gilgamesh Epic are listed in notes 169, 326, and 339.

All translations given are from the original texts. They do not always agree with earlier renderings and we hope on other occasions to present the philological justifications for them.

1 Rudolph Otto, *The Idea of the Holy* (London, 1943).
2 *Gilgamesh Epic* Tablet VII iii 33–34.
3 *IV R*² pl. 9. Cf. *MNS* pp. 165–79. The section quoted is lines 7–14.
4 *OECT* I, pls. 36–39 i. 3–15, 21–26, and duplicates. (See Kramer in *SETP* p. 31.) Thanks are due to Daniel Reisman for making his manuscript edition available to us.
5 *SGL* I pp. 5–79. The section quoted is lines 129–40.
6 *Gilgamesh Epic* Tablet IV iv 10–12.
7 *HRET* no. 22 i 31–35.
8 *CT* XVI pl. 15. v. 37–46.
9 Ibid., pl. 12. i. 1–43.
10 Svend Aage Pallis, *The Babylonian Akîtu Festival* (Copenhagen, 1926).
11 É - s u - š i - h u š - r i - a in unpublished edition of temple list kindly made available by W. L. Moran.
12 *SGL* I p. 15, lines 77–79.
13 Cf. e.g., *SGL* I p. 14, line 74: ᵈE n - l í l i b (thus with variants) - k u g h i - l i -

d u₈ - d u₈ - a - z u, "O Enlil, your holy (cult-)niche laden with attractiveness"; also [K á] - m a h h i - l i d [u₈ - d u₈ - a], "the lofty gate laden with
attractiveness," in the description of Ekur *PBS* I₁, no. 8. i. 18 and duplicate
SK, no. 8. i. 17.

14   é - h a l - l a = *bît piristi*. See the passages cited in *AHw* p. 134 section 19, and
cf. *JNES* 16 (1957), p. 252, line 20 (Nèribtum Gilgamesh fragment) and
Ashurbanipal, *Annals* vi. 30–31.

15   "The Fall of Agade," line 131. *TuMnF* III, nos. 27 rev. 14; 31 obv. 18; 32
obv. 14. Cf. *PBS*₁, no. 8. i. 16 and duplicates *SK*, no. 8. i. 16, and *BL*, no. 44.

16   "Lamentation over the Destruction of Sumer and Ur," line 450. See *UE(T)*
VI₂, nos. 133 obv. 26 and 133 obv. 26. Cf. Kramer in ANET Suppl. p. 182.

17   *TH* p. 26 lines 150, 158, 163.

18   Gudea, *Cylinder A*, x. 24–26.

19   Ibid., x. 19–23.

20   "The Fall of Agade," lines 120–21, 125–26, and 127–28. Cf. Falkenstein, *ZA*
57 (1965), pp. 43–124; Kramer, ANET Suppl. pp. 210–15.

21   For these name forms see, e.g., Gudea, *Cylinder A*, vii. 28 and xi. 3.

22   E. M. Forster, *Anonymity, An Enquiry* (London, 1925), pp. 13–14.

23   See Kramer, *PAPS* 107 (1963), pp. 509–10 (Kramer's interpretation differs
from the one given here) and my article in "The Gaster Festschrift," *Journal
of the Ancient Near Eastern Society of Columbia University* 5 (1973). An unpublished duplicate tablet in the Yale collection, kindly made available by
Professor W. Hallo, shows that the composition begins as here given and not
as we surmised in "The Gaster Festschrift."

24   *TuMnF* III, no. 25.

25   *BE* XXX, no. 4 and duplicates.

26   We owe the reading of this word to an oral communication from B. Alster.

27   *SLTN*, no. 35.

28   *TRS*, no. 70.

29   *SRT*, no. 1 and duplicates. Cf. Falkenstein and von Soden, *SAHG*, no. 18 pp.
90–99, 367–68, and literature there cited.

30   *CT* XLII no. 4.

31   We are aware that "carp-flood" does not exist in English. It is a literal
translation of the Sumerian term for the early flood which was called the
"carp-flood" because carps at that time (spring) swam up the rivers to be
caught by delighted Sumerian fishermen (see above, p. 32). We use it here
because it is so pregnant and illustrative.

32   Kramer, *PAPS* 107 (1963), pp. 505–08. Ni 9602.

33   B. Alster, *Dumuzi's Dream* (Copenhagen, 1972).

34   R A VIII (1911), pp. 161 ff. and duplicates *TRS*, no. 78 and *SK*, no. 2.

35   *SK*, no. 123. ii. 10–21.

36   *CT* XV pl. 18 and partial duplicate, CBS 45 (unpublished)

37   *BE* XXX, no. 1. ii. 3′ to iii. 4′ and its duplicates *HRET*, no. 26 and *SEM*, no.
91.

38   Edited by Kramer, *JCS* V (1951), pp. 1–17 with additional materials *PAPS*
107 (1963), pp. 491–93, 510–16. See also A. D. Kilmer, "How Was Queen
Ereshkigal Tricked?" *Ugarit Forschungen 3* (1971), pp. 299–309. We tend to

think that the motif of obligatory treatment of guests is more relevant to the story of Adapa than to "Inanna's Descent."

39 *CT* XV pl. 19.
40 *IV R*² pl. 27 no. 1. lines 3–13.
41 *OECT* VI, pl. 15, K 5208, rev. 3–11.
42 *TCL* VI, no. 54 rev. 1–6. Cf. the partial duplicate *LKU*, no. 11.
43 *TCL* VI, no. 54. 12–17 and duplicate K. D. Macmillan, BA V₅, no. xxxiv.
44 *ASKT*, no. 16 obv. 13–24 and duplicate Frank, *ZA* 40 (1931), p. 86.
45 *ASKT*, no. 16 rev. 1–16 and duplicates Frank, *ZA* 40 (1931), p. 86 and K 4954 (unpublished copy by F. Geers).
46 K 4954 obv. 1–12. Unpublished copy by F. Geers.
47 *SK*, no. 26. iv. 1–7 which is Old Babylonian in date. The text has suffered badly in the course of its tradition and much in it has been misunderstood and reinterpreted. A late version of the first millennium as given by *IV R*² pl. 30 no. 2. lines 11–31 may be rendered (with omission of the long list of epithets and titles in lines 12–20 and including two further lines) as follows:

If it is required, let me (young) lad
  walk the path of no return!
. . . .

He was walking, he was walking, to the
  breast of the hills (of death)
throughout the day, throughout the day,
  toward the land of his dead,
full of grief over the day he fell,
over (you), Month, who did not safely
  complete your year,
over (you), Road, who made an end of
  your people,
over the wailings on account of the lord —
a (young) brave (walking) into his faraway,
  undiscoverable region.

48 *SK*, no. 26. vi. 14′–20′ and its duplicate *PRAK* II pl. 44 D 41 lines 10′–17′.
49 *SK*, no. 27. v. 7–10.
50 Ibid., lines 11–15.
51 *TRS*, no. 8 and its duplicate versions *CT* XV pls. 26–27 and pl. 30.
52 *CT* XV pls. 24. 14–25. 11 and its duplicates *BL*, no. 71 (K 2485 and 3898), Pinches, *PSBA* XVII (1895), pls. I–II.
53 Oral communication from Robert M. Adams.
54 "Gilgamesh and Agga," edited by Kramer, *AJA* 53 (1949), pp. 1–18, lines 30–39 — cf. 107–11.
55 "Gilgamesh, Enkidu, and the Netherworld." An edition by A. Shaffer is in preparation. For the time being see S. N. Kramer, "Gilgamesh and the Hulupputree," *AS* X; *SM* pp. 30–37; *SLTN*, p. 13; *TuMnF* III, p. 11 to nos. 13–14; and *UE(T)* VI, p. 7 to nos. 55–59.
56 Sumerian version *SK*, no. 196 and unpublished duplicate from Nippur

3N-T 152. An Akkadian version forms the sixth tablet of the Gilgamesh Epic.

57   An edition by A. Shaffer is in preparation. For the time being see S. N. Kramer, "Gilgamesh and the Land of the Living," *JCS* I (1947), pp. 3–46.

58   S. N. Kramer, *Enmerkar and the Lord of Aratta* (Philadelphia, 1952).

59   "The Fall of Agade" — see Falkenstein, *ZA* 57 (1965), pp. 43–124; Kramer, *ANET* Suppl. pp. 210–15.

60   Gudea, *Cylinder A*, viii. 15 to ix. 4.

61   See generally A. Deimel, "Sumerische Tempelwirtschaft zur Zeit Urukaginas und seine Vorgänger," *AnOr* 2.

62   Gudea, *Cylinder B*, vi. 11–23.

63   Uruinimgina, *Cone B + C*, xii. 23–28.

64   Gudea, *St. B*, vii. 36–46.

65   Gudea, *Cylinder A*, cols. i–xii.

66   Cf., e.g., the myth L u g a l - e.

67   *CT* XXI pls. 31 f.

68   "Weltordnung."

69   *Corpus*. Entemena, *Cone A*.

70   See Hans Hirsch, "Die Inschriften der Könige von Agade," *AOF* XX (1963), p. 44 obv. 10 x 1–7.

71   Thureau-Dangin, "La fin de la domination Gutienne," *RA* IX (1912), pp. 111 ff. col. ii. 29 to iii. 3 and duplicate RA X (1913), p. 99 10′–11′.

72   E. Ebeling, *Tod und Leben nach den Vorstellungen der Babylonier* (Berlin, 1931), pp. 86, 127–33.

73   J. Laessoe, *Studies on the Assyrian Ritual and Series bît rimki* (Copenhagen, 1955).

74   See the myth of "Enlil and Ninlil," *MBI*, no. 4; *SEM*, nos. 76 and 77; *SLTN*, no. 19; Pinches, "The Legend of the Divine Lovers," *JRAS* for 1919 pp. 185 ff. and 575 ff.; and *3N-T* 294 (unpublished).

75   More literally: "I could not escape that day in its due time"; "That day's fatality" stands for its "destined occurrence." Similarly below, "I could not escape that night in its due time."

76   The translation of this and the preceding line is tentative only.

77   Kramer, *AS* XII, p. 26, lines 88–112.

78   Ibid., p. 32, lines 152–64.

79   Ibid., p. 34, lines 173–89.

80   Ibid., p. 38, lines 203–04.

81   Ibid., pp. 38–40, lines 208–18.

82   *UE(T)* VI$_2$, no. 131 rev. 45–59.

83   Ibid., nos. 131 rev. 63 and 132 obv. 1–13.

84   *ZA* 32 (1918/19), p. 174 line 58.

85   L u g a l - e Tablet I lines 26–27. An edition of this myth by E. Bergmann(t) and J. van Dijk is in preparation. For the time being see S. N. Kramer in *SM*, p. 117, note 76; *UE(T)* VI, p. 2 to nos. 3–7; *SETP* p. 39 V.(5); and the literature cited by R. Borger, *Handbuch der Keilschriftliteratur* I (Berlin, 1967), pp. 147–48.

86 We consider *urāš* a *purās* form of *erēšu* with resultative force.
87 A n = *Anum* Tablet I lines 25–26. See *CT* XXIV pl. 1.
88 A n = *Anum*, *CT* XXIV pl. 1. 1–2. Cf. A. Deimel, *Pantheon Babylonicum* (Rome, 1914), no. 263.
89 Cf. Lugalzaggesi, vase inscription iii. 27–28, u b u r - A n - n a - k e₄ s i h a - m u - d a - s á, "May he (i.e., An) set to rights the breasts of Antum (i.e., heaven)"; and cf. *CAD* vol. 26 (S), p. 135, section 4a, which we should group with ṣirtu A (ibid., p. 209) "udder, teat."
90 E.g., *SK*, no. 199 abov. 1. 4.
91 *SK*, no. 196. See also the *Gilgamesh Epic* Tablet VI.
92 S. N. Kramer, "Inanna's Descent to the Netherworld Continued and Revised," *JCS* V (1951), p. 5, lines 85–88.
93 *CT* XXXVI pl. 31. 6.
94 Quoted from Otto, *The Idea of the Holy*, p. 227.
95 William James, *The Varieties of Religious Experience*, Mentor Book edition (New York, 1958), p. 67.
96 Thureau-Dangin, "L'elevation d'Inanna," *RA* XI (1914), p. 144, obv. 3–5.
97 Cf. our similar, slightly more detailed characterization in H. Frankfort et al., *Before Philosophy*, Pelican edition (Harmondsworth, Middlesex, 1954), pp. 150–53.
98 *SLTN*, no. 80 obv. 5–9.
99 *SK*, no. 199, obv. 1–28.
100 Cf. "The Creation of the Hoe," *TRS*, no. 72 and duplicates.
101 Note the line: "Ewe and Grain having been settled aplenty in their house Dukug," *MBI*, no. 8 obv. 26 and its bilingual duplicate *CT* XVI, pl. 14. 30.
102 *UE(T)* VI, no. 101, especially lines 12–13 and 32–33.
103 *CT* XV, pl. 10. 18–22.
104 *MBI*, no. 4. iv. 23–31 and duplicate *SLTN*, no. 19 rev.
105 *SGL* I p. 16, lines 96–128.
106 Ibid., p. 17. 129–40.
107 *SBH*, no. 4, lines 100–05.
108 *KAR*, no. 375. ii. 1–8.
109 CNMA 10051; *JCS* VIII (1954), pp. 82 f., col. i. 1–3 and duplicates. See R. Kutscher, *Oh Angry Sea* (a - a b - b a h u - l u h - h a): *The History of a Sumerian Congregational Lament* (New Haven, 1975).
110 *SBH* pp. 130 ff., lines 48–55.
111 Ibid., no. 4, lines 1–21.
112 *TRS*, no. 72 and duplicates.
113 To be edited by M. Civil: see for the time being E. I. Gordon, "A New Look at the Wisdom of Sumer," *Bibliotheca Orientalis* XVII (1960), p. 145, section A. 1 and notes 207 and 208; and Kramer, *UE(T)* VI, p. 6 to nos. 36–37. For the passage referred to see provisionally *UE(T)* VI, no. 36 obv. 11–13; *SLTN*, no. 17 obv. 11–13; and *SEM*, no. 46 obv.
114 See note 74 above.
115 Civil and Reiner, "Another Volume of Sultantepe Tablets," *JNES* 26 (1967), pp. 200–05.

116   *PBS* V, no. 1.
117   W. G. Lambert and A. R. Millard, *Atra-hasîs: The Babylonian Story of the Flood* (Oxford, 1969).
118   *Gilgamesh Epic* Tablet XI.
119   See A n = *Anum* Tablet II. Cf. Deimel, *Pantheon Babylonicum*, no. 365; and see our study "Notes on Nintur," O r i e n t a l i a, n.s. 42 (1973), pp. 274–305.
120   Note the place names H u r - s a ǧ [. . .] (obv. i. 8), A n - z a - g à r - h u r - s a ǧ - ǧ a (i. 20–21), and H u r - s a ǧ (ii. 16–18) in Kazallu and Abiak on the western border of Akkad given in Kraus, "Provinzen der neusumerischen Reiches von Ur," *ZA* 51 (1955), p. 46.
121   See note 113 above.
122   L u g a l - e Tablets VIII–IX. See note 85 above; for the section referred to see especially Borger, *Handbuch der Keilschriftliteratur* I, p. 148.
123   *SK*, no. 198 obv. 12–13.
124   Ibid., lines 18–27.
125   *UE(T)* VI₂, no. 144 obv. 8–14.
126   Ibid., lines 28–33.
127   *BL*, no. 75 rev. 1–4.
128   Gudea, *St. A*, i. 3. The epithet refers to her under her name Ninhursaga; however, Gudea treats that name and the name Nintur as referring to one and the same goddess. See ibid., iii. 5.
129   TU i.e., t u r₅. In its older form it seems to represent the picture of a hut with a decorative reed bundle or bundles at the top. (For the shape cf. Labat, *Manuel d'epigraphie akkadienne* [Paris, 1948], p. 60.) Huts such as that on the stone trough in the British Museum (*British Museum Quarterly* III (1928), pl. XXII) were interpreted as birth huts by P. Delougaz in his article "Animals Emerging from a Hut," *JNES* 27 (1968), pp. 186 and 196, and figs. 2–11.
130   See the incantation VAT 8381. 1–3 published by van Dijk, *VS* XVII, no. 33 and quoted by Hallo and van Dijk, *The Exaltation of Inanna* (New Haven, 1968), p. 53, n. 22. We read and translate: m u n u s - e é - t ù r a m a š - k ù - g a im-da-an-zé-eb-ba-na / é-tu-ud-ǧál é-tùr a m a š - k ù - g a im-da-an-zé-eb-ba-na/numun-zi-nam-lú-uₓ š à - g a b a - n i - i n - r i, "the woman in her gratifying with it (i.e., with the male seed) the birth hut of the sacred sheepfold, in her gratifying with it the house that causes birth-giving to be, the birth hut of the sacred sheepfold, conceived (from) the good human seed in the womb."
131   See Lambert and Millard, *Atra-hasîs*, p. 56, lines 1, 189, and passim.
132   *KAR*, no. 196 obv. i. 65.
133   H. Frankfort, "A Note on the Lady of Birth," *JNES* 3 (1944), pp. 198 ff.
134   *TH* p. 46 lines 500–03.
135   A n = *Anum* Tablet II. See *CT* XXV pl. 12; cf. ibid., pl. 25.
136   *TH* p. 172 lines 77–78. We read: š a g₄ i m - m i - i n - d a b₅ in line 77 and connect it with š a g₄ . . . d a b₅ = *ṣepēru*, "pinch," "make contract."
137   *PBS* X₂ no. 16 obv. i. 25–27 and its duplicates — cf. *SM* pp. 51 ff.
138   A n = *Anum*. See *CT* XXIV pl. 12 line 20 and pl. 25 line 84.

139 *TH* p. 22 lines 96–98.
140 A n = *Anum. CT* XXIV pl. 13 lines 33–35 and pl. 25 lines 92–93.
141 F. Köcher, "Der babylonische Göttertypentext," *Mitteilungen des Instituts für Orientforschung* I (Berlin, 1953), pp. 57–107 obv. iii. 38'–51'.
142 A n = *Anum. CT* XXIV pl. 25 line 88. Note also her epithet š a g₄ - z u - a n - k i, "Midwife of Heaven and Earth," in *TH* p. 47 line 504. Ninhursaga and Nintur are treated as identical in this hymn.
143 "Weltordnung," p. 238 lines 393–99.
144 Gudea, *St. A*, ii. 1–2. Note that the sign DUB is here used as a variant for URUDU.
145 "Weltordnung," lines 400–10.
146 See note 134 above. The lines here quoted are 502–03.
147 "Weltordnung," p. 239 lines 408–09.
148 *PBS* X₂ no. 16 obv. i. 25–26.
149 *PBS* V no. 76 vii. 10'–14'.
150 A. Ungnad, "Datenlisten," in Ebeling et al., *Reallexikon der Assyriologie* II, p. 164, no. 281.
151 "Weltordnung," p. 233 lines 61–70.
152 Ibid., lines 87–99.
153 *CT* XXXVI, pl. 31. 8–10.
154 See, e.g., H. Frankfort, *Cylinder Seals* (London, 1939), pl. xix a., a cylinder seal belonging to a scribe, Adda, of the time of the dynasty of Agade. It shows a scene from the eastern mountains at sunrise. In the middle the sun god rises between two mountains. Over the peak to his right stands the winged goddess of the morning star, Inanna. To her right the god of thunderstorms and floods, Ninurta, with his bow and his lion. Enki mounts the peak at the sun god's left hand, behind him is his Janus-faced vizier, Usmu.
155 A n = *Anum* Tablet II. See *CT* XXIV pl. 14 lines 23–24, 26–27, and 48.
156 "Weltordnung," lines 52–57.
157 A n = *Anum* Tablet II. See *CT* XXIV pl. 14. 19.
158 See generally *CT* XXV pl. 48.
159 Cf. *AHw* p. 672.
160 Frankfort et al., *Before Philosophy*, pp. 159–60.
161 Cf. S. N. Kramer in *ANET* pp. 37–41 and sources there cited.
162 *SM* pp. 69–72 and sources there cited. Also *CT* XLII no. 28.
163 *PBS* V no. 1. Cf. *AS* XI, pp. 58–60.
164 Cf. *SM* pp. 64–68 and sources there cited.
165 "Weltordnung," lines 385–466.
166 See note 38 above.
167 See *SM* pp. 62–63 and sources there cited.
168 Cf. E. A. Speiser, "Adapa," *ANET* pp. 101–03 and sources there cited. See also *TIT*, pp. 48–51 and cf. note 38 above.
169 Lambert and Millard, *Atra-hasīs*. See also particularly the important articles by W. L. Moran, "The Creation of Man in Atrahasis I 192–248," *BASOR* no. 200 (1970), pp. 48–56, and "Atrahasis: The Babylonian Story of the Flood,"

Biblica 52 (1971), pp. 51–61. Another valuable discussion of the story in English is A. D. Kilmer, "The Mesopotamian Concept of Overpopulation . . . ," *Orientalia*, n.s. 41 (1972), pp. 160–77 with bibliography.

170   *MNS* pp. 104–07, lines 8–12.

171   *AGH*, p. 6. 1–3.

172   *UE(T)* I, no. 300. 1–11.

173   This deity, whose name denotes "Lord Earth" (e n - k i) is a chthonic deity distinct from the god of the fresh waters Enki, whose name denotes "Lord (i.e., productive manager) of the earth" (e n - k i (.a k)).

174   *SETP* pl. 96 (emend to 38). Ni 2781 obv. 17–24.

175   Ni 2781 obv. 25–28. Cf. also S. N. Kramer, *Two Elegies on a Pushkin Museum Tablet. A New Sumerian Literary Genre* (Moscow, 1960), p. 54, line 90.

176   Cf. Thorkild Jacobsen, "The Reign of Ibbī-Suen," *JCS* VII (1953), pp. 45 f., (reprinted in *TIT*, pp. 182 f.).

177   Cf. *AGH*, p. 6.

178   *CT* XVI pls. 19–21 lines 1–188.

179   *UE(T)* I, no. 289 i. 23–26.

180   See *UE(T)* VI, no. 133 obv. 25–26 and 134 obv. 3'–4'. Cf. *ANET* Suppl. p. 182 lines 449–50.

181   Cf. *UE(T)* VI, no. 67, esp. lines 45 ff.

182   *MNS* p. 167, line 11.

183   Ibid., p. 166, line 10.

184   Ibid., p. 44, lines 1 ff.

185   *TuMnF* IV$_2$, no. 7. 88; cf. *CT* XXIV pl. 15. 57.

186   *TuMnF* IV$_2$, no. 7. 83; cf. *CAD* vol. 21 p. 136 *zirru* A and *zirru* B.

187   CT XV pl. 5 ii. 5–9.

188   *TuMnF* IV$_2$, no. 7. 67–104.

189   See, e.g., *CAD* vol. 21 p. 136 *zirru* B.

190   See Gadd, "E n - a n - e - d u," *Irak*, vol. XIII (1951), pl. XIV. 7. The first sign of the line seems to us to be ú r.

191   *Tr. D*, no. 16; cf. *KK*, p. 79.

192   *PAPS* 107 (1963), p. 505 rev. iv. 17 ff.

193   *MNS* pp. 80–87.

194   S. N. Kramer in *SM* pp. 47 ff. and 114, n. 50, and in *UE(T)* VI, p. 5 to no. 25. See now also Sjöberg in *MNS* pp. 148–65, and A. J. Ferrara, *Nanna-Suen's Journey to Nippur* (Rome, 1973).

195   See, e.g., *UE(T)* VI$_2$, no. 131 rev. 47–48. Cf. *ANET* Suppl. p. 181 lines 343–44. The first month in the Nippur calendar seems named from this rite.

196   *MNS* pp. 44–46.

197   *MNS* pp. 13–15.

198   *CAD* vol. 1$_2$ p. 348 s.v. *assukku*.

199   Cf. *LE*, pp. 90–111. Note especially lines 100–04.

200   Cf. *JNES* 12 (1963), p. 167, n. 27 (reprinted *TIT*, p. 339).

201   See *Sculptures*, pls. XXXVI–XXXVII and *Stones*, pl. 138.

202   Cf., e.g., L u g a l - e, at end of Tablet III. (See *SEM*, nos. 44 obv. 13, and 45 obv. 11 where the bird is mentioned as one of the foes killed by Ninurta in the mountains.)

203 *CyS*, pl. XXII a. The form shown is that of the bird-lion winged and with talons on its hind legs.
204 Cf. such prayers to him as *AKA*, pp. 254 f. (from the slab picturing his battle with the bird-lion) and *AGH*, pp. 24–26 (cf. *SAHG*, pp. 314–16).
205 An edition by J. S. Cooper is in preparation. For the time being see S. N. Kramer in *PAPS* 85 (1942), p. 321.
206 See note 85 above.
207 L u g a l - e Tablet VIII lines 1–12. See *BE* XXIX, nos. 2 and 3; *SRT*, no. 18.
208 L u g a l - e Tablet VIII lines 13–25. See *BE* XXIX, nos. 2 and 3; *SRT*, no. 18; *SEM*, no. 35.
209 Gudea, *Cylinder A*, iv. 14–18.
210 Ibid., viii. 15–16.
211 Ibid., 23–26.
212 *UE(T)* VI, no. 2.
213 See the bibliography given by Grayson in *ANET* Suppl. p. 78.
214 *UE(T)* VI, no. 2. 48–54.
215 Gudea, *Cylinder B*, iii. 9 and 13–16. Cf. Falkenstein, *AnOr* 30 p. 91 n. 5.
216 *STVC*, no. 34 i. 8–25.
217 For a clear but very late statement see *VAB* IV, p. 260. 33–35 (Nabonidus). An Old Babylonian passage listing Utu's teams is given in G. R. Castellino, "Incantation to Utu," *Oriens Antiqvus* VIII (1969), pp. 6–27, lines 89–102. Unfortunately it is not very clear.
218 Kramer, *Two Elegies on a Pushkin Museum Tablet*, p. 54, lines 88–89, and p. 57, line 174.
219 "Gilgamesh, Enkidu, and the Netherworld" — see note 55 above.
220 *CT* XV pls. 15–16.
221 A n = *Anum*. See *KAV* 172 rev. iii. 10′ and 12′; *CT* XXV pl. 20. 21, pl. 21 rev. 3, 5, and 6.
222 *FTS* p. 106, fig. 6a.
223 *CT* XV pl. 15. 18–20.
224 Ibid., pl. 15. 12.
225 Ibid., pl. 15. 3 and 6.
226 *SBH*, no. 56 rev. 77–78.
227 Kramer, *Enmerkar and the Lord of Aratta*, lines 244–48. We read

> [A r a t t a é]- a n - d a - m ú - a
> ú r - b i ğ i š - r a - à m   p a - b i   ğ i š - b ú r - à m
> [š à] - [b] a [d] I m - d u ğ u d$_x$$^{m u š e n}$ h u - r í - i n - n a
> k é s - d a ^{d} I n a n n a   d ù g   k a   g i b - b a
> u m b i n - h u - r í - i n - n a $^{m u š e n}$ - b i
>   ù - m u n   k u r - r e   k u r - m ù š - e e$_{11}$

> The base of Aratta, the house grown up (i.e., contemporary) with heaven,
> is a stub (lit., "felled tree") its top a sundered tree,
> inside it the eagle's talon of the eagle Imdugud —
> fettered on knee and beak with Inanna's fetter —
> makes blood run down the mountain, down Kurmush.

228   *VAB* IV, p. 274 iii. 14 and p. 276 iii. 33 — both of Neo-Babylonian date; *EI*,
        p. 16, line 14 (cf. *SETP* pl. 8 [= p. 66] iii. 12); *SBH*, no. 53 rev. 13–14.
229   *Gilgamesh Epic* Tablet VI.
230   *SEM*, no. 86, obv. i. 1–2.
231   *EI*, p. 16, lines 17–20.
232   Ibid., p. 17, lines 28–31.
233   *SBH*, mo. 56 rev. 49–52.
234   *JCS* XXI (1967), p. 116, line 203.
235   Cf. A n = *Anum* Tablet I. See *CT* XXIV pl. 1. i. 28–30.
236   *CT* XVI pls. 19–21 lines 1–188.
237   *TCL* VI, no. 51.
238   See Kramer in *UE(T)* VI, p. 4 to nos. 12–17.
239   See B. Landsberger, "Einige unerkannt gebliebene oder verkannte Nomina
        des Akkadischen," *WZKM* LVI (1960), p. 121 b.
240   *SBH*, no. 56 obv. 16–36.
241   *SK*, no. 199 rev. i. 8–24.
242   *SRT*, no. 1 and duplicates.
243   Ibid., i. 1–16.
244   Ibid., iii. 31–32.
245   *TuMnF* III, no. 10. 169–75; and duplicate ibid., no. 11 rev. 11–14.
246   *BE* XXXI, no. 12. 10–20 and dupl. 3N-T 339 iii and *SEM*, no. 87, obv. 21 to
        rev. 4.
247   M. H. Pope in H. W. Haussig, ed., *Wörterbuch der Mythologie* I (Stuttgart), p.
        249.
248   Ibid., pp. 250–52.
249   E. g., in *EI*, p. 14 i. 1.
250   *PBS* V, no. 25 rev. vi 8–9, v 57–58, and v 54–55.
251   J. J. A. van Dijk, *Sumer* XIII, p. 73; IM 51176 obv. 1–6.
252   *BE* XXX, no. 4 and duplicates.
253   *PBS* I₁, no. 1; *PBS* V, no. 25. Cf. *SM* p. 116, n. 67.
254   "Inanna's Descent." See note 89 above.
255   *Gilgamesh Epic* Tablet VI.
256   *TRS*, no. 95 obv. 1–9. Cf. duplicates *SBH*, no. 53 obv. 1–44; ibid., no. 55 on p.
        155 rev. 28–30. The text is broken and also otherwise very difficult, so the
        translation, especially at the end, is given with reservation.
257   See Speiser, "Descent of Ishtar to the Nether World," *ANET* pp. 106–09 and
        sources there quoted. The passage in question is lines 12–20. Cf. the corre-
        sponding passage in the Sumerian "Descent of Inanna," *JCS* V (1951), p. 4,
        lines 72–76, where she is equally impetuous but less threatening.
258   *Gilgamesh Epic* Tablet VI.
259   J. A. Wilson, *The Burden of Egypt* (Chicago, 1951), p. 301.
260   L. W. King, *The Seven Tablets of Creation* II (London, 1902), pls. 75–84, lines
        42–50.
261   Ibid., lines 67–78.
262   *IV R²* pl. 10.
263   Ibid., obv. 58 rev. 8.
264   Ibid., rev. 35–45.

265 *SGL* I pp. 17–18, lines 129–40.
266 Goetze, *ANET* pp. 400–01.
267 Wilson, *The Burden of Egypt*, pp. 297–301.
268 *PBS* l₂, nos. 94 and 134; *UE(T)* VI, no. 173 i. 1′–4′, 174 c, and 180.
269 For this genre see W. Hallo, "Individual Prayer in Sumerian: The Continuity of a Tradition," *Journal of the American Oriental Society* 88 (1968), pp. 71–89.
270 S. N. Kramer, "Man and His God," *Supplements to Vetus Testamentum* III (Leiden, 1955), pp. 170–82.
271 Ibid., p. 173, lines 26–30.
272 Ibid., p. 174, lines 35–39.
273 Ibid., p. 175, line 98.
274 Ibid., p. 176, lines 101–02.
275 Ibid., lines 111–13.
276 Hallo, *JAOS* 88 (1968), pp. 82–84.
277 Ibid., p. 83, line 19.
278 Ibid., lines 20–21.
279 Ibid., lines 25–27.
280 Ibid., p. 84, lines 46–50.
281 *TCL* I, no. 9. Cf. A. Ungnad, *VAB* VI, pp. 80–81 no. 89; and von Soden *AHG*, p. 269 no. 16.
282 *PBS* I, no. 2. ii. 35′–40′.
283 Cf. the materials cited *CAD* vol. 7 p. 101 sec. 5.
284 *CT* XXXVIII pl. 30 line 23.
285 *CT* XXXVIII pl. 17 line 95.
286 *VS* XVI, no. 140. 23–24.
287 *YOS* 2, no. 15.
288 *BWL*, p. 227, lines 23–26.
289 *BRM* IV, no. 22 r. 19.
290 Gudea, *Cylinder A*, v. 19–20.
291 Ibid., xxx. 2–5.
292 *Corpus*, p. 7, Urn. 49 iv. 1 to v. 2.
293 Gudea, *St. B*, iii. 3–5.
294 Gudea, *St. E*, vii. 22 to vii. 10.
295 *Corpus*, p. 25, Ean. 62 Mortier V 3–7.
296 Ibid., p. 58, vii. 10 to ix. 3.
297 *TCL* I, no. 40 20–22. Cf. *VAB* VI, p. 154 no. 186.
298 Cf. *CAD* vol. 7 p. 100, 4′.
299 d i ĝ i r s a ĝ - d u - ĝ u₁₀ = *ilu ba-ni-i* and a m a i m - d í m - e n - n a - ĝ u₁₀ = *um-mi ba-ni-ti*. For references cf. *CAD* vol. 2 p. 94 s.v. *bānû* A.
300 *Šurpu* Tablets V–VI lines 11–12.
301 Lugalzagesi, Vase inscription. *BE* I, no. 87 i. 26–27; cf. *VAB* I, p. 154.
302 *VAB* I, p. 60 a. i. 7–8. Also ibid., p. 62 c. 7–8, e. 6–7, and f. i. 8 (cf. iii. 8–9).
303 *TRS*, no. 12 112–13.
304 *Shulgi, Hymn A*, line 7. See A. Falkenstein, "Ein Šulgi-Lied," *ZA* 50 (1952), pp. 61–81. Cf. Kramer, *ANET* Suppl. pp. 149 f.
305 *STVC*, no. 51 rev. 35. Ibid., no. 50 obv. 22; also *SLTN*, no. 79 line 50.

306   *SLTN*, no. 80. 22–25.
307   Gudea, *Cylinder B*, xxiii. 18–21.
308   Šurpu, p. 50, commentary B i. 19.
309   Cf. the materials and treatments cited *CAD* vol. 7 p. 95 sec. 4'.
310   Kramer, "Man and His God," p. 173, line 9.
311   *Corpus*, p. 41, Ent. 36, Brique B1 iii. 6 to iv. 4.
312   *KAR*, no. 423. ii. 23.
313   E. g., *KAR* no. 148. ii. 22.
314   *TCL* VI, no. 3 line 17.
315   *YOS* 2, no. 141.
316   *BWL*, p. 229, lines 24–26.
317   Ibid., p. 104, lines 135–41.
318   Ibid., pp. 21–62.
319   B. Landsberger, *ZA* 43 (1936), pp. 32–76. See also *BWL*, pp. 63–91.
320   *BWL*, p. 42, lines 71–75.
321   Ibid., p. 46, lines 112–13.
322   Ibid., p. 40, lines 34–38.
323   Ibid., p. 86, lines 256–57.
324   Job 42: 1–6.
325   *AS* XII, pp. 68–70, lines 418–35 and *UE(T)* VI$_2$, no. 139. 59.
326   An edition by W. G. Lambert is in preparation. A preliminary eclectic text by
       W. G. Lambert and S. B. Parker, *Enûma eliš. The Babylonian Epic of Creation.
       The Cuneiform Text* (Oxford, 1966), is at present the most complete available.
       Translations into English may be found in A. Heidel, *The Babylonian Genesis,
       The Story of Creation*, 2d ed. (Chicago, 1951) and by Speiser, *ANET* pp. 60–72,
       with additions by Grayson, *ANET* Suppl. pp. 65–67.
327   A n = *Anum* Tablet I. *CT* XXIV pl. 1. 1–21; cf. ibid., pl. 20. 1–13.
328   See above p. 131 and note 206.
329   See above p. 118 and note 169.
330   *CT* XLVI no. 43. See below p. 231.
331   Cf. Thorkild Jacobsen, "The Battle Between Marduk and Ti'āmat," *JAOS*
       88 (1968), pp. 104–08.
332   We would connect *Lahmu*, as past participle, and *Lahāmu* as infinitive with
       the root l-h-m of *luhāmum, luhummu,* and *luhmu,* "slime," "mud," meaning
       perhaps, "to make soft, slimy." In *Lahmu* = *Lahāmu,* as in *Dûri* = *Dâri*
       elsewhere in the same genealogy, the infinitives (*Lahāmu* and *Dâri*) seem
       originally to have represented the productive aspect, the mothers, the past
       participles (*Lahmu, Dûri*) the product aspect, the sons, of the entities in
       question. In the genealogy of An, however, the pairs clearly are meant to
       represent couples, husbands and wives, rather than (or as well as?) mother-
       son groupings.
333   Note particularly the beginning of the myth of the "Creation of the Hoe."
       (See above p. 103 and n. 112).
334   Note that *mummu,* "archetype," "form," when written without determina-
       tive, is an epithet. When written with divine determinative it denotes a
       hypostasis of "form" personified as the vizier of Apsû.

335   E. Bergmann, *Codex Hammurabi*, textus primigenius, editio tertia (Rome, 1953), obv. 1–22.
336   *UE(T)* VI₂, no. 132 obv. 7–11; cf. *STVC*, no. 25 obv. 18–21.
337   Whether, in the light of this Ti'āmat's spouse Kingu may be thought intended to stand by inept reliance on the written form *Ki-en-gi*ᵏⁱ for *Kengi(r)*, Shumer, we must leave undecided.
338   See B. Landsberger, *JCS* VIII (1954), p. 69.
339   R. Campbell Thompson, *The Epic of Gilgamesh* (Oxford, 1930). For translation and up-to-date bibliography see A. Schott and W. von Soden, *Das Gilgamesch-Epos*, Reclam Universal-Bibliothek no. 7235/35a (Stuttgart, 1970). Cf. also E. A. Speiser, "The Epic of Gilgamesh," *ANET* pp. 72–99, and A. Heidel, *The Gilgamesh Epic and Old Testament Parallels* (Chicago, 1946).
340   The probabilities greatly favor the assumption of an actual Old Babylonian epic rather than a mere epic cycle. In this connection, note that the colophon of the Old Babylonian Pennsylvania Tablet shows it to have been part of a series with three or more tablets, each of some 240 lines if all the tablets were of the same length. That points to a formal composition of very considerable size. I am grateful to Professor Aaron Shaffer for drawing my attention to this point.
341   *The Odyssey of Homer*, S. H. Butcher and A. Lang, The Harvard Classics (New York, 1909), p. 9.
342   Cf. the stone tablet of Anam, *SAK* p. 222. 2. b which dates to Old Babylonian times.
343   We follow here B. Landsberger, "Jungfräulichkeit: Ein Beitrag zum Thema 'Beilager und Eheschliessung,' " *Symbolae iuridicae et historicae Martino David dedicatae* (Leiden, 1968), pp. 83–84.
344   For this view of the dreams and Enkidu's interpretations of them we are indebted to W. L. Moran.
345   See S. N. Kramer, "Gilgamesh and the Land of the Living" (we prefer to translate "and the Mountain where the Man Dwelt"), *JCS* I (1947), pp. 3–46.
346   John Dryden, *Palamon and Arcite*, bk. iii, lines 883 ff.
347   Dietz Edzard, "Enme baragisi von Kiš," *ZA* 53 (1959) pp. 9 ff.
348   See for the time being A. Deimel, "Die Listen über den Ahnenkult aus der Zeit Lugalandas und Urukaginas," *Orientalia* 2 (1920), pp. 32 ff.
349   See S. N. Kramer, *JCS* XXI (1967), p. 115, lines 142–43. We prefer to restore [- g i m] at the end of line 142.
350   E. Ebeling, *Tod und Leben nach den Vorstellungen der Babylonier* (Berlin and Leipzig, 1931), pp. 131–33.
351   S. H. Langdon, *BE* XXXI, no. 43 obv. 11 and *Babylonian Liturgies* (Paris, 1913), pl. VIII rev. line 3–4.
352   *RA* IX (1912), pp. 111 f. ii. 29 to iii. 3.
353   *SLTN*, no. 79. 41–61.
354   For these first written sources see also S. N. Kramer, "The Epic of Gilgamesh and its Sumerian Sources," *JAOS* 64 (1944), pp. 7–23.
355   *SAK* p. 222. 2. b.

356 S. N. Kramer, "The Death of Gilgamesh," *BASOR* no. 94 (1944). Cf. *ANET* pp. 50–52.

357 See note 55 above.

358 An edition by A. Shaffer is in preparation. For the time being see Kramer, "Gilgamesh and Agga," pp. 1 ff. Cf. *ANET* pp. 44–47.

359 Kramer, "Gilgamesh and the Land of the Living," pp. 3–46. Cf. *TuMnF* III, p. 11 to no. 12 and *UE(T)* VI₁, p. 7 to nos. 49–54.

360 *SK*, no. 196 and unpublished duplicate from Nippur 3 N-T 152.

361 *Gilgamesh Epic* Tablet VI.

362 *BASOR* no. 94 (1944), p. 7, line 42.

363 Cf. *Gilgamesh Epic* Tablet XII 90–92.

364 G. van der Leeuw, *Religion in Essence and Manifestation* (Gloucester, Mass., 1967), p. 48.

365 *Palamon and Arcite*, bk. iii, line 885.

366 H. N. Wolff, "Gilgamesh, Enkidu, and the Heroic Life," *Journal of the American Oriental Society* 89 (1969), pp. 392–98.

367 Edward Sapir, *Culture, Language and Personality* (Berkeley, 1960), p. 122.

368 Georges Roux, *Ancient Iraq* (Cleveland, 1964), p. 231.

369 See F. Gössmann, *Das Era-Epos* (Würzburg, 1955). See now L. Cagni, *Das Erra-Epos*, Studia Pohl 5, Dissertationes scientificae de rebus orientis antiqui (Rome, 1970).

370 J. Roberts, "Erra — Scorched Earth," *JCS* XXIV (1971), pp. 11–16, and idem, *The Earliest Semitic Pantheon* (Baltimore, 1972), pp. 21–29.

371 Erra Epic Tablet IV lines 6–12.

372 Ibid., lines 27–29.

373 Ibid., Tablet V lines 5–12.

374 *VAB* II, no. 357.

375 See O. R. Gurney, *Anatolian Studies* X, pp. 105 ff.

376 *VAB* II, no. 357, lines 85–86.

377 O. R. Gurney and J. Finkelstein, *The Sultantepe Tablets* I (London, 1957), no. 28 rev. v 2′–12′ and 18′–27′.

378 W. von Soden, "Die Unterweltvision eines assyrischen Kronprinzen," *ZA* 43 (1936), pp. 1 ff.

379 *CT* XLVI no. 43.

380 Ebeling and Köcher, *Literarische Keilschrifttexte aus Assur* (Berlin, 1953), no. 73 obv. 8–9, 13 and 7; van Dijk, *Sumer* XIII, p. 117, lines 16–18. See *CT* XV pls. 43–44 and K 3476 line 24 for the passage where Anu's extracted heart is played with and cf. *KAR*, no. 307. rev. 11 which deals with representations of the ghosts of Enlil and Anu.

381 *IV R²* pl. 61. i. 19–20 with emendation of last sign in line 20 to ṣa.

382 Ashurbanipal, *Annals* iv. 70–89.

383 *OIP* II, p. 87, 31–33.

384 Ibid., p. 83, 45–48.

385 W. von Soden, "Gibt es ein Zeugnis dafür dass die Babylonier an die Wiederauferstehung Marduks geglaubt haben," *ZA* 51 (1955), pp. 130 ff.

386 W. G. Lambert, "Divine Love Lyrics from Babylon," *Journal of Semitic Studies* IV (1959), pp. 10–11, and idem, "The Problem of the Love Lyrics," in *Unity*

and Diversity, ed. H. Goedicke and J. J. M. Roberts (Baltimore, 1975), pp. 98–135.

387   *OIP* XXXVIII, pp. 132–33; ibid., pp. 130–31.

388   See above p. 137 and n. 237.

389   R. Brünnow, "Assyrian Hymns," *ZA* 4 (1889), p. 246; K 8717 plus DT 363, line 2.

390   *TCL* III, p. 48, lines 314–16.

391   *CT* XXIV pl. 50, no. 47406 obv. 3–10.

392   *KAR,* no. 102 lines 10–19.

393   E.g., Enûma elish Tablet IV lines 4 and 6.

394   *IV R*² pl. 61. iii. 15–26.

395   Ashurbanipal, *Annals* v. 48–49.

396   Ibid., 56–57.

397   Ibid., 63–70.

398   Ibid., 71–72.

399   *VAB* VII part 2, pp. 210–12; K 2867 obv. 15–19.

400   R. Borger, *Die Inschriften Asarhaddons Königs von Assyrien, AOF* supplement 9 (Graz, 1956), pp. 13 44, lines 59 79.

401   *VAB* IV, pp. 122–23, lines 57–72.

Index

Ababa. *See* Dumuzi
abarahhu, 155
abbûtu, 159
Abraham, 159
Activity, forces of, 170
Adad: as personal god, 157; holds back rains, 118–19; Sargon II's prayer to, 233
Adams, Robert M., 78
Adapa, myth of, 115
Agade, period of, 79
Agga, 209; tale of Gilgamesh and, 213
Agriculture: instituted, 85
Akiti: of Nanna, 126. *See* also New Year Festival
Akkad, 226
Alewife: advises Gilgamesh, 204–05; called Sidûri (Si-duri), 217
alu-disease, 162
A m a - d ù g - b a d: meaning of name, 108
A m a - g e s h t i n (n a): name of Geshtinanna, 62, 66
A m a - m u t i n n a: name of Geshtinanna, 62
Amanus, 156
Amarna, 229
Amarna age, 152
amaš, 107.
A m a - u d ú d a: meaning of name, 108
Amaushumgalanna: character of, 36–37; bridegroom of Inanna, 31, 36; different from Dumuzi, 38–39, 138; embodied in Iddin-Dagan, 38–39, 138; meaning of name, 26, 36; peer of Enlil, 31; son-in-law of Suen, 30; to marry Inanna, 30, 31. *See* also Dumuzi
Amniotic fluid. *See* Birth water
Amorites, 168

An (female): cow form of, 95. *See* also Antum, the Akkadian form of the name
An (male): character of authority, 95–98; Adapa and, 115–16; bull-shape of, 95; bull of heaven lent by, 142; calendar and, 95; command of, 77, 91; Damu son of, 69; death of, 73; decapitated in ritual, 231; Dumuzi herdsman of, 35; Dumuzi peer of, 28; Eanna founded by, 79; flayed, 231; god of heaven, 95–96, 169; highest god, 121; Inanna berates him, 137; Inanna instructed by, 136; kingship and, 97; meaning of name, 7, 95; offices conferred by, 85, 110; presides in divine assembly, 86; source of authority, 96; spouse of Ki, "earth," 95; word of, 102; with Enlil, 68, 189; with Enlil and Ea, 234. *See* also Anu, the Akkadian form of the name
A n = *Anum*, 167, 169
Anam, 211
Anarchy: in Enûma elish, 169–72
Anchorite, legend of the hairy, 214
Ancient Mariner, E. M. Forster on, 19
Ancients: difficulties of understanding, 17–19
Andrae, Walter, 36
A n - g i m d í m - m a, 129, 134
Animals, Enkidu lives with, 197
Anshar (god of the horizon): in Enûma elish, 168–69, 174, 178, 182, 185
Antum: identified with Inanna, 137. *See* also An (female)
Anu: Anuship of, 234; bull of heaven lent by, 201; covered during reading of Enûma elish, 231; divides cosmos with Enlil and Enki, 117; Eanna temple of, 198; god of heaven, 168; heart of in ritual,